ALSO BY BERTRAM FIELDS

Royal Blood

The Lawyer's Tale (as D. Kincaid)

The Sunset Bomber (as D. Kincaid)

PLAYERS

THE MYSTERIOUS IDENTITY
OF WILLIAM SHAKESPEARE

Bertram Fields

ReganBooks

An Imprint of HarperCollins*Publishers*

PLAYERS

FIRST PAPERBACK EDITION PUBLISHED 2006.

Designed by Kris Tobiassen

The Library of Congress has catalogued the hardcover edition as follows:

Fields, Bertram.
Players : the mysterious identity of William Shakespeare / Bertram Fields.— 1st ed.
p. cm.
ISBN 0-06-077559-9

1. Shakespeare, William, 1564–1616—Authorship. 2. Dramatists, English—Early
modern, 1500–1700—Biography. 3. Playwriting—History—16th century.
4. Playwriting—History—17th century. I. Title.

PR2937.F54 2005
822.3'3—dc22

[B]   2004064935

ISBN 13: 978-0-06-083417-3 (pbk.)
ISBN 10: 0-06-083417-x (pbk.)

06 07 08 09 10 RRD 10 9 8 7 6 5 4 3 2 1

To B.G. with love

All the world's a stage,
And all the men and women merely players;
They have their exits and their entrances,
And one man in his time plays many parts.

—WILLIAM SHAKESPEARE, *AS YOU LIKE IT*

Oh, what a tangled web we weave,
When first we practice to deceive.

—SIR WALTER SCOTT, *MARMION*

ACKNOWLEDGMENTS

*I*n researching, writing, and editing this book, I had invaluable help from my secretary Roberta Dunner, as well as Ellen Baskin, John Huggett, Dario Dagostino, Anna Grear, Christine Baker (who helped with the illustrations); Melik Kaylan and Giulia Harding (who were kind enough to provide their comments); Frederick Ilchman (my expert on things Italian); Judith Regan and the superb staff at ReganBooks; the British Library; the College of Arms; the Shakespeare Birthplace Trust; the splendid Folger Shakespeare Library in Washington, D.C., and my loving, patient wife.

I have undoubtedly forgotten to mention others, for which I apologize.

B. F.

CONTENTS

Part III: The Other Candidates

Part IV: Summing Up

INTRODUCTION

For centuries, scholars, other professionals, and amateurs have debated the true identity of the author of the magnificent body of poems and plays attributed to William Shakespeare. Most of the literate world thinks of the author as the bearded, balding man from Stratford-upon-Avon. And Stratford has become a prosperous tourist destination as the home of the "great Bard."

Yet some very competent and credible people have questioned this, contending that the vast body of diverse knowledge demonstrably possessed by the author of Shakespeare's works was simply not available to "William Shakspere" of Stratford, who had a grade school education at best, and appears to have had difficulty writing anything, including his own name. They argue that the wisdom and humanity expressed with such perception and elegance in the poems and plays cannot be reconciled with what we know about the crass and selfish behavior of the "Stratford man" (as I will call him). These doubters include such luminaries as Mark Twain, Sigmund Freud, Benjamin Disraeli, Ralph Waldo Emerson, Oliver Wendell Holmes, Walt Whitman, and John Greenleaf Whittier.

Henry James wrote that he was "haunted by the conviction that the divine William is the biggest and most successful fraud ever practiced on a patient world."

But if the Stratford man was not the true author, who was? Here, the "anti-Stratfordians" ("anti-Strats" for short) split into a number of fiercely contending groups, each making the case for its own candidate, be it the earl of Oxford, Francis Bacon, Christopher Marlowe, or even Queen Elizabeth.

The majority of academics and other "authorities" who have written about Shakespeare have tended to dismiss the notion that there is any real issue about authorship of the poems and plays. To these traditionalists (I will call them "Stratfordians") the matter is beyond doubt—the author was William Shakspere, who was born and lived much of his life in Stratford-upon-Avon and who, for a time, appears to have been an actor on the London stage and co-owner of a successful theatre company.

Some Stratfordians have an unfortunate tendency to dismiss all those who even raise the authorship question as cranks and fools. Some no doubt were. But many were not.

One of the first to raise the issue was J. Thomas Looney. Stratfordians have great fun with his unfortunate name. Indeed, the originally intended publisher of Looney's book refused to put it out under that name, insisting that he use a pseudonym. Explaining that the name was pronounced "Loney," Looney found another publisher.

One Stratfordian argument is that the anti-Strats are "snobs," because they claim that only a university graduate of the upper classes could have created these extraordinary works. The attack seems ill-founded. Analyzing the probable results of growing up in a rural English town in the sixteenth century, with a limited education at best, and contrasting that background and the balance of the Stratford man's life, with the broad knowledge and striking perception reflected in the Shakespeare canon, cannot fairly be characterized as snobbishness. Mark Twain was hardly a snob. Nor, for that matter, was Freud.

The most doctrinaire and dismissive Stratfordians tend to see the authorship question as an attack on the value of Shakespeare's works. Of course, it's not. Whether the Shakespeare canon was written by the Stratford man or by some pseudonymous aristocrat, it is monumental and probably the greatest body of literature ever attributed to one author. Questioning the identity of the creator hardly denigrates the creation. After all, when we refer to reading, understanding, or loving "Shakespeare," we mean that great body of work, not the man who bore (or hid behind) that name.

Why do we say "great"? Not because of the plots. Those were primarily taken from earlier sources. Rather, it is the magnificent characters, the fascinating villains, the understandably flawed heroes and the towering historical figures, the perception and intelligence manifested in the way these characters are revealed to us, the extraordinary ability to develop and express timeworn stories in a way that has thrilled audiences and stocked orators with brilliant lines for centuries.

Those lines could illuminate any occurrence with unforgettable poetry. Consider Ariel in *The Tempest* describing in song the physiological transformation of a drowned man, a vision we would ordinarily imagine with horror:

> *Full fathom five thy father lies;*
> *of his bones are coral made;*
> *Those are pearls that were his eyes;*
> *Nothing of him that doth fade,*
> *But doth suffer a sea change*
> *Into something rich and strange.*

At the same time, Shakespeare could pack an extraordinary jolt of candor and wit into a single comedic line. In *As You Like It*, Orlando pleads that, if the object of his love will not have him, he will die. The incomparable Rosalind brings him back to reality: "Men have died from time to time, and worms have eaten them, but not for love."

And it is not only characters and lines. The German literary critic Walter Benjamin distinguished between the subject matter of a work and the basic truths it embodied—if any. In Shakespeare's plays, the basic truths may be subtle, ambiguous, and deeply embedded in the subject matter. There has been vast disagreement over the identity and definition of those basic truths; but, most probably, the Bard held social and political views that he intended to embody in the dialogue and action of the plays, hopefully to be perceived by viewers and readers of intelligence and education.

How were his works different from what had gone before? In many fundamental ways. Most importantly, the characters he portrayed were unforgettable: heroes with discernible, human failings—villains with understandable causes for their villainy. He showed us the human at his best and his worst, but alive, real, and exposed to our perception and understanding.

Apparently, the renowned Elizabethan actor, Edward Alleyn, simply declaimed his lines in a magnificent stentorian voice, while Richard Burbage, who attained fame somewhat later and performed in many of Shakespeare's prime roles, attempted to play the "character," foreshadowing modern theories of acting, such as that of Konstantin Stanislavsky. If so, it was Shakespeare who gave Burbage the characters to play. And unlike the characters in classical plays, whose actions were determined by the gods, Shakespeare's characters had choices; they elected to be as they were and act as they did. And Shakespeare created lines that exposed his character's inner feelings without the artificially staged asides employed by lesser playwrights.

Shakespeare's plays departed completely from the rules of classical drama. They had multiple characters and detailed subplots. They spanned too much time, had too many settings, and combined humor with tragedy. A Greek dramatist would have given him failing grades. Yet for centuries the literate world has enshrined him as a cultural icon. Virtually every part of the political spectrum has claimed him or has at least quoted from his works to support its position. He became and remains a giant; and who he was is less important than what he created.

Nevertheless, the issue of his identity had fascinated us for centuries. Why have so many sincere and intelligent scholars and writers, over so many decades, believed that the Stratford man did not—or at least *probably* did not—write the works for which the world has given him credit? There are several reasons.

The true author appears to have had highly specialized, even esoteric knowledge in many areas, such as the etiquette and practices of the nobility; the workings of the law; military and naval tactics; aristocratic sports; French and Italian courtly and colloquial speech; and Italian and Danish places, names, and customs. He used Latin and Greek classical works with familiarity and ease, in addition to works in Italian and French that had not yet been translated into English. His vocabulary was twice that of the most brilliant men of the time. How was all this possible in a man who never went beyond the sixth grade, if that?

Abraham Lincoln succeeded in educating himself after he was twenty-one by reading the classics and conversing with educated men in New Salem, Illinois. Couldn't the Stratford man have done the same thing? Wouldn't it have been easier to accomplish this in London than New Salem? Not necessarily. Not if the source materials he needed were not yet published or translated. And the writings and speeches of Lincoln, while well crafted and admirable in the principles they advocated, cannot be compared in content with the vast body of diversified information and extraordinary understanding of the human psyche found in the Shakespeare canon.

And how could a man who appears to have been barely able to write his own name have written by hand at least thirty-six plays, two long narrative poems, and 154 sonnets—especially if Ben Jonson was correct in reporting that Shakespeare's manuscripts never contained a blotted line?

Shakespeare's creative focus seems to be on the upper class. His heroes were generally of the aristocracy, and they were carefully defined individuals who spoke and acted as did the members of that class. His common folk tended to be generic bumpkins, whom he caricatured and cursed with a tendency to slaughter the King's English. Generally, although not always, Shakespeare's noble characters speak in iambic pentameter while his common folk speak in prose.

Conceivably, a skilled playwright could accurately portray the nobility, even though he was not highborn. He might even have them speak in verse. But wouldn't he also have three-dimensional, thinking, feeling commoners among his characters? Occasionally, Shakespeare gives us a commoner with "street smarts" and a sense of humor, sometimes with striking loyalty and occasionally with a rough dignity. Sometimes he gives them lines that show common sense and sound judgment, which he will contrast with the hypocrisy and foolishness of a pompous "sophisticate." But this is relatively infrequent, and the common folk are generally not major characters.

At least on the surface, Shakespeare tends to poke fun at these lowborn, one-dimensional characters, with their foolish ideas and mangled grammar. Fools are exceptions. Because they can speak the truth with greater freedom than ordinary commoners, they often do, although usually such truths are cloaked in ambiguous banter. Another exception is Bottom, the honest weaver in *A Midsummer Night's Dream*, who is certainly a major character in that play, if not its protagonist. An even more distinct exception is Falstaff, a drunken, cowardly, yet beloved character. He has rare intelligence and wit, albeit undiluted by morality or courage. But at least Falstaff was a knight.

Was Shakespeare a social-climbing snob? Or was he an aristocrat himself, giving us detailed portraits of individuals of a class he knew intimately and generally gross caricatures of an underclass he encountered only as servants or tradesmen?

Shakespeare's odd sentence structure, his sixteenth-century vocabulary, his plethora of newly minted words and his often oblique references to history, mythology, and people and events of the period make the plays difficult to follow for the average modern reader. Frank Kermode opines that they may even have been difficult for the average theatregoer in the sixteenth century. If so, does this suggest an author who was not dependent for his livelihood on pleasing and entertaining his audience?

Perhaps. But the primarily uneducated groundlings at the public theatre probably enjoyed the performances, even if they could only follow the general plot and missed many of the lines. An eighteenth-century anecdote suggests that this was possible. It seems the well-known actor John Palmer was assigned the title role in *Lord Russell*, a new play. Although Palmer had failed to learn his lines, he was undaunted. In response to every cue calling for a speech by Lord Russell, Palmer simply recited lines he had previously spoken as the earl of Essex in a different play. Evidently, the audience never noticed.

Still, even an Elizabethan audience would seemingly have preferred dialogue they could comprehend. Would an actor and co-owner of a theatre company deliberately write in a manner his paying customers would not fully understand?

Then there is the problem with the name. "Shakspeare," "Shakspere," "Shaxpere," or "Shagspere" (the spellings on most documents that provably referred to the Stratford man) was seemingly pronounced in Stratford with a short *a* as in "shack," not a long *a* as in "shake"—or Shakespeare. Why the difference?

In the case of most authors, significant traces of their own lives can usually be found in their writings. But little in the Shakespeare canon seems relatable to the facts we actually *know* about the Stratford man.

And what of his Stratford will, made after William Shakespeare became famous as a playwright and poet? It carefully delineates various items of personal property—his "second best bed," for example. Yet it makes no mention of any plays, books, manuscripts, or literary property of any kind, or any interest in any theatre company.

And where are the documents that one would expect in the case of such a prolific writer? Where are all the manuscripts, the letters, the notes? All have disappeared—if they ever existed. Even his son-in-law's diary makes no mention of the Stratford man. Did some influential person or group "sanitize" the record?

In 1775, a gentleman named Samuel Ireland came to the rescue. Rejecting the notion that Shakespeare had been a secret Catholic, he produced a "spiritual testament" in the Bard's own hand, which showed that he had remained true to the Anglican Church. Encouraged by the notoriety and praise that followed this historic disclosure, Ireland went on to produce not only the Bard's letters to Queen Elizabeth and Anne Hathaway, but also the missing manuscripts of *Hamlet* and *King Lear*.

Shortly thereafter, the leading Shakespearean scholar, Edmund Malone, proved unequivocally that all of Ireland's "finds" were fakes—and not very good fakes at that. Ireland admitted the deception. No *real* documents have ever been found. Nor is there any record of anyone's ever seeing the Stratford man write a single word except perhaps his name.

Shakespeare does have a monument in Stratford. It portrays him with a quill pen and paper, obviously a writer. But there is evidence that the monument, as originally constructed, showed him not with quill in hand, but clutching what appears to be a sack of grain, which is far more consistent with the wealthy local landowner who was accused of hoarding grain in a time of severe shortage. Someone may have changed the monument, possibly to appeal to the lucrative army of tourists who came to visit the birthplace of the great Bard.

But if the Stratford man did not write the poems and plays, why did someone else write them under the pseudonym *Shakespeare*, rather than under his own name? Most anti-Strats see the true author as a nobleman. They argue, with reason, that it would have been considered most unseemly for an aristocrat or high-level politician to write plays for the common theatre or even to publish poetry under his own name. A highborn person or member of the Royal Council could write poems or even plays to be read or performed privately for his own circle of friends. But to publish or perform such works for the general public under one's own name simply wasn't done.

It wasn't done, in part, because of the disreputable nature of the public theatre. As described by the lord mayor of London, such theatres were "places of meeting for all vagrant persons and masterless men that hang about the city, thieves, horse stealers, whore-mongers, cozeners, cony catching persons, practicers of treason and other such like." ("Cony-catching persons" were swindlers who preyed on those new to the city or otherwise inexperienced.)

And that was not all. Phillip Stubbs described the situation from a different perspective. "... these goodly pageants being ended, every mate sorts to his mate, everyone brings another homeward of their way very friendly, and in their secret conclaves covertly they play the sodomites or worse."

The public theatre was a source of concern to the royal and religious establishment for still other reasons. These were intensely troubled times. England had become Protestant under Henry VIII, with the monarch serving as head of the established Anglican Church. It had shifted back to Catholic under Henry's daughter Mary, and then back to Protestant again under Elizabeth. But there were Catholic plots on one side—sometimes encouraged by Spain—and a growing Puritan movement on the other, plus the ever-present fear of public insurrection fomented by some discontented and ambitious nobleman or by a group of enraged commoners. A theatre audience was, of course, a public gathering; and public gatherings, if exposed to dangerous ideas, could metastasize into rebellion.

At the same time, the crown was ready to use the theatre as a means of entertaining and disconcerting the populace, as well as providing them with desirable ideas such as patriotism and loyalty to the monarch and the established religion. Also, plays were vetted by the queen's master of revels, who would require the deletion of any "dangerous" lines or scenes.

Still, to the royal establishment, the public theatre was always perceived as a source of danger, and writing for that audience was not quite proper. An aristocrat or politician who wished to maintain the favor of the crown might have been well advised not to write for that audience—at least not under his own name.

If the queen was aware of a pseudonymous playwright's true identity, she might look the other way (or even be secretly amused), especially if he was someone she liked or found attractive. But she might fear being seen as too permissive or even weak if she was seen to show favor to a well-known person who wrote plays for public consumption under his own name.

Ironically, the principal theatre companies were all sponsored by powerful aristocrats, one by the lord admiral and one by the lord chamberlain and, later, by King James himself. If the theatre was held in such low esteem, why did these distinguished people lend their names and sometimes their money to the public performance of plays?

Parliament actually *insisted* that actors be enrolled in companies sponsored by distinguished citizens or be branded criminals; in 1572, it passed legislation providing that all "common players ... not belonging to any baron or to any other honourable personage of great degree" shall be "deemed rogues, vagabonds and sturdy beggars" and "shall be stripped naked from his middle upwards and shall be openly whipped until his or her body be bloody." Apparently, the supervision of a "baron or other honorable personage" was thought to be the only thing that could keep an actor from a life of corruption and crime.

Thus, it was proper and even officially approved for a nobleman or other distinguished person to sponsor a company of actors who performed publicly, but not to write plays for such a company. Accordingly, a nobleman or aspiring politician who wished to do so would have had a sufficient motive to hide behind a pseudonym like *Shakespeare* or to use someone else (an actor, for example) as a "front."

Whether this really occurred in the case of Shakespeare is a question that has been debated over the centuries, usually in works that strongly (often stridently) advocate one point of view or the other. It is not the aim of this book to advocate a position, but rather to explore and evaluate the evidence on each side of the many relevant issues, and to set out a scenario that seems best to fit the facts, in an attempt to shed light on the mystery and to come as close as possible to the elusive answer.

I say *elusive* because all the answers in this matter are elusive. Shakespeare is so monumental and complex, and his life and work so full of ambiguity, that virtually any conclusion about him defies provability. T. S. Eliot said that, in dealing with Shakespeare, the best we can hope for is to be wrong about him in a new way. Possibly, Eliot is correct. Possibly, there are no answers and never will be. Still, as rational, curious humans, when we encounter this kind of mystery, we seek a solution.

But there are some caveats. If you're cowed by "authority," this analysis will be disturbing. As I've said, most authorities insist there is no authorship issue at all. My own guide in approaching a subject of this nature is Jeremy Bentham, who said, "Let us not judge on authority; let us seek reason." And, in seeking reason, in evaluating issues centuries old, there is usually no certainty.

If you're looking for certainty, look elsewhere. Look to Stratfordian "authorities" like Samuel Schoenbaum or to committed anti-Strats like Donald Ogden. Schoenbaum is certain the Stratford man was Shakespeare. Ogden is certain he was not. Or look to George Elliot Sweet, who is certain Shakespeare was Queen Elizabeth. What you will find here is questioning, analysis, a weighing of the evidence, an assessment of probability, and what seems a logical scenario.

I'll begin the process with an overview of the brilliant monarchial setting that was background to the events in question and that provided the models for some of Shakespeare's most memorable characters. Then we will explore the facts we really *know* about the Stratford man and compare them with what we know about the great poet and playwright. Next, we will examine and weigh the evidence for and against the proposition that the two were the same. Having considered that overriding issue, we will evaluate the case for each of the principal alternative candidates, assessing the likelihood that one of them, rather than the Stratford man, was the true Shakespeare. Then, finally, we can consider what *might* have happened.

Part I

TUDORS AND STUARTS

✠

I

TUDORS AND STUARTS

Many lines, scenes, and characters in Shakespeare's works are, or at least are claimed to be, references to actual characters and events of the reign of Queen Elizabeth and, to a lesser extent, her successor, James I. An understanding of those characters and events may be a useful tool in attempting to solve the riddle of Shakespeare's identity.

Many such examples exist. Polonius, the ponderous royal councilor in *Hamlet*, may have been patterned after Elizabeth's key advisor, William Cecil, whom she made Lord Burghley. Some commentators have seen Hamlet himself in the mercurial but indecisive earl of Essex. Others, viewing Essex in a different light, see him in the noble conspirator Brutus, in *Julius Caesar*.

We may find clues to the Bard's true identity in the attitudes of Elizabeth and James toward the Catholic minority, in the charges of heresy and blasphemy leveled against Christopher Marlowe, and in Marlowe's strange "death" once those terrifying charges were brought. Other clues may be found in Bacon's prosecution of Essex for treason and in the queen's violent reaction to a performance of *Richard II*.

Sir Walter Raleigh's adventures in the New World; the English defeat of the armada; Essex's Irish campaign; a famous shipwreck near Bermuda, the Catholic "gunpowder plot," designed to blow up Parliament and kill the king; and other events of the Elizabethan and Jacobean ages may be useful in establishing the dates on which the plays were written and thus in including or eliminating particular candidates. Even such intimate matters as the bedroom proclivities of the earl of Southampton, King James's homosexuality, and the possibility that Queen Elizabeth had an incorrectable sexual infirmity may assist us in exploring the evidence of the sonnets and the First Folio.

Moreover, each of the candidates for the Shakespeare authorship lived during Elizabeth's reign and was significantly affected by it. Most also survived into the reign of James I, who, among other things, sponsored the company of actors partly owned by the Stratford man.

A brief summary of the lives and characters of these two monarchs and of the principal events of their reigns may be a helpful key to analyzing the issues before us. Readers already familiar with the reigns of Elizabeth and James may wish to skip to chapter 2.

O n a summer day in 1485, the Wars of the Roses—the long-running series of vicious battles between the great houses of York and Lancaster—finally came to an end. Betrayed by the peers on whom he had counted, the reigning king, Richard III, was defeated by Henry Tudor at Bosworth Field, significantly altering the history of England and the Western world. Richard, the last Plantagenet, died while fighting ferociously against overwhelming odds. Now, Henry Tudor, whose claim to the throne was exceedingly weak, took the throne as Henry VII, founding the Tudor dynasty.

Henry became a shrewd and practical king. Seeking to bolster his tenuous claim, he married Richard's niece, the daughter of his deceased older brother, Edward IV. At least initially, Henry was reluctant to give his wife the public respect customary for a queen, probably because he realized that her claim to the throne was far better than his own.

As Henry grew older, it seemed that the kingdom would be secure in the hands of his oldest son, Arthur, who had married the Spanish princess, Catherine of Aragon. But Arthur died prematurely, and the heir to the throne became his younger brother. This was the handsome, athletic Henry, who married his brother's widow soon after becoming king and went on to become the legendary Henry VIII.

Henry and Catherine had a daughter, Mary, who later became queen. But Catherine's inability to produce a male heir and Henry's obsession with the sensual Anne Boleyn led the king to seek a divorce from Catherine in order to marry Anne. When the Pope refused his support, Henry brought about the English reformation. Severing ties between England—until then a Catholic country—and the Church of Rome, Henry placed himself, as "defender of the faith," at the head of the new Protestant Church of England.

He divorced Catherine and married Anne, the second of his six wives. Like Catherine, however, Anne produced no male heir. She did give birth in 1533 to a daughter, Elizabeth, who was to become perhaps the greatest of all English monarchs. Englishmen were delighted at the birth of this Protestant princess, who was English on both sides, in contrast to her half sister Mary, who was staunchly Catholic and half Spanish to boot.

But Elizabeth's prospects declined significantly in 1536. In that year, when Elizabeth was only three, her mother was beheaded. The charge was committing adultery with her own brother, a claim almost certainly false, and of committing the same offense with a young music teacher, a claim that was probably false as well.

Still Elizabeth survived. She was placed in country manors under the supervision of a governess. She received a superb education and excelled as a student. At an early age, she acquired fluency in several languages, as well as a thorough grasp of classical and medieval history.

Henry VIII's third marriage, to Jane Seymour, finally produced the male heir for whom he had yearned, albeit a physically weak one. Later, when Henry finally married the kindly and caring Catherine Parr, Elizabeth and Mary were often brought to court, along with their half brother Edward. Elizabeth's education was furthered under Catherine Parr's guidance, and she added dancing, riding, and musicianship to her accomplishments.

The Act of Succession provided that Edward, Mary, and Elizabeth, in that order, would succeed to the throne on Henry's death. This order was confirmed in Henry's will.

Henry's death in 1547 began a series of difficulties and dangers for Elizabeth. At first, she resided peacefully enough in Chelsea with the widowed queen, Catherine Parr. Then Thomas Seymour, the lord admiral, married Catherine and became part of the household. The admiral flirted outrageously with his fourteen-year-old stepdaughter, seizing every opportunity to enter her bedroom to tickle, fondle, and kiss her—and, according to gossip, perhaps do more.

Finally, Elizabeth was sent away to a country manor, where she was tutored by the renowned scholar Roger Ascham, who commented on her high intelligence and scholastic aptitude.

When Catherine Parr died in childbirth, there were rumors that Admiral Seymour would marry the teenage princess. But the admiral behaved foolishly. He attempted to overthrow his own brother, who was regent during the minority of Henry's son, Edward VI. Accused of several counts of treason, including scheming to marry Elizabeth, Seymour was confined to the Tower of London. Ultimately, the attractive but foolish admiral was beheaded. Elizabeth later described him as "a man of much wit and very little judgment."

Elizabeth's greatest period of danger came with the death of sickly, young Edward VI in 1553 and the accession to the throne of their half sister Mary. The new queen reestablished Catholicism as the state religion and was betrothed to Phillip II of Spain, the devoutly Catholic king of a staunchly Catholic nation. Her rigorous and often draconian suppression of Protestants led to her historical sobriquet "Bloody Mary."

Elizabeth wisely appeared to be reconciled to the "True Church," although Mary continued to suspect that her conversion lacked sincerity. Mary's concerns were fueled by the fact that Elizabeth was enormously popular and that virtually every Protestant plot was aimed at deposing Mary and placing Elizabeth on the throne. Mary was well aware of this and, at one point, confined Elizabeth to the Tower for eight weeks. Elizabeth feared for her life, but behaved with grace and dignity. Mary had sufficient respect for English law (and English public opinion) that, having no evidence to convict Elizabeth of anything, she ultimately allowed her to go free.

But not entirely free. Elizabeth was sent to a manor in Woodstock, where she was placed under the surveillance of a narrow-minded and stubborn Catholic knight, who allowed her few liberties, even restricting her reading material.

Perhaps Mary's marriage to Phillip of Spain gave the Catholic queen a greater feeling of security. Or perhaps Phillip persuaded Mary to adopt a more liberal policy toward the young sister-in-law he found quite attractive. Elizabeth was finally allowed to return to court, where she professed complete loyalty to Mary. At length, Elizabeth was allowed to reside at Hatfield in the care of Sir Thomas Pope, who was far more intelligent and permissive than her stiff-necked former warden.

Elizabeth's relationship with Mary was now a friendly one, perhaps due to Phillip's influence. Mary even spent midsummer with Elizabeth at Hatfield and visited her there later the same year.

Later, Mary became gravely ill. By this time, her trust in Elizabeth had grown to the point that she made it clear that her younger sister was to succeed her, although she pleaded with Elizabeth to maintain Catholicism as the national religion—and her own.

Finally, on November 17, 1558, Elizabeth received word at Hatfield that Mary had died, that she was now queen of England.

She was not, however, the only claimant. Her cousin Mary Stuart, queen of the Scots, had married the French dauphin and claimed to be the rightful queen of England. When the dauphin became king of France, Mary's claim seemed particularly dangerous. The Scots had long been allied with the French, and French influence in Scotland was extensive. The English crossed the border and, allied with Scottish Protestants, forced the French out of Scotland. The Scots recognized Elizabeth's right to the throne and agreed that Mary Stuart would relinquish her claim—an agreement she refused to accept.

Meanwhile, Elizabeth set about the business of governing. William Cecil had helped administer her properties during her sister Mary's reign, and she turned to Cecil now to assist and advise her in governing the realm. Cecil, who later became Lord Burghley, served the queen faithfully for many years, first as her secretary, then as lord treasurer and first minister.

Despite her sister's deathbed pleas, Elizabeth reestablished the Church of England and stopped all pretense of being Catholic. Nevertheless, she generally followed a policy of tolerance toward Catholics who secretly practiced their religion, so long as they faithfully attended Protestant services and gave the outward appearance of adherence to the English Church. Later, when Elizabeth was excommunicated and theoretically "deposed" by the Pope, her attitudes hardened somewhat; but, generally, she was inclined to resist harsh measures in dealing with nonconformists and to deplore extremism and persecution in religious matters.

Elizabeth was notoriously frugal and sought constantly to avoid costly foreign entanglements. Still, her reign was marked by English accomplishments overseas. Among others, Francis Drake circumnavigated the globe, and Walter Raleigh established the first colony in Virginia.

Elizabeth's court was enlivened with music, drama, and dance. She adored and even wrote poetry, and although theatres were considered disreputable and actors generally considered rogues, legend has it that she even disguised herself and attended the public theatre.

Throughout the first part of Elizabeth's reign, the most significant issue for the Council, Parliament, and the people was the need for Elizabeth to marry and produce an heir. Suitors were plentiful, including Phillip of Spain, who apparently had long fancied his sister-in-law, and whose marriage to her would preserve an English alliance with his powerful nation. Other candidates were the French duke of Alençon and the Hapsburg Archduke Charles. There were even Englishmen who considered themselves potential husbands, notably Robert Dudley and Christopher Hatton.

Dudley, the queen's dear "Robin," was master of the horse and rose steadily in Elizabeth's favor. There were early rumors of an affair between the two and, of course, rumors that he planned to marry her. Those rumors grew into a scandal when Dudley's wife died under suspicious circumstances. Dudley was cleared by a coroner's jury, but he remained a highly controversial figure. His close relationship with the queen continued for many years, and she ultimately made him earl of Leicester. It is doubtful, however, that she ever seriously considered him a potential husband.

Hatton, the handsome captain of the queen's personal bodyguard, wrote her passionate love letters and obviously intrigued her. Although he also received many favors from her and ultimately was made lord chancellor, he was never considered a suitable candidate to be her husband.

At a later time, Sir Walter Raleigh became a great favorite of the queen. Like Leicester and Hatton, however, he was not material for a royal marriage. Phillip of Spain and Archduke Charles were, of course, serious and formidable candidates. Nevertheless, Elizabeth deftly and politely fended off both matches.

The duke of Alençon was another matter. A small but charming man, he seemed to delight the queen, and their courtship fostered a French alliance against Spain, which Elizabeth sought to preserve. She may have turned to the engaging Frenchman for another reason as well. She had discovered that her beloved Leicester, although continuing to profess his love for her, had secretly married Lettice Knollys, one of the queen's ladies in waiting. Elizabeth was outraged and the couple feared for their safety—probably unnecessarily. The queen consoled herself with Alençon. Still, in the end, he too was rejected—perhaps regretfully. Since Alençon was a Catholic, and a French Catholic at that, the English were never enthusiastic about the match.

There are those who contend that Elizabeth had an incorrectable physical defect that would have prevented any sexual union and that this knowledge led her to ward off marriage. There is no real evidence to support this, and it seems more likely that she preferred to rule as the "Virgin Queen," free from any dominance or even significant influence from a royal consort, particularly one with ties to Rome or to a foreign power.

Meanwhile, Mary Stuart, the Scottish queen, had married Lord Darnley, a handsome and daring scoundrel who was ultimately murdered. After Darnley's death, Mary married his enemy, the earl of Bothwell, a man hugely unpopular with the powerful lords of Scotland. Ultimately, they crushed him. Mary was forced to abdicate the Scottish throne and was held captive by Bothwell's conquerors. She escaped to England, where she was placed by Elizabeth in comfortable but close confinement.

But the problem of Mary Stuart would not go away. Over and over again, Catholic and Spanish plots were formed to depose Elizabeth and place Mary on the English throne. As war with Spain became a more serious possibility, the plots grew more dangerous. Ultimately, Mary was discovered to have been personally involved in one such treasonous scheme. Now, Elizabeth had no choice. In 1587, after much hesitation, she finally assented to Mary's execution. After the sentence was carried out, Elizabeth blamed it on her secretary and advisors, calling it "that miserable accident" in a letter to Mary's son James, the Scottish king. Presumably, taking the blame for such "accidents" was part of a secretary's job. No one contradicted the queen.

Relations with Spain grew steadily worse. Hawkins and Drake had openly attacked Spanish colonies in the New World, obviously with Elizabeth's acquiescence. There was also continued pressure on the queen to support the Dutch in seeking independence from Spain. Reluctantly, she permitted an English army to fight there under Leicester's command.

It now became clear that Phillip II of Spain was preparing a mighty armada to effect an invasion of England. In a daring raid on Cadiz, Drake caught much of the Spanish fleet off guard, destroyed many ships, and postponed the attack on England for a year.

Phillip was angry and determined to rebuild the armada and carry out the invasion. About this time, he and Elizabeth, who had been brother and sister-in-law and even potentially husband and wife, appear to have exchanged verses. The originals were in Latin. They are translated here. Phillip's verse was, in essence, an ultimatum:

> *1. I bid you make no armed defense of the Belgians.*
> *2. See that you restore Drake's plundered treasures.*
> *3. Rebuild the (monastic) cells your father emptied.*
> *4. Restore perfectly the religion of the Pope.*

Elizabeth's reply was brief and characteristic:

> *When Greeks measure months by the moon,*
> *Then, Spanish Phillip, thy will shall be done.*

Since the Greeks were known for *not* measuring months by the moon, Elizabeth was saying "never!"

In July 1588, the armada finally came, and, with it, perhaps Elizabeth's finest hour. With the enormous Spanish fleet in the channel, Elizabeth addressed the troops deployed at Tilbury to resist an expected invasion up the Thames estuary:

> Let tyrants fear: I have always so behaved myself that, under God, I have placed my chiefest strength and safeguard in the loyal hearts and good-will of my subjects . . . I am come among you at this time . . . being resolved in the midst and heat of the battle to live and die amongst you all, to lay down for my God and for my Kingdom and for my people mine honor and my blood even in the dust. I know I have the body but of a weak and feeble woman, but I have the heart and stomach of a King—and a King of England too!"

The English ships were smaller but were better manned and more maneuverable and had longer-range guns. They kept at a distance and raked the massive Spanish galleons with cannon fire, causing great damage. When the Spanish fleet took shelter just off Calais, the English sent fire ships among the large and clumsy galleons anchored closely together. The damage was enormous. When the Spanish tried to fight free of the anchorage, further destruction was caused by numerous collisions, as well as by fierce attacks from the small, swift English ships. The great Spanish fleet was broken up and scattered primarily into the North Sea, where storms did further damage, driving many of the Spanish ships onto the rocks and cliffs of Scotland and Ireland. England was saved, and Elizabeth was seen as its savior.

But this glorious triumph was followed by events of great sadness for the now aging queen. Leicester, her dear "Robin," died only a month after the armada's defeat. For a time, Elizabeth was inconsolable in her grief.

Later still, she came to the bedside of the dying Christopher Hatton, whose passing was another grievous personal loss. Then, in 1590, came the death of Sir Francis Walsingham, long her trusted advisor, spymaster, and protector against the numerous plots and schemes that had so often endangered her. Finally, she lost her trusted old friend Burghley, her "partner" in governing the kingdom for forty years. It seemed that all of the men that had supported her personally and politically for so long were falling away one at a time, leaving her alone and unprotected.

But she had one last personal relationship. Maybe it was just a lengthy and ego-building flirtation for the aging queen. Maybe it was more.

Robert Devereaux, the young earl of Essex, was a tall, handsome youth, and a descendent of Edward III. He was Leicester's stepson and the son of Elizabeth's old nemesis, Lettice Knollys. Essex had come to court in 1587 when he was but a teenager. Elizabeth, who was fifty-four at the time, was much taken with the charming, attractive young man. Her beauty had long ago faded. She wore a red wig and used heavy cosmetics in a vain attempt to thwart the ravages of time. But she was still a brilliant and fascinating woman. Perhaps Essex was attracted to her. More likely, he was attracted by her position and the opportunities for advancement it presented.

As time went on, a close relationship developed between the two. Obviously, the queen thrived on the young earl's ardent compliments and attentions. He flattered her outrageously, referring often to her incomparable beauty. She appeared ready to believe whatever he said. Soon, Essex became a "favorite." Lucrative offices and benefits were bestowed on him, which helped him meet the staggering expenses of his lavish lifestyle.

But the young earl was hardly just a drawing-room fop. Brave, adventurous, and skilled in arms, he enjoyed considerable success in tournaments and fought bravely in the lowlands campaign.

He was, however, given to foolish and arrogant behavior, acquiring dangerous enemies in the process. He incurred the enmity of Lord Admiral Howard by signing a joint report on the fighting against the Spanish immediately beneath the text, leaving the proud lord admiral no place to sign but below him.

And, there was a cruel and vindictive side to Essex. Dr. Roderigo Lopez was a Portuguese Jew who had converted to Christianity. Lopez had been Leicester's physician and later became personal physician to the queen. Elizabeth was fond of the doctor, whom she called her "little ape." It seems that Lopez had also been a valuable spy for Walsingham, and thus for the queen. After Walsingham's death, Essex set out to destroy the man. Perhaps this was because of the physician's prior association with Leicester or his unwillingness to serve Essex in spying on Elizabeth, or both. With Walsingham's protection gone, Lopez found himself charged and convicted of trying to poison the queen. The evidence was almost surely trumped up and was probably supplied by Essex and his friends.

The queen was troubled and angry with Essex over the episode; but, for some reason, she was unwilling or felt herself unable to overturn the "legal" process. On June 7, 1594, Lopez was hanged, drawn, and quartered at Tyburn before an enthusiastic crowd.

It appears that, between the physician's trial and his execution, Essex fostered anti-Semitic fervor by encouraging numerous performances of Marlowe's *The Jew of Malta*, in which Barabbas, a Jewish moneylender, is portrayed as a murderous traitor and villain. Perhaps these dramatic events moved Shakespeare to give us the towering and multifaceted Shylock in *The Merchant of Venice*.

But Elizabeth was facing other critical problems. Phillip of Spain was readying a massive second armada with which he was determined to effect an invasion and conquest of England—and with it, the overthrow of Elizabeth and the establishment of the old religion. As she did on many occasions, the queen forgave Essex his part in the Lopez affair. He and Raleigh led another naval and military raid on Cadiz, resulting in the destruction of the Spanish fleet and the frustration—at least for a time—of Phillip's plan.

Although Essex complained that Raleigh was getting too much credit for the Cadiz raid, it was Essex who was becoming enormously popular with the English people. Elizabeth was of two minds about that. Acceptance and praise were fine. Adulation of anyone other than the queen herself could be dangerous, especially if, like Essex, the object of that public adoration could muster a reasonable claim to the throne. Despite this risk, Elizabeth reveled in Essex's company and was less cautious than she might otherwise have been.

Essex developed a circle of enthusiastic friends and supporters, including the brilliant Francis Bacon and his brother Anthony. Repeatedly, Essex tried to use his influence with Elizabeth to further Bacon's career—usually without success. Was he trying to give Bacon greater importance in order to enhance his own position? Perhaps.

Finally, Phillip of Spain assembled another vast armada designed to invade and subjugate England. This time, with the massive fleet in the harbor at Ferrol, Essex sought the queen's permission to lead another preemptive strike like the one at Cadiz. Reluctant, as usual, to take on the expense of such an expedition, she finally relented.

Essex led his flotilla south toward Ferrol, hoping to add to the glory he had achieved at Cadiz. It was not to be. A sudden and violent storm scattered the English ships and prevented any attack. Unwilling to return home to Elizabeth with vast sums spent and nothing accomplished, Essex sailed his fleet toward the West Indies hoping to capture the enormously valuable Spanish treasure ships making their way back to Spain.

What Essex had not grasped was that his diversion of the fleet into the Atlantic left England totally unprotected against the Spanish armada that still lay untouched in the harbor at Ferrol. Realizing the magnitude of Essex's error, the Spanish king gave the order for his new armada to sail at once. He would invade England and finally rid the world of this troublesome, heretic woman.

The Spanish admiral protested vigorously. His ships were not ready. His men were not adequately trained. But Phillip would hear none of it. His enemy lay unprotected and open to invasion. The fleet must sail at once. Sail it did. But not to England. Almost as soon as it left port, the new armada was hit with another major storm. Between the devastation caused by the fierce winds and high seas and the Spaniards' appalling lack of seamanship, much of the great fleet was lost or left unable to fight. What remained of it limped back into the harbor at Ferrol.

Once again, England was saved. But Elizabeth realized the grave peril in which Essex had placed her realm—and herself—through his irresponsible conduct. She was enraged, and the two remained apart for some time.

The public, however, failing to understand his dangerous error, adored the dashing earl even more than before.

The queen found herself in a state of conflict. She realized now how unreliable and even dangerous Essex could be. Yet she missed him. Life without him was insufferably dull.

Ultimately, Elizabeth forgave him, and he was restored to court. Stupidly, he used the opportunity to begin a series of ill-concealed affairs with ladies of the court, humiliating and angering the aged queen. Yet Essex always seemed able to pacify her, until finally an extraordinary scene occurred.

With several courtiers present, Elizabeth was discussing the appointment of a lord deputy for Ireland. The queen indicated her intention to appoint Sir William Knollys, Essex's uncle. But Essex wanted to continue his uncle's influence at court and opposed his being sent so far from the seat of power. He suggested an alternative candidate, whom Elizabeth rejected out of hand.

Soon, tempers were flaring. Essex spoke to the queen in an insolent tone, then turned on his heel, showing his back to her. This was a grave insult. Elizabeth rushed forward and boxed the earl's ears, crying out, "Go to the devil!"

Furious, Essex put his hand on his sword. No one knew what he intended. "This is an outrage that I will not put up with. I would not have borne it from your father's hands."

Before anything further could occur, Lord Admiral Howard placed himself between Essex and the queen, pressing the earl backward. After a moment, Essex turned and rushed from the room to a collective gasp from all present.

Now a long separation ensued. Elizabeth was, once again, torn. She could not be seen to overlook this grievous, public breach by Essex. Still, she did miss his company. The queen turned to Francis Bacon for advice. Despite Essex's unstinting efforts to help Bacon in the past, Bacon cautioned the queen against the mercurial earl. Essex, he said, if free and humiliated, was so popular and so irresponsible as to be dangerous. If the earl was to remain free, it would be prudent to avoid anything he might consider an insult. Bacon didn't say so explicitly, but Elizabeth was certainly bright enough to catch the unspoken thought that perhaps Essex should not remain free.

The queen chose the other alternative. She brought about a reconciliation with Essex. She would try not to humiliate him and would enjoy his presence. But she was alert now to the danger he posed, and their relationship was never the same.

Meanwhile, Tyrone, the leader of the Irish rebels, had defeated or outwitted one English general after another. If the military situation in Ireland seemed favorable, he would fight and inflict a costly defeat on his English opponents. If it did not, he would promise a truce, which he would violate as soon as the danger passed.

Although characteristically concerned about the cost, Elizabeth discussed with her council appointing someone capable of leading an English army into Ireland and destroying this troublesome rebel once and for all. Essex was advised by his friends to feign a willingness to command such an army, but not to accept the position under any circumstances if it was offered. This was sound advice. Tyrone was a skilled commander and could, quite possibly, inflict a humiliating and career-ending loss on whoever undertook the high-profile assignment.

Robert Cecil, Burghley's brilliant, hunchbacked son, had become the queen's secretary. He was well aware of the danger posed by Essex and thoroughly grasped the Irish situation. When Essex made what was probably a feigned offer to lead the Irish expedition, Cecil quickly accepted the offer and flattered the earl with assertions that he was the only man for the job. Always commanded by his ego and ignoring the sage advice he had received, Essex committed himself irrevocably.

The English public was filled with martial spirit, and Essex was the hero of the day. Even Shakespeare's chorus, accompanying *Henry V*, added a tribute to the swashbuckling earl:

> *Were now the general of our gracious Empress,*
> *As in good time he may from Ireland coming,*
> *Bringing rebellion broached on his sword,*
> *How many would the peaceful city quit*
> *To welcome him!*

Essex arrived in Dublin at the head of a large, well-equipped English army. He was ready to meet Tyrone. But the Irish leader had minor allies who would support him against the English. Foolishly, Essex decided to attack these lesser allies first and, only when they were defeated, to turn on Tyrone. The English won some minor and insignificant battles and took some castles of no particular military value. In the process, a significant number of Essex's men were killed or wounded. Even more were lost to disease.

Essex returned to Dublin, where he came to the conclusion that he had insufficient men left to defeat Tyrone's main army. He was horrified at his dilemma. If he attacked Tyrone and lost, he'd be ruined, if not killed. If he returned to London, having spent a fortune, lost a significant part of his army, and accomplished nothing, the queen would be enraged. At the very least, he would be a laughingstock. What could he do? The fact is he did nothing— for months. The queen wrote angry letters urging Essex to attack. Ultimately, she ordered him not to return to England until Tyrone was beaten.

At last, in desperation, Essex led his diminished force out of Dublin to meet Tyrone's army. He was ready to die rather than suffer public disgrace. On the eve of the battle, however, Tyrone asked for a parley. When the two leaders met, the wily Irishman proposed a truce. Perhaps Tyrone did not share Essex's view that the English forces were insufficient. Essex realized this was Tyrone's usual strategy and that the Irish leader was not likely to keep the truce once the English army left. Nevertheless, the very relieved earl accepted Tyrone's terms.

When word reached London, Elizabeth was furious. The vain fool had lost thousands of good men. He had knighted numerous others for no good reason, presumably making staunch supporters of them. Worse still, he had squandered a fortune and had accomplished nothing. There were even rumors that Essex had assured Tyrone that he would soon seize power in England and that their "truce" was really a sort of mutual aid pact.

Defying the queen's orders, a desperate Essex rode hard for London, crossed the river and dashed headlong for Elizabeth's Nonsuch Palace in Surrey. Muddy and disheveled from his long ride, he rushed into the palace. Unannounced, he pushed his way into the queen's own chamber, where her ladies in waiting were helping her dress. Her hair was down, and she was without the heavy makeup she regularly wore.

Frightened at Essex's intrusion and wild appearance, the queen feigned pleasure at seeing him and bantered with him in a frivolous, teasing way. Finally, Essex was eased out, pleasantly surprised that the queen still seemed to love him. In fact, it was their last face-to-face meeting.

Elizabeth knew now that something must be done. She could not continue this charade indefinitely. Bacon's advice remained the same and was delivered with even less ambiguity. If the queen was unwilling to embrace

Essex and ignore his Irish debacle, she must confine him. Essex, still hugely popular, desperate, and free, was extremely dangerous. Elizabeth agreed. The earl was immediately placed under house arrest. After a time, he was induced to make an abject apology for his conduct of the Irish campaign. It was not enough for Elizabeth. His confinement continued.

After ten months of house arrest, Elizabeth finally freed him. Lord Mountjoy had successfully put down the Irish rebellion, shaming Essex even more for his own failure at the same assignment. Perhaps Elizabeth felt that this public humiliation was, in itself, a significant punishment for the vainglorious earl. If so, it was not the only punishment. The queen banned Essex from court and stripped him of his lucrative monopoly in importing sweet wine. Essex pleaded that these punishments be withdrawn. His expenses were great, and losing the wine monopoly was a crushing blow.

On one fateful occasion, hearing a reference to "the queen's conditions," he shouted, "Her conditions! Her conditions are as crooked as her carcass!" The insult was repeated to Elizabeth, who must have been devastated by its cruelty, painfully contrasting it with the ambitious earl's glowing references to her beauty. Undoubtedly, she now grasped fully what a supreme hypocrite he was and how foolish she had been to believe him.

Characteristically, she took no precipitous action. She waited. As Essex grew more desperate, a group of followers—mostly hot-blooded young aristocrats, like the earl of Southampton—gathered around him, urging him to take action. His claim to the throne was better than Elizabeth's, they argued. He should seize it.

Essex's own mind wavered from hour to hour, torn between inertia and rebellion. Even when he thought of rebellion, he was not clear as to whether he intended to seize the throne or merely to protect Elizabeth by ridding her of the "evil men," like Robert Cecil and Lord Admiral Howard, who surrounded and advised her.

Finally, stirred by the vigorous urgings of his followers, he decided to act and, apparently, to seize the throne for himself. The earl's allies arranged for a performance of Shakespeare's *Richard II*, showing the deposition and assassination of that reigning king by Bolingbroke, who became Henry IV. The performance was clearly designed to persuade the public that there are times when even a legitimate monarch must be overthrown.

The next morning, a delegation of notables visited Essex's home to warn him against any act of treason. They were taken hostage by Essex's partisans who were gathered there. There was no turning back now. Armed and shouting their slogans, Essex and his band entered the city hoping to attract a mob of citizens to their cause and then to march on the palace.

But Cecil had anticipated and outwitted them. The citizens of London had been ordered to stay at home behind closed doors. They obeyed. No one joined Essex and his followers as they passed through the empty streets, desperately shouting for the people to rally to the earl's cause. Realizing the game was up, Essex made his way to the river and from there to his home. Ultimately, he and his principal followers were apprehended. This time, there were no half measures. The earl was sent to the Tower.

His trial for treason was one of the great spectacles of the age. Ironically, the prosecution was led by his former friend and ally Francis Bacon, whose career Essex had consistently tried to advance. Now, Bacon had achieved that preeminence—at Essex's expense. In addressing the court, Essex took a line from Shakespeare's *Henry IV*, Part 1, declaring, "I owe God a death."

The earl was convicted and, shortly thereafter, was quietly beheaded within the Tower grounds. It was said that this had been Essex's own last request. More likely, the queen's advisors considered a public execution, before an excited mob, too big a risk.

Many thought that, at the last minute, the queen would grant Essex a reprieve—even forgive him, as she had so often in the past. This time, she did not. Perhaps she could not erase from her mind his cruel remark about her crooked carcass, or perhaps she fully grasped the danger he would always pose if allowed to live. Most likely, it was both.

But Elizabeth was aging and weakening. Her "Golden Speech" of November 30, 1601, was one of her last appearances before Parliament. It is another that has been treasured by Englishmen over the centuries:

> There will never Queen sit in my seat with more zeal to my country, care to my subjects, and that will sooner with willingness venture her life for your good and safety than myself. . . . And though you have had, and may have, many princes more mighty and wise sitting in this seat, yet you never had, nor shall have, any that will be more careful and loving.

In March 1603, it became obvious that the great queen was dying. Unwilling to take to her bed, she lay for days on a pile of cushions heaped on the floor of her chamber. Robert Cecil finally told her that, to content an anxious public, she "must go to bed." The old fire blazed one more time. "Little man," she rasped, "is 'must' a word to use to princes?"

Elizabeth died on March 24, 1603, to the nation's great sorrow and the accolades of virtually every poet, author, and political figure. One famous author said nothing. Inexplicably, the well-known poet and playwright William Shakespeare made no comment on the great queen's death.

Elizabeth was succeeded by James Stuart, who had been James VI of Scotland. While she had not formally designated a successor, she was certainly aware that Robert Cecil had quietly arranged for the Scottish king to assume the throne of England when at last she died. Only with her last breath did Elizabeth supposedly agree to this, whispering so that only Cecil heard. "I will that a king succeed me, and who but my kinsman the king of Scots." Did she really say this? No one will ever know.

The son of Mary, Queen of Scots and her roguish husband, Lord Darnley, James now became James I of England. Being a direct descendant of Henry VII, James had a viable claim to the throne. He had other qualifications as well. He had served for years as king of the Scots, his ancestors had ruled Scotland since the fourteenth century, and he was highly intelligent and well educated.

The Puritan movement grew strong during James's reign. He had been raised a Protestant, but was generally tolerant of Catholics. After the "gunpowder plot" of 1605, however, his attitude and treatment of Catholics hardened. The gunpowder plot was a Catholic scheme to murder James by blowing up the Westminster Palace as he opened the new session of Parliament on November 5, 1605. The plot was uncovered when one of the conspirators wrote, warning his brother-in-law to stay away from Parliament during that session. The recipient of the letter brought it to Robert Cecil, who took immediate steps to protect the king and Parliament. Guy Fawkes was captured in the cellar of the palace about to light the fuse on enough gunpowder to blow up everyone who might be in or near the building. Since then, the holiday commemorating the event has been called "Guy Fawkes Day," and children seeking a holiday gift cry out "a penny for the old Guy."

But the true organizer of the plot was Robert Catesby, who had gathered a group of powerful Catholics in Warwickshire purportedly for a hunt, but actually to effect a takeover of the government once the king and the members of Parliament had been killed.

James resisted strong puritan pressure to abolish the episcopy, uttering his famous line "No bishop, no king." He also directed preparation of a new version of the Bible, still known as the King James Version. Reportedly, Shakespeare revised some of the biblical verses. In the new version of Psalm 46, the forty-sixth word from the beginning is *shake* and, leaving out the word *Selah*, which is a Hebrew notation and not part of the psalm, the forty-sixth word from the end is *spear*. This may or may not be evidence of the Bard's participation. And, even if it is, it doesn't tell us who he was.

James enjoyed plays and was a patron of the theatre. Shakespeare's own company, previously the Lord Chamberlain's Men, became the King's Men in his reign.

Although a homosexual who had a number of male "favorites," James was married to a Danish princess, with whom he produced six children, two sons and four daughters. One of his sons succeeded him as Charles I.

James tried to pursue a policy of peace with Spain, which ultimately proved unsuccessful. James was extravagant and had a running battle with an increasingly powerful Parliament to obtain the funds he needed. He also had trouble with some of Elizabeth's best men, notably Francis Bacon, who was stripped of his offices for taking bribes, and Sir Walter Raleigh, who was executed for conspiring to commit treason.

James died in 1625, nine years after the Stratford man and two years after publication of the famous First Folio containing the complete plays of William Shakespeare. Thus, two of the most important volumes in the English language were created in James's reign: the First Folio and the King James Bible.

Having summarized the events of the reigns of Elizabeth and James, we can now consider how those events affected the life and writings of Shakespeare and can turn our attention to solving the mystery of whether he was, in fact, the Stratford man or, if not, who he really was.

Part II

WAS SHAKSPER SHAKESPEARE?

✠

2.

SHAKSPER'S LIFE

*T*o begin our analysis, we must compare the life of the Stratford man with what we know about the life of "Shakespeare" to determine whether it is probable they were the same person.

The problem is that we know very little about the life of the Stratford man *or* that of the poet and playwright known as William Shakespeare. One note of caution is important here. We must be careful to analyze the two lives separately, avoiding the common error of assuming that the Stratford man *was* the poet and playwright and drawing potentially false conclusions from that assumption.

For example, it is sometimes argued that the Stratford man "must have" served in the army or in a lawyer's office or visited Italy because of the information about the military, the law, and Italy found in Shakespeare's plays.

But that information tells us only that *the author of the plays* may have served in the army or studied law or spent time in Italy. It does not tell us that *the Stratford man* did these things—unless we start with the unproved assumption that he *was* the plays' sole author.

Similarly, it is argued that a particular play "must have" been written at a later date than might otherwise be chosen, because the Stratford man was too young at any earlier date to have written with the depth and maturity inherent in the play. Such reasoning ignores the possibility that the play was written by someone else.

Biographies of "Shakespeare" sometimes fill hundreds of pages. Typically, they expand the few facts we really know by assuming that Shakespeare was the Stratford man. They abound with assertions about what the Stratford man "must have," "would have" or "might have" done, because Shakespeare's writings lead to the inference that *Shakespeare* did those things. But they provide very few hard facts about what the Stratford man actually did. Those things we definitely know about him, as opposed to what we might speculate or assume, can be reported in just a few pages. This might not be strange in the case of other sixteenth- or seventeenth-century figures. In the case of a man assumed to be Shakespeare, it is particularly strange, since armies of scholars, authors, and others have searched for centuries, seeking any fact, any document, any detail or clue they could unearth about his life.

Most of what we know about the Stratford man is gleaned from official records and documents. No letters, diaries, or manuscripts by him have ever been found. Not even a single note, outline, or memo—not a word written in the hand of the Stratford man—exists or, so far as we know, ever existed.

The Stratford man was born Gulielmus (William) Shakspere in 1564, in or near Stratford-upon-Avon, then a provincial market town of about 1,500 people on the north bank of the river Avon, about 100 miles from London. The town was surrounded by open fields. Along with selling goods, sewing, and brewing ale, working in those fields was the principal occupation. Many Stratford households tried to manage all four activities.

Stratford was in the midlands, but it was more like the northern part of England in the slowness with which it adopted the many new developments that were occurring in London. Elizabeth had been on the throne five years when the Stratford man was born. The Elizabethan Age was coming into bloom, but its impact was far less evident in rural Stratford than in the teeming capital.

The Stratford man's mother was Mary Arden, the daughter of a well-to-do farmer. His father, listed on the record of his baptism as Johannes (John) Shakspere, was a glove maker and "whitawer," a dresser of soft white leather.

John Shakspere was probably a secret Catholic. In 1757, a written testament to his secretly following the Catholic faith was found hidden in the rafters of the family home. The reign of Elizabeth was a time of serious danger for Catholics who were open in practicing their religion. Although Elizabeth was generally tolerant, Catholics were required to practice their faith privately; some 200 Catholics were cruelly executed during her reign, primarily for speaking out on the subject or, worse, seeking to convert Protestants.

John Shakspere was not a Stratford native, having been born in nearby Snitterfield. His first recorded appearance in Stratford was in April 1552, when he was fined one shilling for maintaining a dunghill on Henley Street. Defenders of the Stratford man have tended to call this a "muck hill" or to use some other euphemism. But it was, in fact, a pile of manure (*fecerunt sterquinarium*)—and on the town's main thoroughfare. In 1570, when William was six years old, his father was fined forty shillings for twice charging usurious interest of twenty pounds on loans of eighty pounds and one hundred pounds. In 1571, John was fined forty shillings for illegal wool dealings.

Seemingly, Shaksper, Shaxpere, Shackspere, and the like, as the name was generally spelled in Stratford, were pronounced with a short *a* as in *shack*, rather than a long *a*, as in *shake*. But sixteenth-century spelling varied widely and no one seemed to care. Contemporaries of the Stratford man may have pronounced his name Shakespeare (with a long *a*) even when they were spelling it Shaksper, Shaxpere, or something similar.

There is some evidence suggesting this. For example, in 1609, the actor Edward Alleyn noted his purchase of *Shaksper Sonnets*, when the title page plainly stated that they were *Shake-speare's Sonnets*.

Was this merely careless spelling by Alleyn, who certainly knew the Stratford man? Or was the long *a* pronunciation always used, regardless of the seemingly short *a* spelling? We do not know.

The name *Shakspere* is said to have derived from the French name *Jacques Pierre*, with the English, unlike the French, pronouncing the *s* in "Jacques." Another view is that the name stemmed from "Isaac's spear," with the *I* gradually dropping to form "Saacspear," suggesting that the Bard had Jewish antecedents. There is no evidence to support either theory. Both, however, seem consistent with a short *a* pronunciation (as in "shock" or "shack") rather than a long *a* (as in "shake"). A principal character in *As You Like It* is spelled "Jaques," rather than the French "Jacques." Harold Bloom suggests that the Elizabethan pronunciation of "Jaques" was "Jakes."

He cites no authority for this, and, in any event, it doesn't tell us the Elizabethan pronunciation of "Jacques."

Stratford was governed by a bailiff, a council of fourteen aldermen, and fourteen burgesses. The burgesses were originally the owners of allotted land parcels called *burgages*. By the time of the Stratford man, the burgages had long ago been sold off or subdivided. Some men owned more than one burgage, others only a fraction. Most families rented their homes, rather than owning them.

In the 1560s, notwithstanding his brushes with the law, John Shakspere first became an official ale taster and then rose to the position of burgess and alderman. In 1568, he even served as the town bailiff—in effect, its mayor.

Later, however, probably beginning in 1576, John came upon hard times. He accumulated troublesome debts, absented himself from council meetings, and ultimately resigned from the council. He also stopped attending church. It was said that this was to avoid service of process, although why, in a town that small, he could not be served at home or on the street is not explained.

In 1578, John was sued on a thirty-pound debt, and, evidently, things became so bad that the council gave him an exemption from paying his local taxes. In that same year, he had to sell land to raise cash; and, in 1579, he mortgaged his wife's property in nearby Wilmcote and sold her share of her father's property in Snitterfield—apparently for the same purpose.

Most probably, neither John nor Mary Shakspere could read, write, or even sign their names. We know that John Shakspere signed documents with his mark. Stratfordians argue that he may have *chosen* to sign with a mark, even if he could write his name. This is possible, but not likely. It is true that he held responsible public offices in which reading and writing would have been a decided advantage. But it appears that, when John held office, the majority of the town council was illiterate. Judging only by signatures on recorded documents and omitting lawyers and clerics, who almost surely could read, 163 Stratford residents signed their names, while 123 only made their marks. And even the 163 who had learned to sign their names could not necessarily read or write anything else.

We know almost nothing about the first eighteen years of the Stratford man's life. Typically, Stratford boys left home at fourteen to be apprenticed for seven years of service. There is a story that young William worked in a butcher's shop and that he would kill a calf "in high style and make a speech." The tale is most probably apocryphal, although it is conceivable that his father sold meat as an adjunct to his trade as a glove maker and whitawer.

Although William *may* have attended the local grammar school at least part of the time, there is no hard evidence that he had any education at all. The school records are no longer extant.

Writing in the early eighteenth century, Nicholas Rowe, Shakespeare's first biographer, said that he attended the local grammar school "for some time," but that "the narrowness of his circumstances and the want of his assistance at home forced his father to withdraw him from thence and unhappily prevented his further Proficiency in that Language (i.e., Latin)." But Rowe is not always reliable, and, despite his assertion, the Stratford man may have completed the school or may never have attended it at all.

The late Samuel Schoenbaum, director of the Folger Shakespeare Library and a leading Stratfordian, wrote that "we need not doubt that Shakespeare received a grammar school education and the only likely place for it was the King's New School of Stratford-upon-Avon." When Schoenbaum refers to "Shakespeare," he means the Stratford man, and we may indeed have some doubt in the matter. This is a prime example of the "he must have" school of biographical writing.

Of course, if, like Schoenbaum, we begin with the premise that Shakespeare *was* the Stratford man, the scope and magnificence of the Bard's work supports the conclusion that he had a very significant education. But if we cast aside that unproven first premise, the conclusion is wholly without evidentiary support.

It has been argued that Shakespeare's plays contain references to books commonly used in English grammar schools. But this only tells us that *the playwright* had an education, not that the Stratford man had one. Here again, it is only if we assume that the playwright *was* the Stratford man that we can infer from references in the plays that the Stratford man attended an English grammar school.

Regardless of whether or not he attended school, it is generally assumed that the Stratford man could read and write. It would have been difficult (but not impossible) for an illiterate to perform as an actor, as he almost certainly did. On the other hand, we have only six signatures that are supposedly by the Stratford man. In 1612, he gave a deposition in a London lawsuit. It is signed "Willm Shaksp" in a childish, almost illegible hand. A 1613 deed to some London property is signed "William Shaksp_." On the mortgage of that property it is "Wm Shaksp_" with what appears to be a small *a* floating above the *e*. Then, there are three very shaky signatures on his will made in 1616, one on each of the three pages. The first appears to be "William Shakspere," the next "Willm Shakspere," and the last "William Shaks pear," with what might be an *e* following the *r*.

Most people who can write tend to develop regular, virtually fixed forms of signature. The Stratford man's six varying, unsteady signatures suggest someone not accustomed to writing or even signing his name. William Beeston, the son of a London actor who knew the Stratford man when he was active in the theatre, reportedly said, "If invited to writ, he was in paine."

There were, of course, no typewriters in the Elizabethan age. The Stratford man appears, at best, to have had little facility in the physical act of writing. If so, how could he have written *by hand* at least thirty-six plays, two long narrative poems, and 154 sonnets, creating hundreds of manuscript pages in which Ben Jonson reported in *De Shakespeare Nostrati*, "He never blotted out a line."

The Folger Library in Washington, D.C., has a 1568 textbook on law with the difficult name *Apxaionomia*. Inside the book, someone has written the name *Wm. Shakspere*. Tests have indicated that the ink is from the Elizabethan period. The hand seems somewhat different from the six known signatures of the Stratford man. Still, it could be his, and, if it is, it suggests not only the ability to read, but also an interest in the law. On the other hand, if the owner of a book wanted to sell it, writing *Wm. Shakspere* inside the cover might well have increased the price it could command.

Passing the unsolved mystery of the Stratford man's education and ability to read and write, we return to the sparse knowledge about his life. After his birth and baptism, the next thing we really *know* about him is his marriage. There are, of course, many interim possibilities about which many can and do speculate. Anthony Holden and others have the teenage Stratford man serve as a tutor and sometime actor in Catholic homes in Lancashire.

There is a record of a "William Shakeshafte" occupying such a position in 1581. But *Shakeshafte* was a relatively common name in Lancashire; and we know that, only the next year, 1582, the Stratford man was in Stratford getting a local woman pregnant and marrying her.

On November 27, 1582, when he was eighteen, "Wm Shaxpere" of Stratford took out a license to marry "Annum Whateley de Temple Grafton." Curiously enough, the very next day, a bond is recorded for the marriage of "William Shagspere" to "Anne Hathwey of Stratford."

The two men who provided the bond did so by making their marks, not signing their names. Both appear to have been staunch friends of Anne Hathwey's recently deceased father, which suggests that the marriage may not have been altogether voluntary on the groom's part. Other facts may support that inference. The bride was eight years older than her teenage husband, an enormous difference to an eighteen-year-old boy. She was also three months pregnant when the marriage took place.

Did young William intend to marry Anne Whateley only to be waylaid by two angry farmers and forced, the next day, to marry Anne Hathwey instead? Probably not. The two Annes were probably the same woman, and the disparate entries were just a clerical error.

The bride's name was actually Agnes Hathwey, and she was the daughter of a farmer from Shottery, a town near Stratford. To biographers, however, she was "Anne," which apparently was a common variation of the name *Agnes*. To Stratford merchants, she is the now famous "Anne Hathaway," and what is supposed to have been her cottage has become a prime tourist attraction.

The couple went on to have three children: Susanna, born in May 1583, and twins, Hamnet and Judith, born in February 1585. By then, after less than three years of marriage, the Stratford man seems to have grown restless. Following the birth of the twins in 1585, he left his home and family. At some point, no later than 1592, he began a stay of at least twelve years in London, living primarily in rooming houses.

It has been reported by Nicholas Rowe and others that Shakespeare was forced to leave Stratford after being caught poaching deer in a private park owned by Sir Thomas Lucy in Charlcote, near Stratford. There are lines in Shakespeare that could be construed as references to Sir Thomas and to a justice of the peace who might have presided over such a case.

In *The Merry Wives of Windsor*, Justice Shallow complains that Falstaff has broken into his property and killed his deer. Shallow's cousin Slender describes the justice's coat of arms as containing "a dozen white luces" (pike). Another character, the Welsh parson Sir Hugh Evans, misunderstands and refers to Shallow's "coat" having a "dozen white louses."

Sir Thomas Lucy was, in fact, a justice of the peace and a man considered ferocious in defending his rights and point of view. His family arms were recorded as "three luces Lauriant argent." Since the Lucy family arms were "quartered," they actually contained a dozen luces, just like Shallow's.

Despite this intriguing reference, which we will discuss, the deer poaching story is probably apocryphal. The Lucy estate was at Charlcote, but it had no deer park until 1618, two years after the Stratford man's death. The Lucys had once had custody of a royal park at nearby Fullbrook; but, even before the Stratford man's birth, it had been "disparked," so that the locals could hunt there without being prosecuted as poachers.

Like the first eighteen years of the Stratford man's life, the years from the birth of his twins in 1585 to 1592, when he is first mentioned in London, are blank. We have no idea where he was or what he was doing in this seven-year period. It is sometimes referred to as the "lost years," although, aside from his baptism, marriage, and the birth of his children, we know nothing certain about his life in the entire *twenty-eight* years between 1564 and 1592.

Nevertheless, the lost years are a total mystery and one that has attracted vigorous and imaginative speculation. Various Stratfordians argue that, in this period, the Stratford man traveled abroad, was apprenticed to an itinerant company of actors, served on a ship, served in the army, taught school, or worked as a lawyer's clerk—thus acquiring some of the knowledge that appears in his works. These things are all possible, but there is no credible evidence that any of these hypotheses represent the true facts. Indeed, the theories tend to contradict each other. It is unlikely that the Stratford man could have done all of them.

Here again, the Stratfordian logic is to assume that the Stratford man *was* Shakespeare and to infer, from the knowledge displayed in Shakespeare's plays, that the Stratford man "must have" had such employment in the lost years.

Anthony Holden suggests that William left Stratford in 1587 with a touring company of actors that played Stratford. According to this theory, a deadly fight between two actors left them one player short just before arriving in Stratford, and young William filled in. While there is no evidence of this, perhaps the Stratford man did join the itinerant troupe and tour with them until they returned to London. It seems clear that he ultimately became an actor, and this may have been the genesis of that career.

By 1592, the Stratford man certainly seems to have arrived in London. The armada had been defeated, and Elizabeth was in her full glory. Although hugely popular as a monarch, she was aging, and her troubles with Essex were soon to begin.

At the time, London was a bustling port city of more than 100,000 inhabitants. It occupied slightly more than one square mile, intersected by the river Thames. Vessels from many lands tied up by the banks of the great river, loading or discharging their goods and sending their crews drinking, whoring, and brawling in the narrow, filthy streets, which were crowded and, at night, generally unsafe. Robbers and cutpurses plied their trade, often with violence and usually with little interference. In the morning, there was less risk, but a passerby would be lucky to avoid being hit by the contents of 10,000 chamber pots flung from the windows of Londoners greeting the new day.

The river was spanned by a single bridge upon which houses were constructed, and the severed heads of traitors were displayed on pikes. On the north bank were St. Paul's Cathedral and the ominous Tower of London. On the south were the arenas for bear baiting and cockfighting, as well as brothels and gambling dens. Taverns lined both sides of the river, providing ale to Londoners shrewd enough to realize that the water supply was polluted with massive quantities of night soil that washed down the alleys and into the river.

The population was generally in poor health. Rats scurried everywhere carrying plague, which periodically swept the city, killing many thousands. Infant and child mortality was overwhelming. Only about 30 percent of those born survived to their fifteenth birthday. Venereal disease was rampant. Most Londoners had rotten teeth, bad skin, and dysentery or other digestive problems. Few had the means or inclination to wash regularly. For most, life was brutish, smelly, and short.

All the more reason to love entertainment. Bear baiting, cockfighting, hideous public executions, and that less bloody show—the theatre—were all wildly popular. Most of these entertainments, as well as London's numerous bordellos, were confined to areas called *liberties* just beyond the jurisdiction of the city. The London theatre of that era was not only a place where plays were performed. It was also a place where pickpockets and prostitutes were plentiful, and a young man out for adventure could find it.

Perhaps attracted by the color and excitement of the theatre, the Stratford man appears to have become an actor. We know from published remarks supposedly by the dying poet Robert Greene that, by 1592, an actor satirically called "Shake-scene," appeared in *Henry VI, Part 3.* Greene's ambiguous remarks have generally been taken as a reference to the Stratford man and construed to mean that the actor was also the author of the play—or at least that Greene thought so. But his statements are a riddle in themselves, as is the surprising reaction to them—subjects we will analyze later.

Prior to 1592, we have only varied tales about the Stratford man's early days in the theatre. Nicholas Rowe has him begin as a prompter's assistant, a likely start for a youth seeking a career on stage—if the youth could read. Another story, adopted by Samuel Johnson, has young William tending the horses left at the playhouse door and doing it so well that he soon hired other youths to tend the horses while he collected the money. None of these tales is supported by any existing evidence.

When the Stratford man was finally cast as an actor, where and for whom did he perform? We don't know for sure the theatre in which Robert Greene saw a performance of *Henry VI.* It could have been the Theatre, built in the northern suburbs in 1576 by James Burbage, the father of Richard Burbage, the great actor and, at least later, colleague of the Stratford man. Through usage, Burbage's trade name for his enterprise became generic, and all such establishments came to be called *theatres.* Greene could also have seen the performance at the nearby Curtain, built in 1577. Most likely, however, it was at the Rose, built by Phillip Henslowe in 1587 on the south side of the Thames in an area catering to bear-baiting pits, brothels, and similar entertainments.

When the Stratford man began his acting career, the public theatres were open to the elements. The bulk of the audience stood in the uncovered area nearest the stage. These groundlings usually paid a penny for admission. There was elevated and usually covered seating farther back, but these seats were more costly.

In about 1591, Edward Alleyn's company, the Lord Admiral's Men, settled into London headquarters at Henslowe's Rose. Alleyn, a renowned actor, married Henslowe's stepdaughter the following year and became Henslowe's partner. Henslowe had moved from Burbages' theatres and had merged his company with another sponsored by Lord Strange.

If the tale about tending horses outside the playhouse door was true, it suggests that the Stratford man started out at the Theatre or the Curtain, since those playhouses would be reached by horseback, rather than by boat, like the Rose. But, of course, the story may be sheer fantasy. By 1592, when Greene wrote his dying missive, the Stratford man had seemingly graduated from tending horses—if that was ever his occupation.

Shakespearean scholars disagree as to whether the Stratford man would have had to serve an apprenticeship in order to become a member of an acting company. Sir Edmund Chambers opined that acting was not one of the professions that required apprenticeship and that the companies would not have required such an unnecessary formality. Others have disagreed, and there is evidence of some acting companies having apprentices. If the Stratford man served the customary apprentice's term of seven years and began that service after his twins were born in 1585, he would have just completed his apprenticeship when Greene apparently saw him perform in 1592.

Henslowe and his son-in-law, Alleyn, put on numerous plays, including plays attributed to Shakespeare. It is probable that the Stratford man appeared as an actor for their company in his early years in London. In the spring of 1592, a play called *Harey the vi* had a number of successful performances at Henslowe's Rose. It was probably Shakespeare's play and the play to which Greene referred.

Plays were also performed at the inns of court and the universities, as well as at the court of Queen Elizabeth. But it is improbable that, at the time Greene wrote, he was in attendance at those venues.

Titus Andronicus is generally considered one of Shakespeare's very early plays, possibly written even before 1592. In his biography of Shakespeare, Sir Sydney Lee recounted a story originally told by "some anciently conversant with the stage" that *Titus* "was not originally his [i.e., Shakespeare's] but brought by a private author to be acted, and he only gave some master-touches to one or two of the principal parts or characters." Lee's assumption was, of course, that the actor from Stratford was the recipient and revisor of the play. According to Lee, the three parts of *Henry VI*, also among the early plays attributed to Shakespeare, were, in fact, not originally by him and that he simply "revised and expanded other men's works."

If these stories are true, they show the Stratford man at the early stage of what may have been a long career of fronting for a private author, while adding his own theatre-wise "master-touches."

In 1594, the Burbages, along with the Stratford man, John Heminge, Augustine Phillips, William Kempe, Thomas Pope, and George Bryan, formed the Lord Chamberlain's Men. The company went on to perform many of Shakespeare's plays. Later, Kempe, Pope, and Bryan dropped out, and Henry Condell was added. The Stratford man, a "sharer" in the company, almost surely performed as an actor for it as well. After James I took the throne in 1603, he issued a royal patent to the principals of the Lord Chamberlain's Men; and, thereafter, the troupe was called the "King's Men."

By 1594, the Stratford man may have contracted gonorrhea, a malady not unusual in London of this period. *Willowbie His Avisa*, an anonymous work of purported fiction that probably refers to actual people, speaks of "a familiar friend W. S.," described as an "old player," who had been involved "in a like passion, and was not newly recovered from a like infection." We do not know if "W. S." was the Stratford man. Although the average life expectancy was less than fifty, it is difficult to believe that an actor of thirty (the Stratford man's age at the time) would have been described as "old."

Verses preceding *Willowbie His Avisa* refer to "Shakespeare" by name as the poet who "paints poor Lucrece's rape," a reference to *The Rape of Lucrece*, a narrative poem Shakespeare published that same year. If "W. S." was meant to be William Shakespeare, the author of *Willowbie* may have believed that the infected "old player" and the poet were the same. But why call him "Shakespeare" in one place and the cryptic "W. S." in another? Was it because of the derogatory reference to "a like infection"? Perhaps; or perhaps he believed they were two different men—and perhaps they were.

"W. S." is also said to be a "familiar friend" to "H. W.," who might have been Henry Wriothesley, the young earl of Southampton, to whom Shakespeare dedicated *Venus and Adonis* and *The Rape of Lucrece*. If so, and if W. S. was the Stratford man, this would suggest a tie between the latter and Southampton that could be taken as evidence supporting the Stratfordian cause. But, if the Stratford man was secretly fronting for someone else who was the true Bard, and the author of *Willowbie* didn't know it, he would naturally assume that the Stratford man and Southampton were friends, even if that were not the case.

In 1595, "Will Shakespeare" is listed along with Richard Burbage as having been paid for acting in plays before the queen. Anti-Stratfordians, some of whom doubt that the Stratford man was even an actor, argue that this was a false entry, fabricated long after the fact to account to an angry Elizabeth for missing sums of money. They point out that, on the dates on which the company was recorded as performing at court, they were actually playing elsewhere.

There is, however, considerable documentary evidence that the Stratford man was, indeed, an actor and co-owner of an acting company. Anti-Strats who fight this conclusion may do a disservice to their cause, casting doubt on the more supportable position that he was an actor, but maybe not the true poet and playwright.

Even if the questioned entry was correct, it would not resolve the issue of whether the man who acted for the queen in 1595 as "Will Shakespeare" was the same man who wrote the poems and plays that appeared under that name. It would, however, indicate either that the actor (presumably the Stratford man) was, by this time, using the same spelling as the author, or else that whoever made the entry simply misspelled his name.

We do not know for certain what roles the Stratford man actually played. Evidently, he was not one of the leading players. Nicholas Rowe reported that his *best* role was that of the ghost in *Hamlet*, a relatively minor part. One story, not necessarily reliable, has him playing the part of Orlando's faithful old servant Adam in *As You Like It*. There is no indication of his having played any of the major Shakespearean roles, such as Hamlet, King Lear, Othello, or Richard III. But no cast list is extant for any particular Shakespearean play performed during the Stratford man's lifetime.

While in London, the Stratford man was, from time to time, involved in petty litigation and controversy. At least twice, he was cited for failing to pay his taxes. In 1596, William Shakspere, Francis Langley, and others were alleged to have threatened physical harm to a London resident, William Wayte. Wayte sought a bill of peace against such an attack, citing his "fear of death." Presumably, the defendant Shakspere was the Stratford man.

It appears that the petitioner, Wayte, was working for his stepfather, William Gardiner, an unscrupulous and dangerous swindler. Shakspere's co-defendant, Francis Langley, was Gardiner's equally shady rival and enemy. In 1595, Langley had built the Swan Theatre on the south side of the Thames. It may be that this is how he became associated with the Stratford man. Langley and Gardiner had threatened each other with violence; and, evidently, the Stratford man was perceived as one of Langley's circle and thus considered part of the threat against Wayte.

In August 1596, Hamnet, one of the Stratford man's twins, died. We have no record of the effect of this death on the Stratford man or even whether he attended the funeral. Some Stratfordians argue that Shakespeare's plays became darker, more brooding after this. But that change seems to have come much later.

Notwithstanding whatever grief may have been caused by the death of his only son, just two months later, in October 1596, the Stratford man sought to attain the status of "gentleman," an important distinction in class. In that month, he applied for a coat of arms in his father's name. John Shakspere had made such an application years before, describing himself as "Bailiff, Justice of the Peace, the Queen's Officer and Chief of the Town of Stratford." Apparently, after his fortunes changed, John did not pursue the matter, and his application seems to have been neither granted nor denied.

Now, in 1596, William applied again on his father's behalf. To apply for himself while his father was alive would have been unseemly. Arms were drafted for John Shakespeare by the College of Arms in London. Initially, the application appears to have been rejected, based on the lack of sufficiently distinguished lineage. Ultimately, however, it was granted, possibly through bribery.

The grant was issued by two officials of the College of Arms, William Dethick and William Camden. In 1602, another official of the College of Arms formally accused Dethick and Camden of having granted arms to unworthy and base persons. He listed these unworthy grantees, and the list included "Shakespear ye Player." Despite an unpleasant controversy, the grant was never revoked. (Camden, who knew the Stratford man, appears later in our story in another, intriguing way.)

The reference in 1602 to the Stratford man as "Shakespear ye Player," adds to the very strong evidence that he was, in fact, an actor, although not necessarily the poet and playwright of the same name. Indeed, the reference might suggest that he was *not* the poet and playwright. By 1602, William Shakespeare had become a well-known author. It seems odd that, if the College of Arms believed the Stratford man was the author of the poems and plays attributed to William Shakespeare, he would have been described merely as "ye Player," without reference to his writings.

Conceivably, the angry College official thought it more demeaning to describe this base person as "ye Player," rather than "ye Poet and Playwright." He was probably referring to the Stratford man's profession back in 1596, rather than in 1602. But, even by 1596, Shakespeare had become known as the author of a number of plays and two highly successful narrative poems.

The name on the patent for the new coat of arms was *Shakespere*. Thus, even on such a formal document, the Stratford man was now using the same spelling as the poet and playwright. Above the coat of arms as issued was the motto *non sanz droict,* meaning "not without right." This was apparently the Stratford man's own invention. There is no reference to a motto in the text of the grant, and the heralds of the College of Arms did not assign mottoes.

The original draft arms that followed the 1596 application can still be seen at the College of Arms on Queen Victoria Street. At the top, on the right side, someone has written *Non, Sanz Droict,* with a comma after "Non." Immediately under this is a second notation, also *non, sanz droict,* also with a comma, but in lowercase letters. Someone has drawn a line through this second "non, sanz droict." Then, at the top and center of the page is still another *NON SANZ DROICT,* this time without the comma and in uppercase letters.

What did these notations mean? The uppercase notation, without the comma, seems to set out, perhaps for the first time, the words the Stratford man had chosen as a motto—"Not Without Right." Did some disgusted official comment wryly on the actor's pretentious motto by inserting the comma so as to say, "No, without right"?

In *Every Man Out of His Humour*, a play registered in 1600, but probably written a year or two earlier, Ben Jonson has a pompous character claim to have become "a gentleman" because of his newly obtained coat of arms, "a hogs cheek and puddings on a pewter field" with the motto *not without mustard.* Jonson's satirical reference to the Stratford man's proud new arms seems plain.

In any event, from the time of the grant of arms, the Stratford man was generally referenced in documents, and even in his own will as "gentleman" (i.e., "Wm. Shakspere gent."). This was an important social distinction in Elizabethan England. It suggested a status exceeding that of ordinary citizens, yeomen, and laborers. Evidently, it was quite important to the Stratford man.

In 1596, James Burbage purchased space in what had formerly been the

Blackfriars priory near Temple Bar, a fashionable neighborhood, almost directly across the river from the future site of the Globe. The intention was to construct an indoor theatre catering to upper-class patrons willing to pay a higher price of admission. But this wealthy residential area was peopled by a number of influential home owners, who opposed the opening of a theatre in their quiet neighborhood. Curiously, the successful petition of these residents to preclude the theatre was signed not only by George Carey, then the patron of the Burbages' company, but also by Richard Field, the printer of Shakespeare's narrative poems, who, like the Stratford man, had come to London from Stratford.

In any event, the petition seems only to have succeeded in preventing the use of Blackfriars as a public theatre for *adult* actors. Burbage rented the theatre to a company that presented plays performed by children. The venture was successful, and children's performances became quite fashionable, creating serious competition for the adult acting companies.

While continuing to live and work essentially in London, the Stratford man began to manifest an interest in Stratford real estate and business. In 1597, having somehow attained a degree of affluence, he bought New Place, the second largest house in town.

New Place had been previously owned by Stratford's leading citizen, Sir Hugh Clopton, who went on to become lord mayor of London. It is difficult to believe that the purchase price of this splendid residence had come from acting. Actors were generally not highly paid, and this was only five years after the first mention of the Stratford man's appearance on stage. Moreover, during a substantial part of that period, the London theatres had been closed because of the danger of plague.

Was the money from his share in the playhouse? Possibly. But he had been a sharer in Burbages' company for only three years, and during part of *that* time the London theatres had been closed. Other possibilities are that the Stratford man had been paid as a playwright and popular poet or that he had been paid to front for the true poet and playwright.

The next year, 1598, the Stratford man bought and stored a massive quantity of grain in a time of great shortage, apparently hoping to capitalize on dramatic price increases at the expense of his neighbors. More about this later.

Meanwhile, in London, the Burbages' lease to the Theatre expired in 1598, and, after a long period of negotiations, they could not come to terms with the owner. The lease contained a provision allowing the tenant to remove the wooden structure at the end of the lease. But the Burbages knew their difficult landlord would physically oppose any such action—probably with hired thugs.

On December 28, 1598, the landlord was away from London at his country estate. Under cover of night and an intermittent snowfall, Richard Burbage and his brother, Cuthbert, along with their carpenter and a dozen workmen, took down the timbers of the old theatre and rowed them across the river to a new site on the south bank. The old timbers were of excellent quality and each was specifically joined to the theatre's frame. Since they had been carefully marked by the original carpenter, the timbers were easily reassembled at the new site.

When he returned to London, the outraged landlord sued, but the Burbages' actions were upheld, and the case was dismissed.

By May 1599, the Burbages had reassembled the timbers to make the now famous Globe, their new and larger theatre, on the south bank of the Thames. The land, near Phillip Henslowe's Rose, was leased for thirty-one years from Nicholas Brend. The tenants were the Burbage brothers for a one-half share and five actors, John Heminge, Augustine Phillips, Thomas Pope, Will Kempe, and the Stratford man as to one-tenth each. The Stratford man now had a status even beyond that of a sharer in the company. He held a lessee's interest in the new playhouse itself. He and his fellows were now "housekeepers."

The Globe opened in 1599, probably with a performance of *Henry V*, given when Essex was still engaged in his Irish campaign. It became the customary place in which Shakespeare's plays were performed. The Globe, like the Theatre and the Rose, was open to the elements and catered to the general public. Performances took place in the summertime only. They started in midafternoon and were dependent on natural light and good weather.

But the Stratford man's life was not restricted to the theatre. He may have been something of a womanizer. John Manningham, a law student, made the following entry in his diary for March 13, 1601, the year of Essex's beheading:

> Upon a time when Burbidge played Richard III there was
> a citizen grew so far in liking him that, before she went

from the play, she appointed him to come that night unto her by the name of Richard the Third. Shakespeare, over-hearing their conclusion, went before, was entertained and at his game ere Burbidge came. Then, message being brought that Richard the Third was at the door, Shake-speare caused return to be made that William the Con-queror was before Richard the Third. Shakespeare's name William.

We do not know the source of this tale or why Manningham chose to include it in his diary or whether it contains any element of truth. Probably not. It's a bit odd that Manningham found it necessary to explain that Shakespeare's first name was William. By 1601, the poems and plays pub-lished and performed under that name had become quite well known.

In 1601, John Shakspere died in Stratford. Apparently, William was heir to whatever—if anything—was left of his father's estate.

In 1602, the Stratford man paid £320 (approximately a quarter of a mil-lion dollars in today's terms) for a large tract of farmland near Stratford. Certainly, that sizeable sum did not come from John Shakspere's estate. In fact, the price may have been much higher. The prices of real estate were customarily understated to reduce the transfer tax.

In 1603, Queen Elizabeth died and was succeeded by James I. The new king, fond of drama, took the lord admiral's company under his patronage. The company, in which the Stratford man remained a sharer, became known as the King's Men.

In 1604, nine players received an allotment of red cloth from the royal wardrobe to make ceremonial garments for King James's coronation. One player was "William Shakespeare," evidently the Stratford man.

From 1604 on, although still somewhat active in London, the Stratford man seems to have lived primarily in Stratford and to have conducted even more business there. This included money lending; trading in real estate; and, in 1605, buying for £440 (about $350,000 in today's terms) the valu-able right to collect tithes (in essence, taxes) on the produce of his fellow citizens.

He was litigious and apparently quite difficult in local dealings, even failing to pay a debt of forty-one shillings incurred by his wife after he left

Stratford and his family. He sued, and was sued by others, for small sums. In 1604, he sued his neighbor, Phillip Rogers, for one pound, fifteen shillings, ten pence. In 1608, he sued John Addenbroke for six pounds.

In 1605, William Camden, the same man who had approved the grant of Shakespeare's coat of arms in 1596, published a list of "Stratford Worthies." Peculiarly, he did not include the Stratford man. By 1605, the poems and plays of William Shakespeare were very well known. If Camden believed the Stratford man was their author, he would seemingly have led the list of local "worthies." Having been accused in 1602 of betraying his office in granting the Stratford man's application for a coat of arms (and having possibly accepted a bribe for doing so), Camden may have wished to avoid the appearance of granting him still further honors of any kind.

On his trips between London and Stratford, the Stratford man reportedly stayed with friends, John and Jeanette Davenant, the proprietors of an Oxford wine tavern. In 1606, Jeanette gave birth to a son, William. Supposedly, the Stratford man was his godfather. The child, later in life Sir William Davenant, became a writer himself and, ultimately, poet laureate. He was fond of hinting that he was not only Shakespeare's godchild, but his illegitimate son. He was probably neither.

In 1608, the children's company that had been performing at Blackfriars ran afoul of the law for presenting a "seditious" drama insulting to the French king. Worse still, they had performed a play that made fun of King James. The company was closed down. At last, with James on the throne and the King's Men enjoying royal sponsorship, they were permitted to present adult performances at Blackfriars.

Attitudes had changed. This time, the wealthy residents of the area made no complaint. Perhaps, having seen that the children's company had not ruined the neighborhood, they were more willing to accept the adult performances. Or perhaps, given the royal patronage, they were reluctant to voice their opposition.

The government's change of position was based in part on the fiction that Blackfriars was a private theatre, unlike the Globe and the Rose. What made it private was that its admission fees were higher, its clientele were generally upper-class or at least well-to-do Londoners, and its most privileged patrons could sit on the stage. Blackfriars also allowed for lighting effects and more extensive scenery than were possible outdoors at the Globe.

It soon became the winter venue for the company, supplementing their summer runs at the Globe.

The Stratford man, Heminge, Condell, William Sly, and an investor named Thomas Evans became participants with the Burbages in the house itself. The Stratford man was now a "housekeeper" at Blackfriars, as well as at the Globe. Sly died almost immediately, leaving the Stratford man with a one-sixth share at Blackfriars. His share at the Globe was now one-twelfth.

By 1610, the Stratford man seems to have come home to Stratford for good. Still, he maintained some connection with London. In 1612, he gave a deposition as a witness in *Belott v. Mountjoy*, a lawsuit in the London courts. Belott sued his father-in-law, Mountjoy, alleging a 1604 contract to pay money on his marriage to Mountjoy's daughter and to leave the couple money in his will. The Stratford man had been a lodger in Mountjoy's house in 1604. The deposition was signed "Willm Shakp."

In 1613, although primarily residing in Stratford, the Stratford man bought and concurrently mortgaged the old gatehouse of the Blackfriars Theatre. Possibly, this was an investment, rather than a place to live. He (or someone) signed the relevant documents "William Shaksp_" and "Wm Shaksp_."

In the same year, the accounts of Francis Manners, sixth earl of Rutland, show a payment of forty-four shillings to "Mr. Shakspeare in gold about my Lorde's impresa" and a similar payment to "Richard Burbadge for paynting and making it." An impresa was a painted shield made of paper displayed at tournaments and other festivities. Like a fanciful coat of arms, it contained emblems and sometimes mottoes. Stratfordians contend that their man supplied the words, while Burbage did the painting. Possibly; but we do not know if Rutland's impresa contained any written material, and we have no real indication just what "Mr. Shakspeare" did to earn his fee. "Mr. Shakspeare" could also have been John Shakespeare, the royal bit maker, but this seems unlikely. Given his business relationship with Burbage, "Mr. Shakspeare" was probably the Stratford man.

A more historic event also occurred in 1613. During the first act of *Henry VIII* at the Globe, a cannon was fired to mark the king's arrival at Cardinal Wolsey's palatial home. A burning fragment of paper or other material that had been stuffed in the cannon flew up into the theatre's thatched roof. At first, the smoke went unnoticed. By the time the flames broke out, it was too late. Within an hour, the theatre had burned to the ground.

It was the lessee's obligation to maintain and repair any buildings on the leased land. That meant they were obligated to rebuild the Globe after the fire. Insurance did not exist at the time, and the housekeepers were facing a significant financial burden. To make matters worse, the lease had only sixteen years left to run.

Nevertheless, in 1614, the Globe was rebuilt. Whether the Stratford man contributed to the rebuilding and retained his interest is an open question. He may well have thought it was time to bail out. Perhaps he simply released his share to those who undertook the financial burden. Apparently, Heminge gave at least a part of his share to Henry Condell to reduce his part of that burden. But no documentation has been found of any such transfer by the Stratford man.

In 1614, the Stratford man was involved in another controversial matter, somewhat reminiscent of his grain-hoarding episode. Having first made a deal to protect his own interests as a tithe holder, he seems to have acquiesced in an unsuccessful attempt by local associates to enclose common lands in the Stratford area, depriving his fellow citizens of their ancient rights. Later, we will explore this bizarre and rather dramatic episode and consider what it tells us about the Stratford man.

In 1616, the year of his death, the Stratford man made his famous will. Drafted by his lawyer Francis Collins, it was the meticulous will of an obsessive small-town trader. It was signed in three places in what appears to be an attempt at "William Shakspeare." The "William" in two of the places and the "Shakspeare" in one are almost illegible. There is controversy as to whether it was really signed by him at all or someone signed it for him. The will leaves small bequests to his "ffellowes" Burbage, Heminge, and Condell, with which to buy memorial rings. It covers personal property in some detail, specifying individual items, such as his sword and his silver gilt bowl. By a curious interlineation, it leaves his "second best bed" to his wife. The will of this careful, property-conscious man *mentions no books, no manuscripts, no unfinished works, no literary property, no interest in any theatre or theatre company.* It makes no provision for the education of his granddaughter, whom he supposedly adored. She was only eight when he died, and she never learned to write. For that matter, neither did his daughter Judith.

The average life span for Stratford males was forty-seven years. The

Stratford man lived to be fifty-two. On April 23, 1616, William Shakspere of Stratford died and was interred beneath the chancel of Stratford Church. There is no record of a single public tribute or even any public notice of his death. If he was the famous poet and playwright, this is an extraordinary fact.

As we will discuss later, we have no indication that the Stratford man ever evinced in any way the highly evolved philosophy or the deep and passionate feelings expressed in the Shakespeare canon. On the contrary, what we know of his life suggests that he had the mentality and morality of a petty, selfish small-town speculator. But then we have no real evidence of *what* the Stratford man thought or felt—except for his will.

There is also one poem for which he is generally held responsible. It's the one on his grave:

> *Good frend for Jesus sake forbeare*
> *to digg the dust enclosed heare!*
> *Bleste be ye man yt spares thes stones,*
> *And curst be he yt moves my bones.*

Does this clumsy, childish doggerel square with the soaring beauty of the sonnets or the brilliance and wisdom of the plays? Hardly. Stratfordians argue that someone else may have written it, or that, if the Stratford man wrote it, he must have been using language he thought would convince ignorant country folk to stay away. The latter response seems unconvincing, and it appears more likely than not that the Stratford man did, in fact, write the poem.

In any event, the doggerel apparently worked. The bones of the Stratford man have not been moved, although it is not likely that the prosperous merchants and innkeepers of Stratford would have let them go, even if the crude lines had never been written.

3·

THE PLAYWRIGHT'S LIFE

Having set out those limited facts we really know about the life of the Stratford man, we can turn to what we know about the life of William Shakespeare, the poet and playwright. As we proceed, we can compare and contrast the two lives, asking always whether they fit together or are inconsistent in any material respect.

Putting aside the common assumption that he was the Stratford man, we know nothing certain about the poet and playwright until 1592 at the earliest. A number of Shakespearean scholars seem to agree that nine plays were written in the years between 1588 and 1593, a period in which the Stratford man was still in his twenties. These include *Henry VI*, Parts 1, 2, and 3; *Richard III*; *Love's Labour's Lost*; *Two Gentlemen of Verona*; *The Comedy of Errors*; *Titus Andronicus*; and *The Taming of the Shrew*.

They do not *know* that these plays were written in that period. Such scholars generally infer it from the dates the plays were performed, published, or mentioned in writing. For example, since *Henry VI*, Part 3, was performed in 1592 and *Titus Andronicus* was printed by 1594, those plays were necessarily written before that.

Of course, we can't really know how long *before* their first performance or mention the plays were written. Stratfordians tend to infer that they could not have been written too many years before 1590, because the Stratford man would have been too young. But, if someone other than the

Stratford man wrote them, the plays could have been written in 1585 or even earlier. It is unlikely that the Stratford man wrote them in that early a period, unless he was secretly writing plays while still living with his wife in Stratford.

In 1591, Edmund Spenser published *The Teares of the Muses*, which was written no later than 1590, since it was registered in that year. Spenser lavishly praises a playwright named "Willy" who has provided "joy and jolly merriment" and from whose pen flow "honey and sweet nectar." Spenser expresses regret for the cessation of Willy's writing activity, which seemingly had gone on for some time before 1590. Was the reference to Shakespeare? Probably not. There is no indication of any performance of any comedy or other play attributed to Shakespeare prior to 1592. If the reference was to Shakespeare, it would seem unlikely that the Stratford man could have achieved such standing and respect as a playwright so soon after leaving his home and family in Stratford.

We do know that, beginning in or around 1592, several plays were performed that were *later* attributed to "Shakespeare" or "Shake-speare" (not "Shakspeare"). Initially, the plays were produced by Henslowe's company at the Rose Theatre and possibly at other venues as well.

We know of a performance in 1592, because of the report of Robert Greene. When that dissolute playwright lay dying in London, impoverished and terminally ill with syphilis, he (or someone in his name) wrote a piece entitled "A Groatsworth of Wit." The piece, published after his death, contains a warning to unnamed playwrights. They are cautioned in a letter from Greene, included as part of "A Groatsworth," not to trust actors, but particularly to beware of "an upstart crow, beautified with our feathers, that with his tygers hart wrapt in a Players hide, supposes he is as well able to bombast out a blanke verse as the best of you; and, beeing an absolute Johannes fac totum, is in his owne conceit the onley Shake-scene in a countrey."

"Tygers hart wrapt in a Players hide" is an allusion to Shakespeare's *Henry VI*, Part 3, which we know from this had to have been written no later than 1592. In the play, the duke of York is defeated by the Lancastrians at the Battle of Wakefield. He is forced to wear a paper crown and is taunted by his captors with a handkerchief dipped in the blood of his slain young son. The duke rages at their leader, the cruel and vindictive Queen

Margaret, known as "the She-wolf of France." He calls her a "tiger's heart wrapped in a woman's hide."

Most writers on the subject construe Greene's attack as having been directed at an actor who also fancied himself a writer; and view "Shake-scene" as a reference to the actor's being Shake-speare. If that is so (something explored in detail later), it is the first indication of the actor's being perceived as a writer as well. In fact, it would be one of only two times during the Stratford man's entire lifetime that we see Shakespeare, the actor, possibly referred to as a writer as well. Later, we will discuss an ambiguous tribute by John Davies in 1610 which may also be such a reference, as well. If so, it is the only other occasion, unless the gonorrhea-infected "old player," called "W. S.," in *Willowbie His Avisa* in 1594, was also the poet "Shakespeare" mentioned in the verses preceding that supposedly fictional work.

Greene's attack gives rise to one of the intriguing mysteries that abound in dealing with this subject. Someone very powerful seems to have come down quite hard on the publisher of "A Groatsworth of Wit." The publisher, in turn, blamed the printer, Henrye Chettle, for the venomous attack. Chettle was forced to apologize to an unnamed "play-maker" who took offense at what Greene wrote. In his apology, Chettle heaped lavish praise on the anonymous play-maker, adding that "divers of worship" had also praised that writer. Who had the power to force such an apology, and why was that power seemingly exercised on behalf of "Shake-scene," the "upstart crow"?

Could the young man from rural Stratford have brought such power to bear in the relatively short time he had been in the city? Perhaps. Perhaps he had already acquired powerful friends. But, at this early stage of his career, it would not have been easy.

The first time "William Shakespeare" is formally listed as an author is with the publication of the long narrative poem *Venus and Adonis* in 1593. The poem was based on Ovid's *Metamorphoses*. It dealt with the handsome young Adonis resisting the feverish advances of a highly sexed Venus. The printer was Richard Field, a native of Stratford. Field, who was three years older than the Stratford man, had left his home in 1579 to become apprentice to a printer. It is virtually certain that the two knew each other; and Field's selection to be the printer of Shakespeare's *Venus* could be a coincidence, but we must consider it as some evidence supporting the Stratfordian cause.

The dedication of *Venus* is to Henry Wriothesley (pronounced "Rose-lee"), the young and attractive earl of Southampton. The dedication refers to the poem as "the first heir of my invention." The dedication page includes the printed name "William Shakespeare," which does not appear on the title page, as was customary. The poem, considered highly erotic at the time, was an enormous financial success and established Shakespeare's reputation as a poet.

Shakespeare's reference in 1593 to *Venus and Adonis* as "the first heir of my invention" has led to much speculation. Was the poem written even before any of the plays? Possibly. No published play actually bore the name "Shakespeare" until 1598, but plays now attributed to Shakespeare were certainly written and performed before then, as indicated by Greene's attack in 1592. By "the first heir of my invention" Shakespeare may have only meant that it was the first work published, rather than the first written or performed.

There is also the possibility, discussed below, that the Henry VI play seen by Greene in 1592 was essentially the work of Christopher Marlowe. Possibly, "Shakespeare" was acknowledging this by calling *Venus and Adonis* the "first heir of my invention."

Then again, could "my invention" have referred to the idea of having someone else pose as the author? Was Southampton in on the secret? Did the poet mean that this was the first published work using that "invention"? Probably not.

The Rape of Lucrece, another long narrative poem by "Shakespeare," appeared in 1594, again printed by Richard Field. It was based on Ovid's *Fasti* and concerned Tarquin's ravishment of a married noblewoman. *Lucrece* was also dedicated to Southampton and was also a major success.

The London theatres were closed between 1592 and 1594 as a precaution against the plague, which had broken out in the city. Possibly, the absence of a market for new plays in this period led Shakespeare to write the two long poems.

Some Stratfordians have argued that the Stratford man traveled to Italy in this period, thus providing him with the knowledge of Italian names, places, speech, and customs that appear in a number of Shakespeare's plays. Apparently, Shakespeare did turn to the composition of plays set in Italy when the plague was over. But, aside from this, there is no real evidence of an Italian trip in this period, and there is no evidence that the Stratford man was ever in Italy.

Anti-Stratfordians describe the dedications of *Venus* and *Lucrece* to Southampton as fawning and effusive. They find it inconceivable that a commoner—who, at least in the case of *Venus and Adonis,* had not yet attained significant fame—would, without invitation, address such overblown, saccharine words to one of the great—albeit young—noblemen of the day.

An examination of the dedications seems to belie this claim. The dedication to *Venus and Adonis* begins with "I know not how I shall offend in dedicating my unpolished lines to your Lordship" and continues in the same courteous, self-deprecating tone. There is nothing overly obsequious or otherwise inappropriate for a young poet to have written to a great lord.

The dedication to *The Rape of Lucrece* takes a slightly warmer tone, referring to "The love I dedicate to your Lordship." Its suggestion of familiarity indicates that, between the first and second poem, a relationship may have developed between Shakespeare and Southampton. The poet had achieved some degree of fame by reason of *Venus and Adonis,* so that some relationship would no longer seem impossible.

One other problem with the anti-Strat argument is that the dedications are easier to reconcile with the words of a young commoner than with the manner in which the earl of Oxford, or some other nobleman, would have addressed his fellow aristocrat Southampton. Of course, if the aristocratic author were trying to create the false impression that the poems, having been published, rather than merely read to his friends, were the work of a common actor, he would probably have written dedications consistent with that charade.

Given the logical possibilities, the phrasing of the dedications to Southampton does not permit us to rule out the Stratford man or Oxford or any other candidate as the creator of those dedications.

Nicholas Rowe referred to a "story" that Southampton gave Shakespeare £1,000 to make an unspecified purchase. That would have been a huge sum at the time—more than the sum of all the purchases made by the Stratford man in his entire lifetime. The "story" is almost certainly apocryphal.

Following the two epic poems, Shakespeare seems to have written for a different company. Henslowe's records show no further performances of Shakespeare's plays by his company after June 1594. From that point on, Shakespeare appears to have written exclusively for the Lord Chamberlain's Men, in which the Stratford man was a sharer. Thereafter, "Shakespeare" (sometimes "Shake-speare") was credited as the author of numerous plays performed by that company.

The fact that Shakespeare wrote exclusively for the company in which the Stratford man was a sharer has been argued as supporting the view that they were the same person. But it is equally consistent with the opposite view. If the actor from Stratford was fronting for someone else, the plays would *have* to be written for the actor's own company. Once he became a sharer in the Lord Chamberlain's Men, the Stratford man could hardly appear to be writing plays for a rival company.

In 1598, the name *William Shake-speare* first appeared on printed, quarto editions of his plays. In a quarto, each sheet was folded twice, making eight pages from a single sheet and resulting in a small booklet. A folio was different. Each sheet was folded only once, making four pages per sheet and a larger book.

Between the successful publication of *Venus and Adonis* in 1593 and the quarto editions of plays in 1598, naming Shakespeare as the author, a number of his plays were published anonymously, including *Richard II*, *Henry VI* (Parts I and II), *Richard III*, *Romeo and Juliet*, and *Titus Andronicus*. *Titus* was first printed in 1594, followed by *Romeo and Juliet*, *Richard II*, and *Richard III* in 1597 and *Love's Labour's Lost* in 1598.

After *Venus and Adonis* was published in 1593, Shakespeare was a well-known name, likely to attract buyers and increase sales. Why was the name not used in publishing these anonymous plays? If Shakespeare had already arranged for an actor to front for him as the purported author of his works, why not use that promotable name when the plays were published? Did the author initially consider it proper to publish poetry under the name Shakespeare, but not plays for the common theatre? Did he later change his mind?

Perhaps the anonymous plays were published by "pirates" acting without authority. If so, the pirates may have been ready to steal the plays, but were afraid to appropriate the playwright's name. If the plays were pirated, there is no indication that either the Stratford man or his acting company or anyone in the name of Shakespeare ever objected. Does that square with the combative and litigious character of the Stratford man? He was involved in considerable petty litigation about other things, but there is no record that, at any time in his life, he ever attempted to protect or assert any rights in or in connection with any poem or play. And, if the Lord Chamberlain's Men owned the plays, would they have stood by while others published them without authority and without paying for the right?

Later, plays written by others were passed off as Shakespeare's, presumably to capitalize on his fame. Yet Shakespeare, whoever he was, made no complaint about this either.

In 1598, Francis Meres wrote in *Palladis Tamia* that "the sweet, witty soul of Ovid lives in the mellifluous and honey-tongued Shakespeare, witness his Venus and Adonis, his Lucrece, his sugared sonnets among his private friends . . ." This is the first recorded reference to the sonnets.

Meres also lists twelve plays that he attributes to Shakespeare. There were six comedies, *Two Gentlemen of Verona*, *The Comedy of Errors*, *Love's Labour's Lost*, *Love's Labour's Won* (probably *Taming of the Shrew*), *A Midsummer Night's Dream*, and *The Merchant of Venice*; four histories, *Richard II*, *Richard III*, *Henry IV*, and *King John*; as well as two tragedies, *Titus Andronicus* and *Romeo and Juliet*.

Meres omits *Henry VI*, which we know from Greene had been written no later than 1592, probably in all three parts. Meres did not complete his university education until July 1593, and perhaps *Henry VI* was no longer playing at the time, or perhaps Meres, like some Shakespearean scholars, believed that Shakespeare had merely revised the Henry VI plays and that they were written by someone else—perhaps Marlowe.

In any event, we know that, by 1598, Shakespeare had written *Venus, Lucrece*, at least some of the sonnets, and at least twelve plays. Assuming that the Stratford man started writing around 1588, three years after leaving Stratford, this would have been a sizeable body of work to create in ten years—more than a play a year, plus two long poems and some sonnets. Creating that body of work while, at the same time, performing as an actor, would be a difficult task. Is it impossible? By no means, even assuming that he did no writing in the first three years after leaving Stratford or even before he left.

If we assume that Shakespeare wrote nothing before the appearance of Greene's "Tyger's Heart" allusion in 1592, then his output in the six-year period before 1598 was even more striking, although still not impossible. Besides, that assumption may be unwarranted.

In 1599, William Jaggard published a collection of poems called *The Passionate Pilgrim*. It included two of Shakespeare's sonnets (138 and 144) plus three others from *Love's Labour's Lost*, along with the work of another poet. The entire collection was falsely attributed on the cover page to "W. Shakespeare." There is no indication, at the time, of any complaint by the Stratford man or by anyone else purporting to be, or speaking for, "W. Shakespeare."

Around 1600, one of the Parnassus plays, put on each Christmas at Cambridge, had as a character a patently uneducated actor, who recited the following lines:

> Few of the University men pen plays well; they smell too much of the writer Ovid and that writer Metamorphosis and talk too much of Proserpina and Jupiter. Why, here's our fellow Shakespeare puts them all down, [aye] and Ben Jonson too. O that Ben Jonson is a pestilent fellow; he brought up Horace giving the poets a pill, but our fellow Shakespeare hath given him a purge that made him bewray his credit.

This has been taken by Stratfordians as a serious statement that, like Ben Jonson, the real Shakespeare the playwright was not a "University" man, and, therefore, that he must be the Stratford man. But, the character who speaks the quoted lines is portrayed as an ignorant fool. By this time, Shakespeare was known for his use of Ovid and, of course, "Metamorphosis" was not a writer. The passage seems clearly intended as satire—a send-up of uneducated actors. It does not allow us to conclude with certainty even that the man *perceived* by the students to be the author of the plays was believed not to be a "University" man. And, of course, it does not demonstrate that the *perceived* author of the plays was, in fact, their real author.

At another point in the Parnassus plays, there are references to "Mr. Shakspeare." This has also been taken as another recognition that the playwright referred to was the Stratford man. It might have been—or it might simply have been a misspelling. The use of "Mr." may have been a jibe at the Stratford man's newly acquired status as a "gentleman." But, again, his being *perceived* by the student playwright as the author of the poems and plays does not make it so.

Stratfordian scholars tend to date *Hamlet* in 1601, when the Stratford man was thirty-seven. They could be correct. The play was not mentioned by Meres in 1598 and was registered in 1602 and printed in 1603. Stratfordians also support their date with the contention that the play is the work of a mature author, so that thirty-seven fits.

But there remains a problem in dating this landmark drama. In 1589, Thomas Nash referred to "Hamlets" and "Tragical speeches." In 1589, the Stratford man was only twenty-five and had been away from his family in Stratford for no more than four years. Is it possible that he wrote this extraordinary and insightful play that early? Phillip Henslowe's records show that a play called *Hamlet* was performed in 1594; and Thomas Lodge, writing in 1596, refers to a "ghost which cried so miserably at the theatre like an oyster wife 'Hamlet, revenge.'"

Some Stratfordians deal with the improbability of the Stratford man's having written *Hamlet* so early in his career by asserting that the *Hamlet* performed and mentioned prior to 1601 was another play altogether, which they call the "Ur-Hamlet," and assert that it was the work of Thomas Kyd, rather than Shakespeare. They contend that Shakespeare used Kyd's "Ur-Hamlet" as the source of his own later play.

But Shakespeare's *Hamlet* comes from Belleforest's *Histoires Tragiques* and from Saxo-Grammatica's twelfth-century retelling of a Danish legend about Prince Amleth who feigns madness to outwit his murderous stepfather. There is no printed or written *Hamlet* by Kyd and no persuasive evidence that Kyd ever wrote any version of that play.

If the Stratford man was too young and immature to have written a *Hamlet* that was seen in 1589, it would be just as reasonable to assume that someone else wrote both the earlier and later versions as to assume that Thomas Kyd wrote the earlier version and that, years later, the Stratford man wrote the version now known to the world. From the derisory comment by Thomas Lodge about the "oyster wife" crying "Hamlet, revenge," one could infer that the earlier version may not have been well received. Perhaps a younger Shakespeare wrote a crude and melodramatic version in or before 1589, but, with experience and added maturity, revised it years later to create the play as we know it today or, more accurately, to create the much longer version of that play that has been cut down over the centuries.[1]

One might expect Shakespeare's writing in 1601 to have been quite different from his writing in 1589. As John Dryden put it, discussing the improved writing of Jonson, Fletcher, and Shakespeare as they matured, "A slender poet must have time to grow, and spread and burnish as his Brothers do." Shakespeare may have written both plays twelve or more years apart.

In Shakespeare's play, Rosenkrantz and Guildenstern tell Hamlet about the commercial success of "little eyases" who carry away even "Hercules and his load." Those who date the play in 1601 claim that this was a reference to the child actors who performed at Blackfriars no earlier than September 1600, and whose competition was felt even across the river at the Globe, that theatre's emblem having been Hercules with the world on his shoulders. It has been argued that the reference to "little eyases" might have been to a rival company of child actors who had been performing for some years in the cloisters of St. Paul's Cathedral. But the Globe wasn't built until 1599, so that its losing business to any children's company would not have been included in a *Hamlet* written before that. On the other hand, the "little eyases" passage appears to have been added in a later printing and apparently did not exist in the play as originally written. If so, we cannot draw any conclusions from its presence in the text as to when Shakespeare's *Hamlet* was originally written.

In 1601, on the eve of Essex's rebellion, his supporters paid members of the Lord Chamberlain's Men to stage a performance of Shakespeare's *Richard II* at the Globe. Queen Elizabeth was enraged. Her crown and her life had repeatedly been threatened by plots on the part of Catholics, Spanish, Scots, disaffected noblemen, and others, to put Mary, Queen of Scots, Phillip II, and finally Essex on the throne in her place. Some years before,

---

1. So far as basic storyline is concerned, there is some reason to prefer that of the ancient legend. Amleth is confronted with the threat of being murdered by his stepfather. His feigned madness makes sense as a device to lessen his stepfather's reason for killing him. King Claudius in the Shakespearean play appears to have no intention to harm Hamlet until *after* Hamlet has pretended to be mad. He has killed Hamlet's father and married his mother, but he seems perfectly willing to recognize Hamlet as his heir until later in the play, when he comes to fear Hamlet's revenge. Of course, the greatness of Shakespeare's *Hamlet* does not lie in the basic plot, but in the fantastically complex character and magnificent, insightful lines.

in 1594, a tract had been written by the Catholic priest Robert Persons, praising Essex, urging his right to participate in deciding the succession, and pointing out, as precedent, that Richard II had been deposed.

Given the threat posed by Essex, the queen viewed the scene in *Richard II* in which a reigning monarch is deposed as a call for her own overthrow. After all, Richard II, like Elizabeth, was accused of establishing and relying upon favorites, and he was overthrown by Bolingbroke, who, like Essex, had become the darling of the common people. Elizabeth, whose statements about the play's performance were recorded by the antiquary William Lambard, cried out "I am Richard II. Know ye not that?"

The deposition scene deplored by the queen had been previously stricken from the play. The first quarto edition published in 1597, with the deposition scene missing, can be seen at the Huntington Library in San Marino, California. On the eve of Essex's rebellion, however, the scene was reinstated and performed. Apparently, there were other performances as well. The queen told Lambard, "This tragedy was played forty times in open streets and houses." Perhaps she was exaggerating, but she was plainly upset and angry.

The scheduling and performance of the play were investigated. One might have expected the playwright to have been in serious trouble, or at least to have been the subject of considerable scrutiny.

The question of the seditious play was explicitly raised at Essex's trial. The actor Augustine Phillips testified that Sir Charles Percy, Sir Joscelin Percy, Lord Monteagle, and others, all participants in Essex's conspiracy, asked for "the play of the deposing and killing of King Richard the Second" to be played "the Saturday next." The actors were promised "forty shillings more than their ordinary to play it."

According to Phillips's testimony, the actors were initially reluctant, not because they realized the play was potentially treasonous, but because it was "so old and so long out of use as that they should have small or no company at it." Phillips added, however, that the extra forty shillings overcame these objections, and that the play was performed as requested.

Sir Gilly Meyrick, one of Essex's supporters who crossed the river to speak to the actors that fateful night, testified that the play the actors were asked to perform was "Kyng Harry the iiiith" (*Henry IV*). Even Edward Coke, who presented the crown's argument against Meyrick at the trial, contended that "the story of Henry IV being set forth in a play, and in that play there being set forth the killing of the king upon a stage . . . Sir Gilly Meyrick and some others . . . must needs have the play of Henry IV . . ."

Oddly, Meyrick and Coke both had the wrong play. Richard II is not deposed and killed in the play *Henry IV*. He was deposed and killed by the man who became Henry IV; but this occurs in the play *Richard II*. In any event, Bacon and the queen knew which play was which and where the guilt lay.

After Essex's execution, Bacon was instructed to prepare a public state-ment of the treasonous acts for which the earl had been beheaded. The charges included arranging for the performance of *Richard II* "in the hope that the spectacle of the murder of a king might encourage the people to revolt." Yet, curiously, the playwright was never questioned or called as a witness. Nor was the name "Shakespeare" mentioned even once in the pro-ceedings.

Elizabeth could be harsh and extreme in her punishment of writers who expressed what she considered dangerous ideas or thoughts she felt were contrary to her own best interests. For example, she decreed that a man named Stubbs have his right hand cut off for writing a tract opposing her possible marriage to the duke of Alençon. And, in an act even more closely related to Shakespeare's "crime," Elizabeth had Sir John Hayward impris-oned in the Tower for years with a death sentence hanging over his head. His offense? He wrote a biography of Henry IV, which, of course, referred to that usurping king—previously Bolingbroke—seizing the throne from Richard II. Would that same queen, virtually obsessed by any reference to a reigning monarch's being deposed, have allowed a common actor to have written *Richard II* with impunity? It is difficult to believe.

One explanation is that the playwright was not a common actor at all, but a powerful nobleman close to the queen herself, to whom she might al-low more latitude, especially if he wrote under a pseudonym, so that a per-son of such eminence would not appear to have endorsed such dangerous views.

But the explanation might be just the opposite—that neither Sir John Hayward nor, even more so, a peer of the realm, would have been forgiven for writing such a play, but that, like the actors, a playwright who was a comparatively uneducated commoner could be considered to have written the scene innocently, without realizing its relevance to Elizabeth. He may not have known of the "criminal" performance, and even if he had, he might be considered to have been duped by Essex and his fellow conspirators, who, of course, were well aware of the scene's relevance.

Also, George Carey, son of the late lord chamberlain, had, by this time, taken over as patron of the actor's company. In the year after his father's death, Carey had also become lord chamberlain. Carey's father had been closely allied with Elizabeth and was her first cousin. Carey, himself, was a man of considerable influence. A persuasive word from him might have achieved a royal willingness to overlook the innocent, albeit misguided, acts of common actors and a common playwright. There is, however, reason to doubt that Carey interceded. Although the patron of Burbages' acting company, he was not particularly active in its affairs, and he had even signed the petition that successfully prevented the company from using the Blackfriars Theatre for many years.

There may be another factor that helped the playwright (whoever he was) avoid royal vengeance in 1601. Since the play had been written at an earlier time, the queen may have considered the playwright less likely to have perceived a serious threat of rebellion.

And, although *Richard II* did show the reigning king being overthrown by Bolingbroke, it also had the king and other characters argue forcefully against the propriety of such usurpation. In addition, it contained one of the most stirringly patriotic speeches in all English literature, the one in which John of Gaunt invokes:

> *This royal throne of Kings, this scepter'd isle*
> . . . .
> *This happy breed of men, this little world,*
> *This precious stone set in the silver sea*
> . . . .
> *This blessed plot, this earth, this realm, this England . . .*

Moreover, by the time of Essex's trial, Elizabeth would have seen Shakespeare's *Henry V*, in which the playwright portrayed that legendary warrior king (Bolingbroke's son) as fully conscious of his need to pay for his father's guilt and showed England itself as having suffered grievously by reason of his father's usurpation.

Henry V is depicted about to go into the battle of Agincourt with a fervent prayer that God not use that critical moment to exact revenge for his father's murder of a rightful king:

> *Not today, O Lord,*
> *O, not today, think not upon the fault*
> *My father made in compassing the Crown!*

And Shakespeare reminds us, at the end of the play, that Henry V died prematurely and that Henry VI, the usurper's grandson, "lost France and made his England bleed."

Thus, the queen may have concluded that the fault did not lie with the playwright, who, after all, had issued arguments against deposing a reigning monarch and had told the public in a later play that usurpation doesn't pay. Rather, the fault lay with Essex and his supporters, who dredged up the earlier play, restored the previously omitted deposition scene, and had it performed for the express purpose of urging the crowd to support Essex in deposing Elizabeth, just as Bolingbroke had deposed Richard II.

As the old queen reached the end of her long reign, Anthony Munday wrote a play about Sir Thomas More, who had been executed for his uncompromising defiance of Elizabeth's father, Henry VIII, in the matter of religion. Naturally, anything about More was a sensitive subject, and the master of revels insisted on substantial alteration of Munday's text. A number of writers made handwritten changes to the original manuscript.

It has been claimed that one of the unnamed writers, whose addition to the text is called "Hand D," was Shakespeare. If so, this would be the only writing that we know is the Bard's, other than possibly the six signatures we have discussed (if he was the Stratford man). The original manuscript is at the British Library in London. The writing called "Hand D" may be Shakespeare's; but, since we only have the six shaky signatures as possible samples of the Stratford man's writing, it is difficult, if not impossible, to say whether "Hand D" is his. The author of the lines attributed to "Hand D" dotted his *i*'s. In his six signatures, the Stratford man did not. Also the Stratford man's pen seems to move stiffly and irregularly even in signing his own name. "Hand D," by contrast, is smooth and free flowing, suggesting great facility with the pen. Not only the letters, but many of the words are connected by a thin, continuing line as if the writer wrote in a swift and fluid movement, most unlike the Stratford man, who was said to be "in paine if called upon to writ." And the lines in "Hand D" are filled with words crossed out and blotted, a state that does not fit Jonson's report that Shakespeare "never blotted out a line."

Stratfordians point out that "Hand D" misspells *silence* in the same manner as Shakespeare did in *Henry IV*, Part 2. But, at most, this is merely evidence that "Hand D" might be Shakespeare, not that it was the writing of the Stratford man.

The substance of the lines written in "Hand D" are consistent with the views expressed elsewhere by Shakespeare. Thomas More, employing his logic and oratorical skills, quells the passions of a mob rioting against foreigners trading in the city. As he shows us in such plays as *Coriolanus*, *Julius Caesar*, and *Henry VI*, Part 2, Shakespeare distrusted the common mob.

Is it possible that "Hand D" was Shakespeare? Yes, but we have insufficient evidence to say one way or the other. Was "Hand D" written by the Stratford man? Looking at the actual text in that hand, and comparing it to the Stratford man's six shaky signatures, it seems unlikely. Indeed, if "Hand D" was Shakespeare, it might be considered evidence that Shakespeare was *not* the Stratford man.

Whether or not anything can be inferred from the fact that Shakespeare was not even mentioned in connection with Essex's rebellion, there is certainly something very strange in his silence on the death of Queen Elizabeth in 1603. This was a momentous and emotion-charged event throughout England. Virtually every well-known poet spoke out, mourning the great queen's death. But William Shakespeare issued neither a eulogy nor any other public utterance. Even the apologist Henrye Chettle chided him, albeit obliquely, for his silence.

There could have been a number of reasons for this seemingly odd behavior, some of which would not be consistent with Shakespeare being the Stratford man.

For example, Shakespeare may have had reason to resent Elizabeth. This would not fit the Stratford man; but, as we will see later, there were other candidates for authorship who were threatened or punished in Elizabeth's reign and who may have had such feelings.

Or, if Shakespeare was not the Stratford man, he may have eulogized the queen under his own name, or, in his private capacity, saw no need to make any public statement. Even if he had to use the name *Shakespeare* on poems and plays, there was no reason to use a false name on a tribute to the deceased queen or even to issue a public tribute.

Another possibility is that Shakespeare reasoned that too much praise for Elizabeth might not please the new king. That kind of cynical thinking might fit the Stratford man at least as well as the other candidates. He may already have been considering the possibility that James I could be induced to sponsor his theatre company, as the new king actually did.

Those brave few who believe that Queen Elizabeth *was* Shakespeare see this silence as proof of their case. Shakespeare couldn't comment on the queen's death, they argue, because it was "Shakespeare" who had died. For a number of reasons we will discuss later, the queen is a doubtful candidate.

Between 1598 and 1604, a dozen Shakespearean plays had been published in quarto form. Between 1604 and 1608, no new plays were published. In 1608 and 1609, three were published: *King Lear; Pericles, Prince of Tyre;* and *Troilus and Cressida.* Was this gap in publishing attributable to the Stratford man's leaving London for a bucolic semiretirement? Or was it due to the death of the earl of Oxford in 1604? Or to the death of the queen herself in 1603?

We do not know that it resulted from any of these events. Shakespeare may have continued to write after 1604, even if the pace of publication had slowed. Most scholars date the creation of some ten plays (including the disputed *Pericles*) to the period between 1604 and the death of the Stratford man in 1616. Of course, some or all of these could have been written in 1604 or earlier, but were not published or performed until later.

During the reign of James I, who succeeded Elizabeth, it became the fashion to present elaborate and costly masques to celebrate various events, such as weddings, holidays, and the visit of a foreign monarch or dignitary. Often, these were presented by the court, but sometimes by others such as Robert Cecil, who continued serving James as he had Elizabeth.

The principal creator of these masques was Ben Jonson, often in collaboration with the great architect Inigo Jones, who provided the scenery and special effects. Masque making paid far more than writing plays. Yet there is no evidence of Shakespeare's having engaged in this lucrative work. Was he no longer alive?

A watershed event occurred in 1609. In that year, eleven years after Francis Meres mentioned Shakespeare's "sugared sonnets among his private friends," Thomas Thorpe published an entire collection of *Shake-speare's Sonnets,* 154 in all. Apparently, these extraordinary poems were published without the participation of Shakespeare himself and probably without his permission. The poet wrote no dedication, as he had for *Venus and Adonis* and for *The Rape of Lucrece*, and it is most unlikely that he would have failed to catch the numerous typographical errors that plagued the work.

Significant evidence may lie in the curious wording of the sonnets' dedication. Shakespeare is described there as "our ever-living poet." This seems almost surely a reference to a poet already dead, but immortalized by his works. It is not a phrase that fits a poet who is still alive. But the sonnets were published in 1609. The Stratford man was not to die for seven more years.

The fact that someone other than the poet himself wrote the dedication also suggests that "our ever-living poet" may have been dead. And, even the title, *Shake-speares Sonnets*, rather than "Sonnets by Shake-speare," could imply that these are *all* the sonnets he wrote, and that there will be no more.

In 1610, John Davies paid tribute to the Bard, prefacing his lines with "To our English Terence, Mr. Will. Shake-speare." Some anti-Strats have asserted that Terence was a Roman author who allowed his name to be used on works written by others, particularly aristocrats reluctant to publish under their own names. Thus, the argument goes, Davies was telling us that "Mr. Will. Shake-speare" engaged in the same kind of conduct.

But, if Terence allowed his name to be used on the works of others, it is not a commonly reported fact. Terence is widely known as a freed Roman slave, who became famous for writing comedies in the second century. It seems far more likely that Davies was alluding to Shakespeare's being a successful writer of comedies than to his fronting for pseudonymous aristocrats.

Davies continued his tribute with the following highly ambiguous lines:

> *Some say (good Will) which I in sport do sing,*
> *Hads't thou not plaid some Kingly parts in sport,*
> *thou hads't bin a companion for a King,*
> *And beene a King among the meaner sort.*
> *Some others raile; but raile as they thinke fit,*
> *Thou hast no rayling, but a raigning Wit.*
> *And honesty thou sow'st which they do reape,*
> *So, to increase their Stocke which they do keepe.*

These lines have been the subject of much controversy. They seem to say that, if "Mr. Will. Shake-speare" had not chosen to act the part of kings on stage, he would have been a fit companion for actual royalty and been considered like royalty himself among the common people. And Davies uses the present tense "hast" and "sow'st," apparently referring to a man still alive.

Davies's words seem a point for the Stratfordians. But, they would tell us only that the man Davies referred to as "Mr. Will. Shake-speare" was an actor, and, given the line about Terence, that Davies probably thought he was also the author of the plays. It does not tell us he really was the author. If the Stratford man was fronting for someone else, the whole point of the scheme was that people were to believe the actor from Stratford was the poet and playwright. The fact that Davies and others did believe this may be *evidence* that supports the Stratfordian cause, but it is hardly conclusive.

In 1612, William Jaggard evidently perceived the popularity of the sonnets. In that year, he published a new edition of *The Passionate Pilgrim*, once again attributing the entire work to Shakespeare. This time, Jaggard included five sonnets. Thomas Heywood, the other poet whose works had been included under Shakespeare's name, published a sharp criticism of Jaggard for attributing his own poems to Shakespeare. He included the claim that Shakespeare was also "much offended" by Jaggard's conduct. Evidently, this worked. Jaggard promptly removed Shakespeare's name from the title page. This would seem an indication that Shakespeare was still alive. Of course, it may have been the Stratford man who was offended, and Heywood, like John Davies, simply assumed he was Shakespeare. Or Heywood may simply have made up the part about Shakespeare's being offended, since that would carry more weight than Heywood's own complaint. We may wonder why, if Shakespeare was really "much offended," he didn't complain directly. Perhaps he did, but we have no record of it.

Toward the end of 1612, King James's son Henry, the prince of Wales, died at eighteen. There was a funeral of enormous pomp for the handsome heir to the throne. Even though there were tributes and outpourings of grief from virtually every English author of note, there was, once again, nothing from Shakespeare. Contrary to the inference we might draw from Davies's verse and Heywood's complaint, this curious silence on the death of the prince could support the inference that Shakespeare was no longer alive.

But then Shakespeare said nothing on the death of Queen Elizabeth in 1603; and all of the principal characters for Shakespeare authorship were alive at that time, except (possibly) Christopher Marlowe and the queen herself. As we will discuss, Marlowe was either dead or pretending to be.

Neither feelings of resentment toward the Queen Elizabeth nor fear of displeasing King James could explain silence on the occasion of this royal death. An explanation that might fit is that the real Bard eulogized the prince under his own name or, not being known publicly as Shakespeare, he was not expected to make a public statement and chose not to. That explanation would not, of course, fit the Stratford man. But, by 1612, even he may have found a reason for silence in retirement to Stratford.

If Shakespeare was the Stratford man, a far more striking anomaly arises on the latter's own death in 1616. By then, the plays and poems attributed to William Shakespeare had become quite famous. He had become a major figure in the English literary world. Yet, the death of the Stratford man in 1616 brought on no national mourning or public eulogies. There's no evidence of a single word written at the time by any fellow writer, such as Ben Jonson, or even from fellow actors such as Heminge or Condell, who were certainly aware of Shakespeare, were left money in the Stratford man's will to buy memorial rings, and obviously knew he had died. So far as we know, when the Stratford man died in 1616, not a single person wrote or said a word about the death of William Shakespeare, the famous poet and playwright.

On the passing of such writers as Francis Bacon, Edmund Spenser, Ben Jonson, and Sir Walter Raleigh, there was widespread public mourning and an outpouring of poetic tribute. Even the death of the actor Richard Burbage put the city of London in mourning. Why not the death of the Stratford man, if he *was* Shakespeare? Was it known that he was really just a retired actor and not really the author of the great poems and plays?

Perhaps, at the time, the public at large did not connect the author with the Stratford grain and real estate dealer who had once played small parts on the London stage. But if they were perceived as the same person by those in the English literary or theatrical scene, such as Ben Jonson, Leonard Digges, Francis Bacon, John Heminge, Henry Condell, and Richard Burbage, surely there would have been notice taken of the passing of the Stratford man, and surely there would have been some mention of the fact that the great poet and playwright had died.

Even William Camden, who had praised Shakespeare in his book *Remaines* and had approved the grant of the Stratford man's coat of arms in

1596, said nothing about the death of the Stratford man (or of "Shake-speare") in the volume of *Annals* Camden published for 1616. If Camden believed that the Stratford man was really the well-known poet and play-wright, how could he have omitted his death from the principal events of that year? This, taken with Camden's omission of the Stratford man from his list of "Stratford Worthies" published in 1605, suggests that at least Camden, who knew the Stratford man, did not believe he was William Shakespeare, the great poet and playwright.

Until 1623, seven years after the death of the Stratford man, no one seems to have written anything to the effect that the poet and playwright had died. In that year, however, those who had previously been strangely silent about the great Bard's passing seemed suddenly to remember that he was the actor from Stratford who had died back in 1616, and to grieve retroactively by lavishing upon his memory the most extraordinary and ef-fusive praise.

In 1623, the First Folio was published, containing thirty-six plays, repre-sented to be "all" of Shakespeare's dramatic works. It is preceded by intro-ductory letters purportedly written by the Stratford man's fellow actors, Heminge and Condell, as well as laudatory poems by Ben Jonson and Leonard Digges, both of which contain allusions that seem quite clearly in-tended, seven years after the fact, to tie Shakespeare to the Stratford man.

The First Folio did not include *Pericles, Prince of Tyre*, a play that appar-ently the compilers (like a number of subsequent authorities) did not con-sider to be Shakespeare's work.

Then, in 1634, eighteen years after the Stratford man's death, a play called *The Two Noble Kinsmen* was entered in the Stationer's Register and subsequently published. The title page describes the play as a "Tragi-Comedy" authored by "the memorable worthies of their time, Mr. John Fletcher, and Mr. William Shakespeare, Gent." It adds that the play "had oft been presented at the Blackfriars by the King's Majesty's servants with great applause." There is also evidence that, in 1619, *The Two Noble Kinsmen* was being "considered for performance at court" and that it had been per-formed in the mid-1620s.

Whoever Shakespeare was, he seemed clearly to have collaborated with another playwright on a few of the plays in the Shakespeare canon. Inter-estingly, these appear to be the less admired works, *Titus Andronicus, Timon of Athens, Pericles, Henry VIII*, and *The Two Noble Kinsmen*.

Brian Vickers's *Shakespeare, Co-Author*, provides substantial evidence of the collaborative efforts of George Peele in *Titus Adronicus*, Thomas Middleton in *Timon of Athens*, George Wilkins in *Pericles*, and John Fletcher in *Henry VIII* and *The Two Noble Kinsmen*.

But Vickers's fine work doesn't aid us in determining who wrote the portions of those plays attributed to Shakespeare. Vickers believes it was the Stratford man; and we certainly cannot assume the contrary just because Shakespeare had collaborators on these few plays.

In a knee-jerk reaction, however, some Stratfordians have resisted Vickers's well-reasoned conclusions, apparently viewing any suggestion of co-authorship to impugn the greatness of the Bard and to undermine what to them is the unassailable principle that he was the Stratford man.

One reason there are so many riddles surrounding Shakespeare is that he left no manuscripts, notes, diaries, letters—nothing in his hand. We have manuscripts by other writers of the period, such as Jonson, Marlowe, Beaumont, Fletcher, and even Greene. But none by the great Bard. Not a page. Not a scrap. Thirty-six handwritten play scripts, two manuscripts of long narrative poems, handwritten versions of 154 sonnets—all of them gone.

And there would have been at least three manuscripts for each play. Typically, the playwright would create a handwritten manuscript called the "foul papers," because they were usually replete with corrections, additions, and deletions. That version was delivered to a scribe who would make a "fair copy." But more than one fair copy was needed. One would be cut into pieces and made into scrolls giving each actor his own "part." Another was needed for the prompter.

If, as was reported, Shakespeare never blotted a line, no scribe might have been needed to convert his "foul papers" into a fair copy. But it is unlikely that he would have taken the time to make handwritten copies for the actors and the prompter.

In any event, whether there were once three copies in Shakespeare's own hand or only one, with two others done by a scribe, there are now none. And thousands of scholars and historians have searched for them for hundreds of years.

In 1630, John Milton wrote a sonnet praising Shakespeare for representing nature, as opposed to art. Later, he took the same tack in distinguishing the "learned" Ben Jonson from Shakespeare, whom he described as "fancy's child," who warbles "his native wood notes wild."

By the beginning of the eighteenth century, Shakespeare was a widely praised poet and playwright, but during that century, his stature in England grew to that of genius and national treasure. This was a century of conflict with France, and the French literary establishment was highly critical of Shakespeare as one who violated all the rules of classical drama. Among other flaws, they asserted that he had too many subplots, too many characters, and too many settings, and that he mixed tragedy and history with low comedy. Perhaps out of patriotic fervor, the English literary world rallied to his side. He represented the unique natural talent of genius, as opposed to worn-out, stereotyped French neoclassical "art." He did not imitate the classics. He embodied natural human (and English) thought and feelings.

Through the nineteenth and into the twentieth century, his reputation grew and was adopted in many countries. Actors became famous playing his monumental roles, such as Shylock, Richard III, Hamlet, Lear, and Othello. He had become "the great Bard."

And yet, we might wonder. If the armada had succeeded and England had been conquered by Spain, would the world today be celebrating the works of Lope de Vega, rather than those of William Shakespeare? I think not. I think that, in a world dominated by any literate culture, Shakespeare's works would have emerged as the greatest of literary achievements. His greatness is beyond dispute. His identity, however, remains a mystery—one to which we can now turn.

4.

THE KEY ISSUES

Having set out the few facts we really know about the life of the Stratford man and having contrasted them with what little we know about the author of the poems and plays, we can turn to the critical issues that bear on whether they were really one and the same.

We must contrast the arcane and specialized knowledge manifested in the poems and plays with the Stratford man's limited education, if any. Just how limited *was* that education? And how esoteric and unavailable was the information in the poems and plays? Was it impossible for the Stratford man to have written the Shakespeare canon? Could it have been the product of diligent research or sheer genius—or both?

Could the Stratford man even write beyond shakily signing his name? And if, as it appears, he had difficulty writing, how did he write by hand many hundreds of manuscript pages on which he reportedly never blotted a line?

Do the attitudes and actions of the Stratford man fit what we can infer about Shakespeare from his poems and plays? What about his political and religious views? His sexual preferences? Can these be squared with what we know about the Bard?

Are the sonnets mere fictional musings about imaginary characters, or do they represent events and feelings from the life of the poet? If the latter, how do the sonnets fit the life of the Stratford man? Why did the author of the dedication refer to "our ever-living poet," a phrase inappropriate for someone still alive, like the Stratford man?

Does the difference in spelling between "Shaksper" and "Shakespeare" constitute significant evidence that they were different men?

And what of the famous will? How can we explain why he included his "silver gilt bowl" and "second best bed" while omitting mention of any books, manuscripts, literary property, and interest in theatre companies?

Does the First Folio prove beyond a doubt that the Stratford man was the author of the Shakespeare canon? Why would it say so, if it wasn't true?

And, what about the Stratford monument? Doesn't it also prove that Shakespeare was the Stratford man? Or was the monument mysteriously altered to create that impression?

We will examine each of these issues in turn and then try to see where they fit and what conclusions we can draw from them.

5.

A STRATFORD
EDUCATION

Stratfordians assume that their man attended the town grammar school. They argue that it provided him with a good basic education, including a study of Latin and maybe even Greek. As we have seen, those assumptions may or may not be correct. But if the Stratford man did attend the school and completed his studies there, it is probable that he did receive a good basic education in classical language and literature.

Dr. Levi Fox's *The Early History of King Edward VI School Stratford-upon-Avon* gives us some insight into the grammar school the Stratford man may have attended. The actual records of the school no longer exist. We know there was a school at Stratford in 1295 and probably even before that. Like most such schools, the Stratford grammar school was initially affiliated with the Catholic Church. The register of the Bishop of Worcester in 1295 shows the ordination of deacons at the Stratford Church, one of whom is designated "rector scolarum" (schoolmaster).

A new "scolehaws" was built in 1427–1428 by the Guild of the Holy Cross, the organization that employed the town's priests. In 1482, one Thomas Jolyfe gave "all his lands" to the Guild administrators to "find a priest fit and able in learning to teach grammar freely to all the scholars coming to him to school in that said town."

In 1547, just seventeen years before the Stratford man was born, the

Guild of the Holy Cross was suppressed, as a part of the laws that followed Henry VIII's reformation of the English Church. All of the Guild's properties were taken over by the crown. The school, however, continued. In 1553, it was placed by Henry's son, Edward VI, under the management of the Stratford Town Corporation. The school was renamed the King's New School of Stratford-upon-Avon.

William Smart was appointed schoolmaster on December 20, 1554. His contract still survives and provides for him to "teche in the said gramer scole all such . . . chylder as shall forten to cum thither to lerne godly lernynge and wysdom" who were "reddy to enter into their accydence and princypalles of gramar." "Gramar," as used in the master's contract, probably meant *Latin* grammar. Latin was, of course, the language of the church. But it was also the language of the law, of diplomacy, science, medicine, civil service, teaching, and other disciplines.

Some of the subsequent Stratford schoolmasters had university degrees. Simon Hunt held that office from 1571 to 1574, the early years in which Shakspeare might have attended the school. But we cannot be sure that Hunt ever obtained such a degree. Hunt was followed by Thomas Jenkins, who apparently did have an Oxford degree, and who may have taught the Stratford man, if he continued at the school.

Urging the Stratfordian cause, Samuel Schoenbaum cites the lines in *The Merry Wives of Windsor* in which Shakespeare seemingly alludes to Latin grammar lessons set out in William Lily's *Short Introduction of Grammar*, a text prescribed for grammar schools by Henry VIII. According to Schoenbaum, this shows that the Stratford man must have studied Lily's text in school. Of course, it shows nothing of the kind. It simply indicates that *whoever wrote the works attributed to "Shakespeare"* probably studied from or was aware of Lily. It does not prove that *the Stratford man* read Lily's text or attended school and certainly not that he wrote *The Merry Wives of Windsor*.

Here again, Schoenbaum starts with the assumption that Shakespeare *was* the Stratford man and, based on that unproven assumption, infers, from *Shakespeare's* reference to Lily's work, that the Stratford man studied Lily.

Similarly, Schoenbaum cites Shakespeare's references in *Richard III* and in *Love's Labour's Lost* to the "hornbook" used by English schoolboys as evidence that the Stratford man used that book in the Stratford grammar school. Again, this indicates only that *the author of these two plays* was once a schoolboy and used a hornbook, not that the author was the Stratford man or that the Stratford man attended the Stratford grammar school or used a hornbook. Only if we start with the unproved assumption that the Stratford man wrote the plays can we draw Schoenbaum's conclusion.

If the Stratford man did attend the local grammar school and did complete his studies there, he probably received a fairly good knowledge of Latin and Latin authors. The Stratfordians certainly claim this, and they are probably correct. Indeed, Anthony Holden goes so far as to assert that even a university education would have added little to the competency in Latin and familiarity with Latin authors provided at the Stratford grammar school.

Although we do not have the records of the school at Stratford, we do have those of other grammar schools in similar communities, and it is a reasonable inference that the curriculum at the Stratford school was generally similar. School was attended six days a week and most of the year. The school day was a long one, beginning at six or seven in the morning, with a break for lunch and then continuing until five or six in the evening.

The usual age for starting the grammar school was seven or eight, although the boys often started earlier in a kind of preschool under a tutor appointed by the master. Grammar school entrants were usually required to read and write. These skills were usually taught at the preschool level even before entry to the grammar school. We do not have a record of any such preschool in Stratford. But it probably existed.

The modern concept of a high school between grammar school and university did not exist. At fourteen or fifteen, after completion of grammar school, the "best witted children" were supposed to be ready to attend a university. But these children were a distinct minority. The overwhelming majority of boys in a provincial town would have started work or been apprenticed at or before that age. Girls in such towns did not attend school at all and had to attain what education they acquired in other ways.

According to Dr. Fox, the Stratford grammar school was available only to the sons of the town burgesses. This might seem inconsistent with Master Smart's contract requiring him to teach "all such . . . chylder as shall forten to cum thither." But perhaps only the sons of prosperous burgesses were inclined to "cum thither," rather than to start work and provide labor or revenue at a young age. Although John Shakspere ultimately gave up his position on the town council, he apparently was not deprived of his status as a burgess.

The first two or three years at a typical grammar school were spent learning Latin grammar. This was taught by undermasters called *ushers,* using Lily's *Short Introduction of Grammar* (actually written by Lily in collaboration with John Colet and the multitalented Erasmus). At the end of this period, the pupils were expected to write and speak Latin.

The higher forms, boys of eleven or twelve, were taught by the master himself. These forms read Latin works, progressing from the easier to the more difficult authors. Cicero, Terence, Ovid, and Horace were among the authors typically studied, with the boys required to write essays in the style of Cicero or some other classical author on subjects given by the master.

In the higher forms, Greek was frequently introduced, through the reading of Greek authors. In some schools, even a little Hebrew was taught.

There is another issue to be faced concerning the Stratford grammar school. The masters and the ushers were expected to be Protestants, and Protestant rituals were strictly observed. Queen Elizabeth herself issued the order "that all teachers of children shall stir and move them to the love and due reverence of God's true religion, now truly set forth by public authority." This meant the Protestant *Book of Common Prayer* and accompanying Protestant texts.

If, as has been contended, John Shakspere was secretly a Roman Catholic, would he have turned his son over to such a Protestant regimen? Possibly. Since John himself attended church in Stratford, accepting (or pretending to accept) the Protestant ritual, he may have been willing for his son to participate in the same charade. Probably, no other education was available.

Putting aside the question of whether the Stratford man was ever enrolled in the Stratford school at all, we have the report of Nicholas Rowe that he started the school but was withdrawn when his father suffered the reversal of his fortunes. If this is true, and if he began school at the customary age of seven or eight, he was one or two years from completing his studies, when his father's financial situation began to deteriorate.

At best, we are left with a series of "ifs." *If* the Stratford grammar school followed the typical pattern of English grammar schools of the period, and *if* the Stratford man attended that school, and *if* he completed the upper forms, he would probably have had a good working knowledge of Latin and of the works of Latin authors and possibly of Greek and Greek authors as well.

The playwright Shakespeare certainly had that knowledge. For example, *The Merchant of Venice* was written no later than 1598, the year it was registered. The play contains a line taken verbatim from Ovid—"The moon sleeps with Endymion." But the English translation of Ovid containing that line was not published until 1599. If Shakespeare took it from Ovid, he had to read it in the original Latin and translate it himself. Could the Stratford man have done this? If he attended the local school and completed its curriculum, it is probable.

But all of this remains speculative. We do not know the actual curriculum of the Stratford grammar school or whether the Stratford man was ever enrolled there and, if he was, how long he remained. In fairness, however, as the son of a town official, he probably was enrolled and probably finished at least four or five years there before his father's finances turned sour.

But, if he did attend that rural school, would it give him the ability to acquire the vast body of diverse knowledge displayed in the poems and plays? Could all of that information, all the places, the languages, the jargon, the massive vocabulary, have been acquired by this young man who, at best, attended the Stratford grammar school and was never, so far as we know, outside of England?

It is hard to accept. Still, in 1615, the year before the Stratford man's death, Ben Jonson received a letter from "F. B.," whom scholars have assumed was Francis Beaumont. The letter contained the following passage:

> Here I would let slip (If I had any in me) scholarship, and
> from all learning keep these lines as clear as Shakespeare's
> best are, which our heirs shall hear preachers opt to their
> auditors to show how far sometimes a mortal man may go
> by the dim light of Nature . . .

Stratfordians point to this as positive proof that Shakespeare was a man of limited education, whose writing was lit solely "by the dim light of Nature," rather than the bright illumination of formal education. They assume that as a fellow playwright, Beaumont knew the truth about Shakespeare and, in writing privately, would have had no reason to depart from it.

On the other hand, the letter doesn't actually *say* Shakespeare was lit only by nature. It says that, in the future, *preachers will make that claim.* While it may be taken to support the Stratfordian claim that the true author was relatively uneducated, the letter can also be construed as merely a recognition that the public may simply be fed that tale. Although it seems unlikely, it is also possible that, if the Stratford man was fronting for some-one else who really wrote the poems and plays, F. B. did not know it and therefore presumed that the relatively uneducated actor had written these monumental works "by the dim light of Nature." It would be more difficult to believe that Ben Jonson was unaware of the truth, but then we don't know what reply Jonson made to F. B.'s letter.

Similarly, the Stratfordians construe a statement by Ben Jonson in the First Folio as an assertion that Shakespeare had "small Latin and less Greek," a position difficult to square with their argument that he "must have" attended the Stratford school, and so had a knowledge of Latin and Latin authors rivaling that of a university scholar. We will explore this in our analysis of the First Folio and Ben Jonson's role in creating it.

The Stratfordians' position on the Stratford man's education is not con-sistent. Some argue that he obtained a solid classical education at the Strat-ford grammar school, which, according to Holden, was virtually as good as that of a university graduate. Yet others seize on "F. B.'s" letter and Jonson's comment in the First Folio as proving that Shakespeare's splendid works are not the product of education at all, but rather of the unique ability of one with "small Latin and less Greek" to create by "the dim light of Nature."

In the next chapter, we will contrast the Stratford man's education in Stratford (assuming he attended the local school) with the enormous body of knowledge seemingly possessed by the author of the Shakespeare canon. We will do this in continuing our search for the answer to our fundamental question: Were they the same man?

6.
WHAT SHAKESPEARE KNEW

*T*he poems and plays contain a vast store of diversified knowledge that would not only suggest a highly educated author, but also one of broad experience, extremely well read and traveled. The subjects apparently mastered by the Bard include English, French, Greek, and Roman history; Italian, French, and Danish locales, places, names, customs, and events; legal and medical principles; military and naval science and tactics; the etiquette and usages of the nobility; French and Italian courtly and colloquial speech; biblical and mythological lore; falconry; horsemanship; tennis; lawn bowling; and even insider terms used by students at Cambridge University.

Could this extraordinary amount of diverse information have been the product of a Stratford education aided by diligent research, or was it necessarily the result of an upper-class life, a superb education, and wide experience of the world outside of England?

Thomas Kyd and Ben Jonson were both successful playwrights of the period, and neither had a university education. But then neither displayed the immense and wide-ranging knowledge found in Shakespeare.

Samuel Schoenbaum tells us that, at some point, the Stratford man occupied lodgings a short walk from the stationer's stalls in London and that "he must there have thumbed books which provided him with sources for his plays." Here again, we have "he must have" speculation. There is no *evidence* that he actually did any such thing. Besides, unless the thumbing continued for an unimaginable length of time, thumbing through books at a sidewalk stall would probably not even reveal the complete storylines embodied in the thumbed volumes, much less the vast scope of information and understanding found in Shakespeare's extraordinary body of work.

KNOWLEDGE OF FOREIGN PLACES, PEOPLE, AND EVENTS. The plays contain numerous references to Italian places, names, and events that the anti-Strats claim are too detailed to have been obtained through research or questioning others.

On the other hand, Stratfordians counter that Shakespeare's knowledge of Italy was indeed simply the product of research, and careless research at that. They accuse the Bard of demonstrable errors, which they assert show that he had no real familiarity with Italy, but merely did some casual reading on the subject. Three of the supposed mistakes they cite are characters traveling between Verona and Milan by water, a reference in *The Taming of the Shrew* to the making of sails in inland Bergamo, and describing Giulio Romano as a sculptor in *The Winter's Tale*, when, in fact, Romano was a painter.

But the Stratfordians appear to lose this round. As Joseph Sobran points out, in the sixteenth and seventeenth centuries, it was possible to travel between Verona and Milan by way of connecting rivers and canals. Indeed, it was the most comfortable way to make the journey. And Bergamo, although an inland city, was famous for sail making. Also, Giulio Romano was a sculptor as well as a painter. Contrary to the Stratfordian position, these references from Shakespeare seem to indicate a greater, rather than lesser, knowledge of things Italian.

Stratfordians also point out that in *Romeo and Juliet* (act 4, scene 1) Shakespeare refers to "evening mass," while mass is celebrated in the morning. Here again, the playwright was better informed. The play was set in Verona, where mass was said in the evening well into the nineteenth century.

Instead of suggesting shoddy research, these supposed "errors" demonstrate what appears to be a more intimate knowledge of Italy than was probably available in books when Shakespeare wrote.

It has also been argued by Stratfordians that there is no such place as "Belmont," where Portia has her home in *The Merchant of Venice*. But

Montebello (which, like Belmont, means "beautiful mountain") lies between Padua and Venice, at about the same distance from Padua that Shakespeare places Belmont. On the other hand, Portia seems to send Balthasar on an errand from Belmont to Padua and back *by way of Venice*, which would make no sense if Belmont were between the two cities. Possibly, Portia is planning to meet Balthasar in Venice rather than Belmont or, possibly, Belmont was simply a fanciful place, created in the mind of the Bard.

Some of the "Italian evidence" may not be quite so powerful as anti-Strats make it out to be. For example, the descriptions of Venice and Venetian people and practices in *The Merchant of Venice* are cited as examples of Shakespeare's intimate knowledge of Italy. Yet those descriptions are rather general and nothing that Shakespeare could not have gleaned from English travelers to Venice or from travel books.

Yes, Shylock speaks of "the Rialto" and his "ducats" and threatens that the laws of Venice will have no meaning if his bond is not enforced. But this is not proof that Shakespeare had been to Venice. Available books could have told him about such things as the Rialto and Venetian coinage, as well as the policy of rigorously enforcing Venetian commercial law. Conversations with English travelers to Italy could have provided the same kind of general information. Anti-Strats have emphasized Portia's reference to the "traject" as showing the playwright's knowledge of the *traghetto*, the Venetian ferry. But, it was "tranect" in the original version, and has been changed by subsequent editors to "traject." Either the original word was a misprint, or the playwright was not that familiar with Venetian terminology or, perhaps, he is referring to some other means of transportation entirely. Portia is directing Balthasar to bring her legal disguise from Padua. She tells him, "Bring them I pray thee with imagined speed unto the tranect, to the common ferry which trades to Venice." Perhaps the "tranect" means something other than "the common ferry which trades to Venice" (i.e., take the disguise on the tranect *and then* to the ferry).

Englishmen frequently traveled in Italy during the Elizabethan period, and travel guides to Italy written in English were readily available. John Hale in his *England and the Italian Renaissance* tells us that "[t]he late Elizabethan tourist had at his disposal books giving charts of distances, telling him how, if necessary, to calculate his latitude and longitude, even telling him how to write home. The number of works dealing with the technique of travel—where to go, where to eat, how to dress, what money would be required, was not matched again until the expansion of the tourist industry in the nineteenth century." In 1542, for example, Andrew Borde wrote such a guide covering, in separate chapters, Sicily, Calabria, Naples, Rome, Venice, and Lombardy.

There were also histories of the various cities and areas of Italy that provided information about the laws and customs of those places. William Thomas, a colorful character, wrote such a work in 1549 called *Historie of Italie*. It had separate chapters for Rome, Venice, Naples, Florence, Genoa, Milan, Mantua, Ferrara, Piacenza, Parma, and Urbino. Thomas toured Italy when he was literally "on the run," having embezzled his employer's money in England. Later, he returned to England, seemingly forgiven. But, as a well-known Protestant, he was suspect during the reign of "Bloody Mary" and ultimately was hanged, drawn, and quartered—not for writing his travel guide.

Taking the Italian plays as a whole, while they do contain some general information that might have been readily available, they also contain detailed "inside" information about Italy that research and conversing with travelers would probably not have provided.

This knowledge of things and places Italian is explored at length by Professor Ernesto Grillo, an Italian scholar. Although he does not question that Shakespeare was the Stratford man, Professor Grillo *assumes* that he must have traveled extensively in Italy, because of his "profound knowledge of the country in general and of our cities in particular."

An alternate explanation for this knowledge is John Florio, language tutor to the young earl of Southampton and author of an Italian language manual. If the Stratford man had become a regular visitor to Southampton's estate, he could have learned from Florio at least a general knowledge of Italian places and things and even a smattering of Italian colloquial phrases. Of course, as in so many aspects of this puzzle, we have no hard evidence of the Stratford man's ever being in Southampton's home, much less having conferred extensively with Maestro Florio.

Shakespeare's extensive use of European people, places, and events was not limited to Italy. Ben Jonson, often mean-spirited about Shakespeare during the Bard's lifetime, claimed that Shakespeare had a flawed knowledge of geography because he referred to Bohemia as having a seacoast. But it was Jonson whose knowledge was lacking. In the thirteenth century, when *The Winter's Tale* was set, Bohemia did have a seacoast. Under Ottocar II, Bohemian conquests reached the shores of the Adriatic, although Ottocar's gains were ultimately lost to the Hapsburgs.

Jonson was referring to *The Winter's Tale*. Jonson does not point out what seems at first blush to be an instance of erroneous geography in the same play and even in the same scene. When Antigonus's ship lands on the Bohemian coast, we are told they have arrived at the "deserts of Bohemia." While Ottocar's dominions extended to the sea, I am unable to find any reference to their ever including any area that could reasonably be called a "desert." But Shakespeare may have used the term simply to mean an uninhabited area. In *Two Gentlemen of Verona*, for example, he refers to "This shadowy desert, unfrequented woods" in describing an uninhabited part of the forest. And, in *The Tempest*, the admiral says, "This island seems to be desert," meaning uninhabited. The "deserts of Bohemia" was probably used in the same sense (i.e., an unpopulated part of the Bohemian Empire)— and Jonson probably knew it.

Shakespeare's detailed knowledge of actual characters and happenings involving the court of Navarre are depicted in *Love's Labour's Lost*. His inside references to those characters and events and accurate descriptions of the manners and behavior at the court make it improbable that this was just the product of research or the questioning of travelers who had been there.

For example, King Ferdinand in the play was Henri of Navarre, who, in 1593, became the legendary Henri IV of France. To accomplish this, Henri converted to Roman Catholicism, making the famous cynical remark, "Paris is worth a mass." The attendant lords in the play were actual noblemen. Biron in the play was the duc de Biron, Dumain was the duc de Mayenne, and Longaville was the duc de Longaville. Maria and Katharine were the wives of de Mayenne and Longaville.

The Princess was Marguerite de Valois, daughter of the French king. In act 2, King Ferdinand refers to her father's "payment of a hundred thousand crowns," which, if received, "there remains unpaid a hundred thousand more; in surety of which, one part of Acquitaine is bound to us." One hundred thousand crowns was the actual sum repaid by the French king on a loan of twice that amount, which was, in fact, secured by the territory of Acquitaine.

The play even depicts "Fantastical Spaniard" Don Adriano deArmado, who seems to have been based on a Spanish adventurer, Antonio Perez, at one time Phillip II's foreign minister. In Spain, Perez was involved in various shady intrigues. Suspected of serious crimes, he defected to France, where Henri IV sent him on a mission to England. While there, he moved in powerful circles, became an ally of Essex, and stayed at Bacon's home. Unable to resist bold and nefarious schemes, however, he was soon viewed as wild and unreliable. Ultimately, he returned to France. While in England, he wrote books under the pseudonym *Peregrino*. In what appears to be a punning allusion to Perez, Shakespeare describes Don Armado, in act 5, scene 1, as being "too peregrinate," a word he never used again.

Such inside references may not have been understood by the groundlings at the public theatres, but they would have been quickly recognized and appreciated when the play was performed at court, as it was.

Could all this have been the product of scholarly research? It is improbable—not the speech and manners, and possibly not even the characters and events. These were fairly recent events involving Navarre and France, not likely to have been recorded in any histories that existed in England at the time.

Love's Labour's Lost is generally thought to be a relatively early play written in 1594 or even before. The Stratford man was still in his twenties and had been in London only a few years.

Could he have obtained the information by the close questioning of some well-informed nobleman? Possibly, but this seems unlikely. Even if the young man from Stratford had the luck to meet such a highborn traveler, it seems improbable that their relationship would have permitted the kind of detailed interrogation necessary to ferret out the inside knowledge reflected in *Love's Labour's Lost*.

The printer, Richard Field, who had come to London from Stratford, was married to a French Protestant. Field published pamphlets on affairs in France and Navarre that mentioned the names de Longaville, Mayenne, and Biron. The Stratford man could have learned the names from Field and his wife, and possibly even a general description of certain events. But it is most unlikely that he would have known and absorbed the aristocratic speech and manners found in the play.

If the Stratford man wrote *Venus and Adonis*, which was published in 1593 and dedicated to the earl of Southampton, he might possibly have spent time with the earl and members of his household before writing

Love's Labour's Lost. If so, they conceivably might have provided him with the gossip and inside information about France and Navarre. But we have no evidence supporting this possibility.

In the play, the aristocratic men take an oath to abstain from the company of women, only to break their oath when a group of attractive young ladies arrive at court. It has been argued that this is a subtle allusion to the Protestant Henri of Navarre having received English aid to fight the Catholics, and then cynically deciding to become Catholic in order to take the French throne as Henri IV. But the argument seems unfounded. If anything, the point of the play is that the men were foolish and sophomoric to take the oath in the first place and, while much fun is made over their quickly breaking it, the playwright seems reasonably sympathetic to their very human conduct. At no point are the men who took and then broke the silly oath shown to have violated any serious moral or religious principle or to have betrayed anyone other than themselves.

As in the case of the Venetian references in *The Merchant of Venice*, the general references in *Hamlet* to the castle at Elsinore (Helsingör) are not proof that the playwright had actually visited Denmark. In 1586, William Kempe, George Bryan, and Thomas Pope, who later became fellow actors with the Stratford man, actually performed at the Castle of Helsingör as part of a European tour with the earl of Leicester's men. They could well have given the Stratford man such general information.

But there are other elements in *Hamlet* that do indicate a knowledge of local matters that would seem to exceed the bounds of whatever research tools were available to the Stratford man or of what his fellow actors might have remembered from playing the castle. For example, Hamlet's classmates at the University of Wittenberg are Rosencrantz and Guildenstern. The sixteenth-century records of that university show the registration of students named "Rosencrantz" and others named "Gyldenstjerne."

How could the Stratford man have acquired this information? It is not likely that he found it in any book available to him in England or that this would have been information known to his fellow actors. Conceivably, he could have been given those names by someone familiar with the university and its students. But is it likely that friends of the common Stratford actor would have possessed such unusual data about the names of actual Danish students at the University of Wittenberg?

In act 2 scene 1, Polonius refers to *Danskers,* the Dane's own word for themselves; and, later, a priest speaks of allowing the dead Ophelia her *crants,* the Danish term for wreaths.

In act 4 scene 5, the king of Denmark, hearing a threatening noise, demands, "Where are my Switzers? Let them guard the door." Like the Vatican, the Danish court employed Swiss guards. They were called "Switzers."

Did Shakespeare insert Danish terms just to show that he knew them? Or did they come naturally to him as a result of having been in Denmark or among Danes for a considerable period? And, if he were an actor and theatre operator interested in the commercial success of the play, why would he use Danish terms that were probably incomprehensible to his audience?

Again, the playwright may simply have picked up such facts and terms from someone who was Danish or had spent considerable time in Denmark. We cannot necessarily conclude that he had been there himself. But it does seem unlikely that the Stratford man would have acquired such esoteric local knowledge and terminology and that, if the choice were his, he would have chosen to include such material in the play.

Some Stratfordians argue that the name *Hamlet* comes from Hamnet, the Stratford man's deceased son. But the origin of the name seems, instead, to have come from de Belleforest's version of a thirteenth-century tale by Saxo-Grammaticus, a Danish historian, about "mad Prince Amleth," whose uncle murders his father.

OTHER LANGUAGES. Shakespeare relied on Plutarch's *Lives,* but he apparently used an English translation published by Sir Thomas North in 1579. In other instances, he had to have known Latin and Greek. He employed Ovid, Virgil, Plautus, Horace, Seneca, Plato, and other classical writers, including works not yet translated into English when he wrote, such as Ovid's *Fasti* and Sophocles's *Ajax.*

The ability to read Latin and Greek could be attributed to a Stratford education. But Shakespeare also used French and Italian works which had not yet been translated, such as de Belleforest's *Histoires Tragiques,* published in French in 1576, on which he probably based *Hamlet;* and Cinthio's *Ecatommiti,* published in Italian in 1565, the source of *Othello.* Orlando Pescetti's *Il Cesare,* published in Italian in 1594, appears to be one source of *Julius Caesar.*

The Merchant of Venice is taken from *Il Pecorone* by the Florentine Ser Giovanni. This fourteenth-century story, first printed in 1558, contains the essential plot of Shakespeare's play. There is no record of any English translation of *Il Pecorone* when Shakespeare wrote his play. *Measure for Measure* is also taken from Cinthio's *Ecatommiti*. Although a version of the story had been written in English by George Whetstone, Shakespeare appears to have worked from Cinthio's original Italian.

There are other such examples. Hamlet asks if his players can perform *The Murder of Gonzago*. The reference appears to be to an account of the murder of Alfonso Gonzaga, written in Italian by Antonio Possevino and not translated into English.

Nor was Shakespeare limited to the formal aspects of such languages. Professor Grillo provides examples of his ready use of Italian colloquialisms, as when, in *All's Well That Ends Well*, he refers to Florence and Sienna's being "by the ears," meaning in continuing conflict, or when he describes a character as being "sound as a fish."

Shakespeare not only appeared to use untranslated French sources, but he uses French seemingly with ease and wit, as in *Henry V*, where many lines are in French and where he even plays with French double entendre and colloquial speech. For example, when Henry is wooing the French princess, with the assistance of her maid, who speaks some English, the maid tells him, "I cannot tell vat is *baiser en* Anglish." While the noun *baiser* means a kiss, when used as a verb, *baiser* can have a very different meaning. In French argot, it means to have sex. Evidently, Shakespeare knew this and was having fun with it. This fits with act 3, scene 4 of *Henry V*, a scene almost entirely in French. Princess Katherine's mispronunciation of *gown* and *foot* are "de foot et de coun." She exclaims that these new words are "mauvais, corruptible, gros and impudique," since, as she pronounces them, they approximate the French words *foutre* (fuck) and *con* (cunt).

It has been argued that the Stratford man learned French while residing in the Mountjoy home in London, since Mountjoy had been born in France. This seems a considerable stretch, particularly since Shakespeare's 1612 deposition testifies to having lived at the Mountjoy's "ten years or thereabouts" earlier (i.e., around 1602). Yet most scholars place the creation of *Henry V* in early 1599.

Henry VI, Part 2, was probably written in 1590 or 1591, long before the

Stratford man resided with the Mountjoys. Yet in act 4, scene 7 of that play, Shakespeare has Jack Cade demand of Lord Say, "What cans't thou answer to my majesty for giving up of Normandy unto Monsier Basimecu, the Dauphin of France." *Basimecu* is a contraction of the French *Baise mon cul* (kiss my ass). Thus Cade refers to the dauphin as "Monsieur Kiss My Ass." But, given the ambiguity of the verb *baiser* in French argot, Cade may have had a cruder meaning—essentially "Monsieur Bugger Me."

Whichever the intended meaning, the lines certainly suggest a playwright quite familiar with the language of the French streets, as well as the French court.

No one suggests that the Stratford man learned Italian and French at the local grammar school. Yet how would this apparent fluency be possible for someone who, so far as we know, never left England?

ARCANE AND METAPHORICAL USAGE. Not only does Shakespeare use hundreds of esoteric terms from various fields that would have been difficult for the Stratford man to acquire, but he used these references as if they came naturally to him. One could argue, as traditionalists do, that Shakespeare could have boned up on these subjects and inserted them into the plays to add a note of authenticity. But, often, that was not how he used his amazingly diverse information. Often, it became a part of his descriptive text by metaphor and analogy.

For example, one area in which Shakespeare used esoteric terminology in a natural way was falconry, the use of falcons, hawks, and other fierce birds to hunt small game. In falconry, a set of bells is attached to the bird's tether. When the bird is ready to fly to the attack, he will begin to move, and the bells will sound. In *Henry VI*, Part 3, Shakespeare wrote that neither King Henry nor any other Lancastrian "dares stir a wing if Warwick shake his bells."

Warwick, of course, was the mighty earl called the "king maker" for his part in supporting the Yorkist Edward IV and defeating the Lancastrian Henry VI and his "she-wolf" queen. Shakespeare doesn't insert the reference to the Lancastrians' timidity should Warwick "shake his bells" in a literal sense, as would a writer who had acquired a few such terms to give a scene about falconry the appearance of authenticity. He uses the phrase metaphorically, as if the terminology of falconry was a working part of his vocabulary. The scene has nothing to do with falconry, and much of the London audience probably failed to understand the reference, since falconry was generally restricted to the upper classes and their country estates.

We see the same metaphoric use of falconry terms in *Othello*. The great general says of Desdemona, "If I do prove her haggard, though that her jisses were my heart strings, I'd whistle her off, and let her own the wind to prey at fortune." A bird that proved *haggard* was one that flew away never to return; and *jisses* were the leather straps by which the falconer held the bird before releasing it to fly.

A number of universities have "insider" terms, used only by students and faculty at those particular institutions. Another example of Shakespeare's unusual knowledge is evidenced by his natural and metaphoric use of terms particular to Cambridge University.

In act 2, scene 1 of *Hamlet*, when Polonius asks "What Danskers there are in Paris," he also inquires "where they keep." At Cambridge, the word *keep* meant "reside."

In act 2, scene 4 of *King Lear*, the king mistakenly says it would not be like his daughter Regan "to scant my sizes." At Cambridge, *sizes* were allowances granted to needy students or "sizars." To scant a student's sizes meant to reduce his allowance, usually as a punishment.

Here again, this was not the employment of unusual terms researched and artificially inserted in a play to show the playwright's erudition or to add authenticity to a scene. The terms are used comfortably and in a natural context by an author seemingly accustomed to their use as a part of his regular vocabulary. It would be difficult to imagine the Stratford man asking a Cambridge graduate, "How do you fellows say 'reside'?" or "What's a Cambridge term for cutting your allowance?" or even "Give me some inside terms I can throw into a play."

Was Shakespeare a Cantabrigian? His use of these inside terms may suggest that he was. Yet there is no evidence at all that the Stratford man ever attended Cambridge—or any other university. His name is not listed anywhere as a student, and he had no reason to use an alias, even in the unlikely event that he won a scholarship and was able to attend.

A work called *Polymarteia* was published at Cambridge in 1595. It lists a number of honored writers, including Shakespeare. The other listed writers are all Cambridge or Oxford men. Does this mean that Shakespeare was also a university graduate? Perhaps he was, but his being on this particular list isn't convincing evidence of it.

MILITARY AND NAVAL MATTERS. Although a number of writers in the field have insisted that Shakespeare must have seen military service, the case for that proposition is not overwhelming. To argue that the Bard was necessarily a man of military experience because he has described typical military characters, such as Falstaff, the cowardly knight; Pistol, the swaggering ensign; and Bardolph, the rascally corporal, is to overlook the fact that these are typical characters *in life*, not just in the military.

In *Love's Labour's Lost*, Biron advises his companions to deal with the women as if facing a battle, telling them to make sure "in conflict, that you get the sun of them." That is, attack with the sun in your enemy's eyes. This certainly indicates some knowledge of military tactics, although it doesn't necessarily establish Shakespeare as a military veteran.

In *Henry V*, he does appear to display some military knowledge, particularly with respect to the siege of Harfluer. The siege described in the play is inconsistent with the historical facts about Harfluer itself, but it is entirely consistent with events that might have occurred in such a siege; and it suggests that Shakespeare *may* have had military experience. But, here again, we cannot do better than "may."

The military campaigns portrayed in the *Henry VI* plays are essentially marchings on and off the stage, accompanied by speeches not particularly indicating military experience on the part of the playwright. Nor does any other play appear to contain inside military knowledge that could not be acquired through research or discussion with the veterans of military campaigns. Moreover, although "get the sun of them" in *Love's Labour's Lost* is an exception, Shakespeare's military terms are generally used in a military context, adding a note of authenticity to the scenes in which they appear. This is more consistent with their being the product of deliberate research than in those many instances in which Shakespeare uses esoteric terms metaphorically in unrelated contexts.

In *Julius Caesar*, Shakespeare describes how Brutus's troops, flushed with apparent victory over Antony, race ahead, out of control, uncovering the flanks of Cassius's adjacent formation and allowing Cassius to be encircled by the forces of Antony's ally Octavius.

This could, of course, be the work of a writer of military experience. But it is a fairly simple concept, readily understood by virtually any intelligent person, even without a military background. It doesn't take a Napoleon or Clauswitz to know that, if two allied wings of an army are fighting side by side and one wing advances much faster than the other, a gap will be created between them, leaving the flank of both wings exposed to enemy attack.

Besides, the situation was described in Plutarch's life of Brutus, and Plutarch was the source of Shakespeare's play. Indeed, Plutarch describes the battle in much greater detail than Shakespeare. If one were to decide which of the two authors had military experience, it would be Plutarch— and, in fact, he had none.

In *Richard III*, the night before the Battle of Bosworth Field, the king inquires whether his "beaver" is "easier than it was." And in *Hamlet*, Horatio says that he could see the face of the ghost, because "he wore his beaver up." A military man would have known that a *beaver* was the face guard of a helmet. But a nonmilitary playwright might well have learned the term, perhaps having asked some old soldier for examples of military terms that would add a note of authenticity.

Similarly, in *Hamlet*, the ghost is described as armed "cap à pé" (i.e., from head to foot). Once again, this suggests military knowledge but could be the product of research or questioning.

Just before the fighting begins in *Richard III*, the king announces the order of his forces:

> *My foreward shall be drawn out all in length,*
> *Consisting equally of horse and foot;*
> *Our archers shall be placed in the midst;*
> *John Duke of Norfolk, Thomas Earl of Surrey,*
> *Shall have the leading of this foot and horse.*
> *They thus directed, we will follow*
> *In the main battle, whose puissance on either side*
> *Shall be well winged with our chiefest horse.*

In other words, the forward ranks would be formed in a long line comprised of both cavalry and infantry with archers placed in their midst. These front ranks would be led by Norfolk (who actually died in the battle) and his son Surrey. Just behind the front ranks would be the main body of troops led by the king himself, with the principal elements of the loyalist cavalry stationed on each wing.

These certainly are military concepts. But, again, they are relatively simple ones, probably known in Elizabethan times to men who had never fought a battle. Moreover, as in the case with Plutarch, Richard's order of battle can be found in Hollingshed's *Chronicles*, Shakespeare's source.

Even considering the realistic aspects of some military scenes, there is insufficient evidence in the plays to draw the firm conclusion that Shakespeare had military experience. All we can say is that it is not unlikely.

Entire books have been devoted to the thesis that Shakespeare used terms known only to experienced seamen and used them, in every instance, correctly. One such work is W. B. Whall's *Shakespeare's Sea Terms Explained* (1910).

In *The Tempest*, for example, the boatswain reports that the ship "is tight and yare and bravely rigged." Here again, *tight* and *bravely rigged* might be known to nonseafarers; but *yare,* meaning a craft that responds quickly to the helm, would seem fairly esoteric. *Yare* is used again in *Antony and Cleopatra* to contrast the mobility of Octavius's ships with Antony's "heavy" vessels.

But these are instances in which Shakespeare uses nautical terms in describing the qualities of ships. More interesting are those passages in which characters use such terms metaphorically or as analogies in contexts entirely unrelated to ships, fleets, or navies. For example, in *Measure for Measure*, the clown tells the executiener that, if he will accept the clown as an associate, "you shall find me yare."

And, in *The Merry Wives of Windsor*, Pistol tells Falstaff that, in seeking romance, he should "clap on more sails; pursue; up with your fights; give fire; she is my prize; or ocean whelm them all."

"Clap on more sails," "pursue" and "she is my prize" seem the kind of nautical phrases an intelligent nonseaman might know. But "give fire" seems to have been the correct phrasing of the command to fire the ship's guns and might not have been widely known. "Up with your fights" is an even more arcane phrase. *Fights* were the heavy canvas sheets raised in a naval battle to screen the men on deck from enemy snipers.

In *Othello*, Iago describes himself as "be-lee'd and calm'd," because

Othello has chosen Cassio as his lieutenant, rather than Iago. A ship "be-lee'd" was one whose sails were blocked from the wind so that it was unable to move.

Perhaps, with the defeat of the armada, common Englishmen had become more familiar with such naval expressions. And, of course, Shakespeare, even if he had never been to sea, might have inquired about such terms from others who had. But the way he uses them, in such speeches as those quoted from *Measure for Measure*, *The Merry Wives of Windsor*, and *Othello*, is metaphorical and natural and not at all as if he had inquired about nautical terms that he could work into his plays to provide authenticity.

Here again, we cannot draw a definite conclusion that Shakespeare had naval experience. However, it seems more probable than not. And there is no evidence that the Stratford man had any such experience.

LEGAL KNOWLEDGE. Another area in which Shakespeare displayed significant inside knowledge was the law. Over and over again, he employs legal terminology in a natural and relevant context.

In *Othello*, for example, Iago refers to "non-suiting" other claimants, that is, dismissing the plaintiff's case without the necessity of even hearing the defendant's evidence. In *The Merry Wives of Windsor*, Mrs. Page says that the devil may have Falstaff "in fee simple with fine and recovery" (i.e., absolute ownership with damages in the event of interference).

In *Henry VI*, Part I, the king tells his son that Richard II "enfoeff'd himself to popularity," that is, surrendered absolute ownership of himself to the quest to be popular.

In *Hamlet*, Shakespeare refers to poor Yorick's being beaten about the head but not threatening to bring an "action of battery." Then, in discussing whether Ophelia has the right to receive a Christian burial notwithstanding her suicide, Shakespeare uses the identical argument advanced by the defendant's counsel in the case of *Hales v. Petit* as reported by Plowden in 1571. Shakespeare's words are quite close to those in Plowden, even though that report is in legal French.

Stratfordians contend that, in the Elizabethan Age, many ordinary people had knowledge of legal terms and that the Stratford man would have gained an even greater familiarity with such terms through his own legal proceedings and those of his father. As an example, they cite Ben

Jonson, Shakespeare's contemporary, who they claim used even more legal terminology in his plays than Shakespeare.

But Shakespeare used legal terms naturally and in proper context. As Lord Campbell, the lord chief justice (and, later, lord chancellor), put it, Shakespeare demonstrated "a deep technical knowledge of the law" and exhibited "an easy familiarity with some of the most obtrusive proceedings in English jurisprudence." By contrast, Jonson tended to interlard his character's speeches with legal terms that were not necessarily given their proper meaning but were used to make the character appear foolish or perhaps to show off the playwright's erudition and versatility.

For example, in *The Staple of News*, Jonson's character Picklock simply spews out a list of unrelated legal nonsense:

> *In all languages in Westminster-Hall.*
> *Pleas, Bench, or Chancery. Fee form, fee-tail,*
> *Tenant in dower, at will, for term of life.*
> *By copy of count-roll, knight's service, homage.*
> *Fealty, escuage, soccage, or frank almoigne.*
> *Grand serjeantry, or burgage.*

Jonson, although not a "university man," had an excellent education at the Westminster School, where he studied with the noted scholar William Camden. This would not have taught him legal terms. But, later, Jonson served as a secretary to Sir Francis Bacon, the leading lawyer of his day. Jonson would, of course, have learned numerous legal phrases.

It has been suggested in some biographies that the Stratford man served as a clerk in a lawyer's office. There is not the slightest evidence of this. And, if he had worked as such a clerk, one would expect to find his signature as a witness on numerous legal documents. Not one such document has ever been found. To argue that the Stratford man must have had legal training, because Shakespeare used legal phrases, is, once again, to beg the question by assuming that Shakespeare *was* the Stratford man.

Over the centuries, there has been controversy as to whether Shakespeare's use of legal terms and principles was, in some instances, inaccurate. Lord Campbell, certainly an expert on the subject, opined that the Bard "uniformly lays down good law." Sir George Greenwood, a London barrister and member of Parliament, agreed and wrote books defending Shakespeare's legal usage. Moreover, some errors in jurisprudential usage might be consistent with the legal knowledge of a nobleman who studied law at the Inns of Court but had never actually practiced as a lawyer. Among the anti-Strat candidates, only Bacon was a skilled legal practitioner, and any legal mistakes in the Shakespeare canon might militate against the Baconians. The others, who studied at the Inns of Court, but never practiced, such as Oxford, Stanley, and Rutland, would probably have had a working knowledge of legal terminology and the ability to use it in the proper context, but might make an occasional error.

Shakespeare did, in one instance, use a plot device that, arguably, ignores the applicable law. In *The Merchant of Venice*, Shylock seeks to enforce Antonio's pledge of a pound of flesh. In effect, this security device would allow the creditor to kill or severely maim the debtor if the loan was not repaid. Seemingly, such a pledge would have been unenforceable as against public policy in every European jurisdiction, including Venice. This was a simple and straightforward legal argument available to the supposedly brilliant Portia and yet overlooked by her. However, even if Shakespeare saw the argument, he would probably have considered it dull, preferring the clever "twist" of his lawyer-heroine conceding that Shylock can take his pound of flesh, but arguing that, in doing so, he must not shed one drop of blood—lest he exceed the pledge.

ENGLISH VOCABULARY. Shakespeare employed a plethora of words far, far in excess even of writers credited with genius. The average sixteenth-century yeoman or artisan in an English country town—the kind of men with whom the Stratford man was raised—is said to have had a vocabulary of probably 300 to 400 words. Today's university graduates average far more, probably 3,000 to 4,000 words. The entire Old Testament contains 5,642 words. Marlowe, a brilliant and highly educated poet and playwright, used about 7,500. John Milton, considered a genius, used an extraordinary 8,000. By contrast, Shakespeare used over 21,000 words, many of which he created himself from Latin and Greek roots. Hundreds of words that he coined remain in common usage today. As Alexandre Dumas put it, "After God, Shakespeare created most."

He was a "genius," say the Stratfordians. But so was Milton. Yet Milton's vocabulary was less than half of Shakespeare's. Even given extraordinary intelligence, it would seem highly improbable that the young man, newly arrived from rural Stratford, could have accumulated the massive vocabulary and volume of information, much less the maturity of outlook, required to write even the early poems and plays, much less the full Shakespeare canon.

That amazing vocabulary and enormous quantity of varied information must be considered strong evidence supporting the conclusion that Shakespeare was not the Stratford man—or at least that he was not the Stratford man working alone. This evidence may not be conclusive, but it does point our way toward a likely scenario.

7.

LOCAL REFERENCES

Quite frequently, authors use the names of places familiar to them and make references in their work to such places and to people in the area—albeit by other names. This permits a greater and more relaxed feeling of familiarity and accuracy. Shakespeare mentioned a myriad of English place names. For example, the plays contain many references to the places in which Bacon and Oxford had homes. *Yet, Shakespeare never mentions Stratford. Not in one line of one poem or play.* Is that absence conclusive? No. For some unknown reason, Shakespeare may have deliberately avoided mentioning his hometown. Other authors have. But given the volume of Shakespeare's work and the numerous references to other English places and names, the paucity of references to people and places in Stratford is unusual.

Even though there has been widespread research for centuries on the issue of local references in Shakespeare, the Stratfordians have found little that is convincing. E. K. Chambers points out that a man named Fluellen and another named Bardolfe, both characters in *Henry V*, were once on a list of those absent from Protestant services in Stratford, along with John Shakspere. Samuel Schoenbaum points to a reference in *The Taming of the Shrew* to "Marian Hacket, the fat ale-wife of Wincot" in a speech by Christopher Sly "of Burton Heath." Schoenbaum argues that Barton on the Heath is a tiny village fifteen miles from Stratford, while Wincot (it's really

"Wilmcote") is another small place only four or five miles from Stratford. He adds that a family of Hackets lived in the parish, and there were Slys in Stratford itself. "Burton" could, of course, be "Barton," just as "Wincot" could be "Wilmcote."

But the names cited by Chambers and Schoenbaum are fairly common ones. Sir William Phillips, hardly a provincial Stratfordian, was, for example, Lord Bardolph. Fluellen is a relatively common Welsh name. And, certainly, Hackets, Hacketts, and Slys lived in many English parishes. In fact, Christopher Sly is a character in *A Shrew*, a play that is a source for *The Taming of the Shrew*.

Virtually all of the action in *As You Like It* takes place in the Forest of Arden. Arden was the maiden name of the Stratford man's mother. But, in the play, the Forest of Arden is in France, and it seems likely that it was an anglicized version of the French Forest of Ardennes, through which the German Panzers attacked in World War II's Battle of the Bulge.

We have already discussed the possibility that Justice Shallow and his coat of arms of a dozen luces in *The Merry Wives of Windsor* refer to Sir Thomas Lucy of Charlcote near Stratford, who was a justice of the peace and who had just such a coat of arms. Could someone who hadn't come from the Stratford area have possessed such information? Probably. Sir Thomas Lucy was a member of Parliament who gained considerable notoriety as a fanatical Protestant, ferocious in pursuing Catholics and even in pursuing Protestants whom he considered too soft on Catholics. Indeed, Sir Thomas urged his fellow members of Parliament to execute one of their number who, although a Protestant, had suggested that certain anti-Catholic legislation might be unduly harsh.

If the real "Shakespeare" was a well-connected aristocrat or politician, it would not be surprising if he knew Lucy or at least knew *of* him, and was aware of Lucy's arms and Sir Thomas's unique "enthusiasm" in pressing his point of view.

On the other hand, the reference to Lucy might well suggest an author from the Stratford area or at least that someone from the Stratford area made suggestions to the author.

Just as the anti-Strats cite references to the widely diversified information in Shakespeare's plays that might not have been known to the Stratford man, the Stratfordians cite references in the plays to information about agriculture and animal husbandry. They argue that this rural information would have been known to the Stratford man, whose father was also a farmer and wool dealer, but would not likely have been known to his aristocratic rival candidates.

Most of these references provide a general sort of information, probably known to most Englishmen at the time, such as Antonio's speech in *The Merchant of Venice*: "I am the tainted wether of the flock, meetest for death: the weakest kind of fruit drops earliest to the ground."

There are more references to such matters, particularly to the slaughtering of calves, the breeding of sheep, and the selling of wool. Probably the most telling for the Stratfordians is Clown's speech in *The Winter's Tale*: "Let me see:—every leven wether tods; every tod yields pound and odd shilling; fifteen hundred shorn, what comes the wool too? . . . I cannot do it without a counter."

A *tod* was a weight used in the wool trade. Clown, a shepherd's son, is saying that every eleven sheep produce a tod, which yields a little over a pound, but that the yield from fifteen hundred sheep cannot be computed in his head.

Even this rather arcane bit of rural speech would not have been outside the ken of the owners of rural estates, such as the earls of Oxford, Derby, and Rutland. The terminology is not used metaphorically as in the examples previously discussed. Possibly, it could have been obtained by Marlowe or Bacon, through inquiry, in order to add a note of authenticity to a rural scene.

Stratfordians also argue that a number of Shakespeare's plays contain lines showing a familiarity with John Shakspere's trade as a maker of fine gloves and other leather goods. In *The Merry Wives of Windsor*, for example, he speaks of "a glover's paring knife" and, in *Romeo and Juliet*, there are references to *cheverie*, which is kidskin used in making fine gloves. Other plays contain references to various kinds of animal skins being used for varying purposes. But none of these references seems so arcane as to have required familiarity with a glover's workshop.

The references cited by the Stratfordians fall short of demonstrating that the playwright was the Stratford man. There are certainly considerable references to rural matters and to various trades in which John Shakspere engaged; but they are not sufficient to make the Stratfordian case. On the other hand, the absence from the plays of more local references or clearer ones does not compel us to the conclusion that the Bard was *not* the Stratford man.

In a thoughtful and imaginative book, Stephen Greenblatt takes a different approach. Rather than focusing on physical references to Stratford or explicit references to events of the Stratford man's life, Professor Greenblatt suggests that the plays reflect "Shakespeare's" personal reaction to the events of his life, such as his father's dramatic loss of status, his own striving to become a "gentleman," his relationship with his daughter Susanna, and his feelings on leaving his career in London and retiring to Stratford. For example, Greenblatt tells us that Prospero's putting aside his magical powers to become the duke of Milan reflects what must have been "Shakespeare's" feelings on leaving his career as a playwright to retire to Stratford, and "Shakespeare's" seemingly unhappy marriage may be reflected in the fact that, with the possible exception of the Macbeths and the marriage of Claudius and Gertrude in *Hamlet*, the marriages in the plays tend to be loveless, if not troubled.

Greenblatt assumes that Shakespeare was the Stratford man, and his references to events of that man's life tend to be of the "he must have," "may have," "undoubtedly did" school. But his insights are more profound than most. He is forthright in conceding that his assumptions often skate on thin factual ice, but his book is still a fine piece of work and a pleasure to read. Could his hypothesis be correct? Possibly. Is it compelling? Perhaps to some, not to me.

8.

THE "GROATSWORTH OF WIT"

*A*mong the significant pieces of evidence cited by the Stratfordians is Robert Greene's reference to an actor he calls "Shake-scene," and his use of language that may suggest that "Shake-scene" was a playwright as well.

But how seriously should we take whatever Greene had to say? Drunk, diseased, and destitute, Greene tended to rage at his ill fortune. Near death, he called for a "penny-pot" of malmsey wine, sending a pitiful note to the wife he had abandoned, pleading with her to reimburse the shoemaker who took him in, "for if he and his wife had not succored me, I had died in the streets." As Gabriel Harvey put it, "Who in London hath not heard of his dissolute and licentious living" and "his scandalous and blasphemous raving." Greene wrote his "Groatsworth of Wit" as he lay dying in the shoemaker's house—if he really wrote it at all. It is entirely possible that someone else wrote it after Greene's death.

Despite all this, what Greene appears to have written is evidence of a sort, and we must consider it with the rest. His embittered letter was directed to unnamed playwrights, warning them against an "upstart crow, beautified with our feathers, that with his tiger's heart wrapped in a player's hide supposes he is well able to bombast out a blank verse as the best of you; and being an absolute *Johannes fac totum* is in his own conceit the only Shake-scene in a country."

Assuming, as I think we must, that the Stratford man became an actor and, at least on stage, used the name *Shakespeare*, Greene's reference seems, at first blush, directed at him and appears to consider him not only an actor, but also an actor who at least claimed to be a playwright.

Struggling to avoid that connection, anti-Stratfordians have argued that Greene's reference is not to a playwright who also acts, but to an actor who takes it upon himself to ad-lib additions to the playwright's lines. This might seem inconsistent with the reference to "Johannes fac totum," which meant a jack of all trades (from the Latin *facere*, "to do," and *totum*, "all") and with the plain allusion to Shakespeare's line from *Henry VI* ("a tiger's heart wrapped in a woman's hide").

But there is a possibility we should not ignore—that Greene's diatribe was directed to the actor Edward Alleyn, who played the duke of York and spoke the line to which Greene was alluding; and that the term *Shake-scene* is a spiteful reference to Alleyn's boisterous overacting, rather than a play on the name *Shake-speare*. Apparently, Greene envied and resented Alleyn, and the two had quarreled bitterly over business dealings. The use of "Johannes fac totum" fits Alleyn quite well, since he not only acted and wrote some plays, but was also a partner of his father-in-law Phillip Henslowe in owning the theatre. The fact that Shake-scene is capitalized may suggest that Greene's reference was to the name *Shake-speare*. But sixteenth-century capitalization was hopelessly inconsistent, with many midsentence words capitalized that would not be capitalized today. The possibility that Shake-scene meant a "ham" actor whose loud overacting "shakes the scenery" cannot be ruled out, but it is generally treated as less likely than the alternative.

The anti-Strats may be overly concerned about what can be inferred from Greene's warning. True, its most likely construction does indicate that Greene *believed* that Shakespeare, the actor, also wrote the play or at least claimed to be the playwright. However, this does not tell us that he *did*, in fact, write the play, rather than serve as a front for the actual playwright. That, of course, is another and more difficult question. Greene may not have known who really wrote the lines to which he referred; and, if, as has been contended, someone else (such as Henrye Chettle) actually wrote "Greene's" letter, that person may have been even more distant from the London theatre scene and even less likely to know the truth.

There is a clue suggesting that, whomever Greene was really attacking, Shakespeare believed himself the subject of the attack. Sonnet 112 includes the following curious lines:

> Your love and pity doth th' impression fill
> which vulgar scandal stamped upon my brow;
> For what care I who calls me well or ill,
> So you o'er-green my bad, my good allow?

"O'er-green" is one of those numerous words coined by Shakespeare. He uses it again in act 4, scene 14 of *Antony and Cleopatra*, where a beaten Antony describes how he did once, "O'er-green Neptune's back with ships." In Sonnet 112, however, the fanciful verb may well be an allusion to Greene's attack, particularly since the spelling in the original version of the sonnet appears as "o'er-greene," with an *e*, just as Greene spelled his name. Moreover, these lines are followed by the poet's assertion that his concern is only for the opinion of his love and that he discards "all care of other's voices," his senses being "stopped" to "critic and to flatterer." The confluence of "o'er-greene" and the professed lack of care for "who calls me . . . ill" or of what a "critic" might say lend support to construction of the sonnet as a reference to Greene's attack on "Shake-scene," the "upstart crow."

Perhaps years later, when he wrote *Hamlet*, Shakespeare was still smarting from what he perceived to be Greene's accusing him of being "beautified" with the "feathers" of other playwrights. When Hamlet's letter described Ophelia as "beautified," Shakespeare had Polonius say "That's an ill phrase, a vile phrase, 'beautified' is a vile phrase."

Even if the author of the sonnets *perceived* Greene's attack to have been aimed at him, this does not demonstrate that it was or that he was the Stratford man. Even if Shakespeare were someone else, for whom the Stratford man "fronted," it was still his play that Greene lampooned. Moreover, Greene's attack seems to contain an accusation of plagiarism. In writing that the "upstart crow" was "beautified with our feathers," Greene may have been accusing the playwright of "stealing" the play itself from one of the university-educated authors Greene considered "us."

On the other hand, "beautified with our feathers," could simply refer to Edward Alleyn's performing in a play written by one of Greene's fellow playwrights.

What can we infer from the apparently powerful person who took umbrage at Greene's remarks, forcing poor Henrye Chettle to apologize? It is commonly assumed that Shakespeare was both the "upstart crow" attacked by Greene and also the unnamed "play-maker" who took offense and received Chettle's fawning apology. That common assumption makes little sense.

In his apology, Chettle wrote that Greene's warning against the "upstart crow" had been addressed to "divers play-makers" and that "one or two of them" took offense. Chettle then apologized to one of these two offended "play-makers" and praised him and his work. The apology and praise seem addressed to one of the writers that Greene had warned against the "upstart crow," rather than to the "upstart crow" himself.

If Shakespeare was the "upstart crow" and the "Shake-scene" against whom the "divers play-makers" were being warned, it would seem impossible that he was also one of the "divers play-makers" to whom the warning was addressed. If Greene was warning the play-makers *against Shakespeare*, it would follow that Shakespeare could not have been one of the unnamed "play-makers" Greene was warning against the "upstart crow." Otherwise, Greene would have been in the bizarre and illogical position of warning Shakespeare against Shakespeare.

On the other hand, when Chettle characterized Greene's warning as having been addressed to "divers play-makers" and added that "one of the two *of them*" took offense, he may have meant one or two *play-makers* took offense, but not necessarily the particular play-makers who were being warned by Greene. That would be a somewhat strained construction of Chettle's language, but not an impossible one. It is supported by the balance of Chettle's apology in which he refers to one of the offended playwrights "whom at the time I did not so much spare, as wish I had" and adds that he had "moderated the heat" of writers in the past and was "sorry" that he had not done so in this case.

Those words in the apology suggest that the offended playwright to whom Chettle apologized was the person Greene had attacked as an "upstart crow," but was not necessarily one of the playwrights Greene was warning *against* the "upstart crow."

But there are alternative explanations. One is that Chettle's apology was directed to a "play-maker" who was not the person Greene meant to attack, but who incorrectly believed he was or feared that the public might think so. In that case, the play-maker who took umbrage at Greene's words could have been Shakespeare, who, because of the reference to "Shake-scene," *believed* he was the subject of the attack, when perhaps he was not.

Even if Edward Alleyn was actually the intended subject of Greene's verbal abuse, Shakespeare may have erroneously believed it was intended for him, and others may have construed it as criticism of Shakespeare and his work. After all, his lines were parodied and the ambiguous reference to "Shake-scene" would likely have been taken as a play on his name, just as most scholars construe it today.

But whether or not Greene was attacking the playwright, the person he was attacking was certainly an actor. Otherwise, "tiger's heart wrapped *in a player's hide*" makes no sense. If Shakespeare construed the attack as meant for him, wouldn't that tell us that Shakespeare was an actor? And, if so, wasn't he the Stratford man?

No, because there is still another alternative explanation—that Shakespeare was *not* the Stratford man but was already using him as a front for his plays. If so, when Greene attacked "Shake-scene" as an "upstart crow," particularly with a parody of Shakespeare's lines, the real Shakespeare might well have considered this an attack on his writing and taken umbrage, even if Greene had meant to attack the Stratford actor, who Greene *believed* had written the play, because the actor had kept his part of the bargain by taking credit for having written it.

That scenario might be more consistent with Chettle's apology. If the apology was meant for Shakespeare, and he was really the Stratford man, it would be difficult to imagine the young actor, at that early stage of his career—even before *Venus and Adonis*—having enough clout to force an abject apology from an experienced businessman like Chettle. Wouldn't it suggest someone with much more power and influence?

Can we draw any firm conclusion about the identity of Shakespeare from the Greene/Chettle episode? Not really. There are too many alternative possibilities. Maybe Greene thought the Stratford man wrote the play. Maybe he didn't. Maybe he meant to attack someone else entirely, such as Alleyn; and even if he thought the Stratford man wrote the play, that doesn't make it so. Maybe Chettle's apology was forced by

Shakespeare. Maybe not. And if it was, it still doesn't tell us who Shakespeare was.

Since Greene was dead by the time his attack was published, there is no way of knowing with certainty the person he meant by "Shake-scene," the "upstart crow." We can only try to formulate a reasonable hypothesis, and I will try to do just that as we proceed.

9.

THE PUZZLE
OF THE SONNETS

*I*n the sonnets, and only in the sonnets, do we obtain what seems a glimpse of Shakespeare speaking for himself as a real person, expressing his own intense feelings, as opposed to his beautifully expressed insights into the behavior of others. Only in the sonnets do we sense what appears to be his own pain and anguish, his very human fears and doubts, his consciousness of advancing age, his imperfections, his ill-concealed jealousy. As William Wordsworth said of the sonnets, "With this key, Shakespeare unlocked his heart."

Wordsworth was right. If, as seems likely, the sonnets are not mere fiction, but reflect the inner musings of the poet himself, they are an extraordinary window into his soul. Still, almost everything about them creates a puzzle. Who is speaking, and to whom and about whom? Beyond one strange and beautiful poem, very little in the sonnets seems to fit anything in the life of the Stratford man.

The sonnets are preceded by a dedication written by someone other than the poet. It is repeated here in its entirety.

TO . THE . ONLIE . BEGETTER . OF .
THESE . ENSUING . SONNETS .
MR. W . H . ALL . HAPPINESSE .
AND . THAT . ETERNITIE .

PROMISED .
BY .
OUR . EVER-LIVING . POET .
WISHETH .
THE . WELL-WISHING .
ADVENTURER . IN .
SETTING .
FORTH .
T. T.

We have already seen that at least three things about the dedication suggest that Shakespeare was no longer alive in 1609 when the sonnets were published. First, the use of "our ever-living poet" seems almost surely a reference to a dead poet given immortality by his works. Second, the publisher, Thomas Thorpe ("T. T.") wrote the dedication, rather than the poet himself, as would be customary. And, third, the publication was entitled *Shake-speare's Sonnets*, rather than "Sonnets by Shakespeare," perhaps implying that these are all the sonnets there will ever be. Is this conclusive proof that the Bard was dead? No. But it must certainly be considered significant evidence supporting that conclusion. And, of course, the Stratford man was still very much alive.

The dedication creates further questions. Who was "Mr. W. H.," described as "the onlie begetter" of the sonnets? That odd phrase would seem to describe either the author of the poems or the person who inspired them. One theory is that "W. H." is a misprint and was meant to be "W. SH.," an abbreviation of William Shakespeare. As the poet, he could certainly be considered the "onlie begetter."

But it would be rare to dedicate a collection of poems to the poet himself. And, given the way the terms are used, the "onlie begetter" seems to be someone different from "our ever-living poet."

Another theory is that the reference was to the earl of Southampton, to whom both *Venus* and *Lucrece* had been dedicated. Young Southampton may have been the "beauteous and lovely fair youth," who is the subject of most of the sonnets. Elizabethans sometimes placed a man's family name before his given name, so that "W. H." could have stood for "Wriothesley Henry," Southampton's name. If he was the person who inspired the majority of the sonnets, he could seemingly qualify as the "onlie begetter."

As we have seen, "H. W." was a character in *Willowbie His Avisa*, described as "a familiar friend" of the actor, "W. S." That "H. W." has also been thought to be Southampton.

The wording of the dedication is consistent with "the onlie begetter" being the "lovely youth." The "well-wishing adventurer"—evidently Thomas Thorpe—seems to wish "the onlie begetter" the "eternitie" that was "promised" him by "our ever-living poet." And the sonnets do promise a kind of "eternitie" to the "lovely youth" through the poet's words.

An alternative candidate for both "Mr. W. H." and the "lovely youth" is William Herbert, the earl of Pembroke. But Pembroke was born in 1580. Since the sonnets appear to have been written in the 1590s, he would seem too young to have engaged in some of the actions attributed in the sonnets to the lovely youth, such as having an affair with the poet's mistress. Of course, by 1609, when the sonnets were published, Pembroke was certainly old enough to be the "W. H." of the dedication, even if he was not the "lovely youth" of the poems.

One problem with either Southampton or Pembroke being "W. H." is the use of "Mr. W. H." Gentlemen, including even knights, were sometimes addressed as "Mr," but it was not a proper mode of addressing an earl.

Others argue that the reference was not to the poet or some inspiring nobleman, but to plain William Hall, who physically brought the manuscript to Thorpe, and that the word *ALL* was meant to be connected to the preceding letter *H* to spell "HALL." But the spacing does not support that contention. Nor does Hall's mundane connection to the manuscript seem to fit the sense of the dedication or to warrant his being called the "onlie begetter" of the sonnets. And nothing in the sonnets suggests that the "ever-living poet" promised "eternitie" to William Hall.

These are not the only candidates whose names have been advanced as "Mr. W. H." Another is Sir William Harvey, Southampton's stepfather. Harvey had been bequeathed the personal property of Southampton's mother upon her death. This may have included the manuscript of the sonnets, if Shakespeare had given it to her or to Southampton. It has been suggested that a wish for "all happinesse" to "the well-wishing adventurer" could be a reference to Harvey's having just set out on a new marriage. But that construction doesn't square with the context. It is "the well-wishing adventurer" who wishes "the onlie begetter" "all happinesse" and the "eternitie" promised by the "ever-living poet." The "well-wishing adventurer" is not the recipient of the wish.

Other candidates are William Hammond, William Hathaway, and William Hughes. Those advocating Hughes find, in Sonnet 20's "a man in hue all hues," a pun on their candidate's name.

We do not know the answer; and the identity of "Mr. W. H." remains another of the mysteries surrounding Shakespeare's life and works. The most likely solution is that "Mr. W. H." was the lovely youth to whom most of the sonnets are directed; and the most likely person to have been the lovely youth was Southampton.

Most of Sonnets 1 through 126 are addressed to that unnamed youth, described as beautiful and much younger than the poet (e.g., Sonnet 18, "Shall I compare thee to a summer's day? Thou art more lovely"). At first, the youth is repeatedly urged to marry and beget children (e.g., Sonnet 3, "Die Single and thine image dies with thee"). Then, the sonnets become far more personal—even intimate. While indicating in one sonnet that their relationship is not sexual, the poet repeatedly speaks of his love for the youth (e.g., Sonnet 20, "thou, the master-mistress of my passion"). It is not clear whether they are equals in class and status, or the poet is of a lower class.

It seems odd that the poet was so emphatic about urging another man to marry and have children. Did he have some motive of his own in push-ing marriage on the youth? It is difficult to find any such motive that fits the Stratford man. Indeed, if the Stratford man was the poet and young Southampton was the lovely youth, as well as the poet's patron, the Strat-ford man would seem to have embarked on a very unwise campaign. He would have been aggressively pushing his wealthy benefactor into doing the very thing he was most adamantly resisting—marrying Burghley's granddaughter, a match being urged on Southampton by Burghley himself. Surely, Southampton would have resented such pushy behavior from a common actor. We will revisit this issue in considering the candidacy of the earl of Oxford. Southampton's potential bride was Oxford's daughter, as well as Burghley's grandchild. Oxford had a motive for urging marriage. The Stratford man did not—at least not one we know.

There is a suggestion in the sonnets that the poet has suffered some public disgrace or at least criticism, but that he is consoled by the youth's

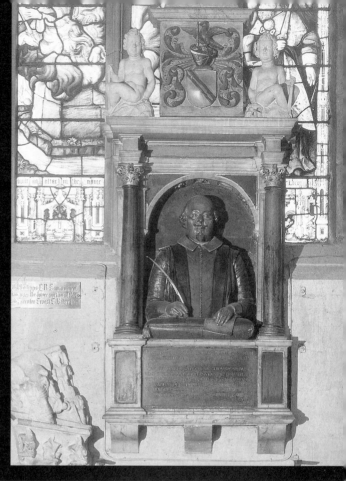

Monument to William Shakespeare (1564–1616) c. 1616–23 (stone & marble) by Gheerart Janssen (1600–23). (HOLY TRINITY CHURCH, STRATFORD-UPON-AVON, WARWICKSHIRE/ REPRINTED BY PERMISSION FROM BRIDGEMAN ART LIBRARY INTERNATIONAL.)

Engraving of the original Monument to William Shakespeare in Holy Trinity Church, Stratford-upon-Avon. (FROM ANTIQUITIES OF WARWICKSHIRE ILLUSTRATED, BY SIR WILLIAM DUGDALE (1605–1686), 1656, P.520. REPRINTED BY PERMISSION FROM THE FOLGER SHAKESPEARE LIBRARY: D2479.)

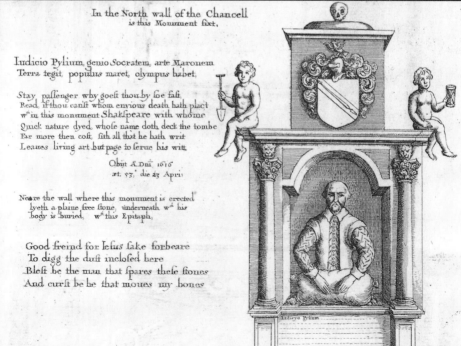

In the North wall of the Chancell
is this Monument fixt.

Iudicio Pylium, genio Socratem, arte Maronem
Terra tegit, populus maret, olympus habet.

Stay, passenger why goest thou by soe fast,
Read, if thou canst whom envious death hath plact
w.th in this monument Shakspeare with whome
Quick nature dyed, whose name doth deck the tombe
Far more then cost, sith all that he hath writt
Leaues living art but page to serue his witt.

Obijt A.Dni 1616
æt. 53, die 23 Apri:

Neare the wall where this monument is erected
lyeth a plaine free stone, underneath w.ch his
body is buried, w.th this Epitaph.

Good freind for Iesus sake forbeare
To digg the dust inclosed here
Blest be the man that spares these stones
And curst be he that moues my bones

Iudicio Pylium

TO.THE.ONLIE.BEGETTER.OF.
THESE.INSVING.SONNETS.
Mr.W.H. ALL.HAPPINESSE.
AND.THAT.ETERNITIE.
PROMISED.

BY.

OVR.EVER-LIVING.POET.

WISHETH.

THE.WELL-WISHING.
ADVENTVRER.IN.
SETTING.
FORTH.

T. T.

Dedication page from *The Sonnets*.
(REPRINTED BY PERMISSION FROM THE FOLGER
SHAKESPEARE LIBRARY: STC22353.)

**Title page of The First Folio with the
Droeshout engraving.** (REPRINTED BY PERMISSION
FROM THE FOLGER SHAKESPEARE LIBRARY: STC22273.)

Ex dono Will Iaggard Typographi. a° 1623

Mr. WILLIAM

SHAKESPEARES

COMEDIES,
HISTORIES, &
TRAGEDIES.

Published according to the True Originall Copies.

Martin Droeshout sculpsit London.

LONDON
Printed by Isaac Iaggard, and Ed. Blount. 1623.

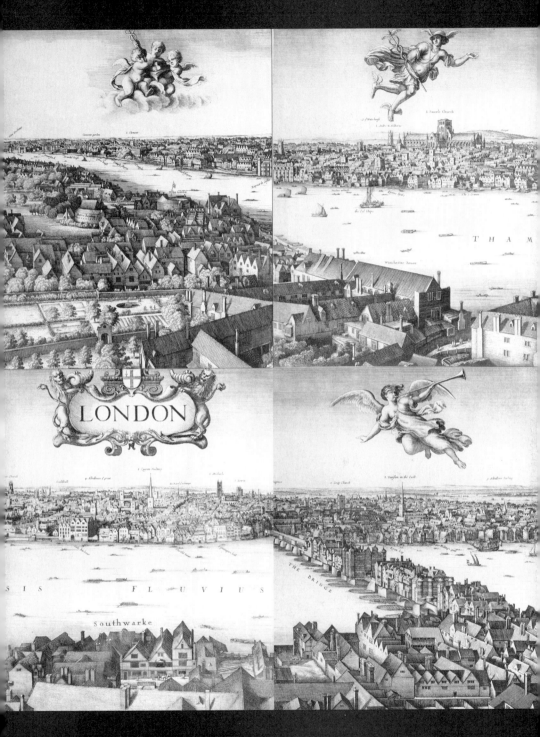

View of London, 1647 (copperplate) by Wenceslaus Hollar (1607–77) [detail showing the Globe Theatre, Blackfriars, and the London Bridge]. (GUILDHALL LIBRARY, CORPORATION OF LONDON, UK/REPRINTED BY PERMISSION FROM BRIDGEMAN ART LIBRARY INTERNATIONAL LTD.)

Shakespeare's will (1) (TNA: PROB 1/4 F.1)

Will (2) (TNA: PROB 1/4 F.2)

Will (3) (TNA: PROB 1/4 F.3)

First page of the Stratford Man's will. The writing is not Shakespeare's.

(REPRINTED BY PERMISSION FROM THE NATIONAL ARCHIVES: TNA: PROB 1/4 f.1)

Draft grant of arms to John Shakespeare. (REPRINTED WITH PERMISSION FROM THE COLLEGE OF ARMS, LONDON: MS SHAKESPEARE GRANTS 1.)

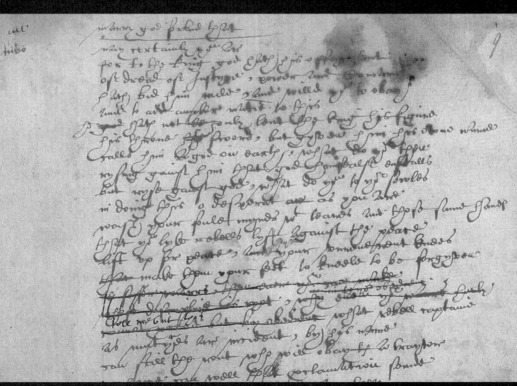

"Hand D" in the manuscript of "The Booke of Sir Thomas More."

(REPRINTED BY PERMISSION FROM THE BRITISH LIBRARY; SHELFMARK: HARLEY 7368 F.9.)

Portrait of Henry Wriothesley (1573–1624), Third Earl of Southampton, c. 1590–93 (oil on panel), attributed to John de Critz (1555–1641). (PRIVATE COLLECTION/REPRINTED WITH PERMISSION FROM BRIDGEMAN ART LIBRARY INTERNATIONAL LTD.)

Queen Elizabeth I (1533–1603) being carried in Procession (Eliza Triumphans) c. 1601 (oil on canvas), attributed to Robert Peake (fl. 1580–1626). (PRIVATE COLLECTION/REPRINTED WITH PERMISSION FROM BRIDGEMAN ART LIBRARY INTERNATIONAL LTD.)

love. There is also the suggestion that somehow the relationship with the poet may come to shame the fair youth.

The poet contrasts his own "tanned antiquity" with his love's youthful beauty. He chides the boy for what appears to have been his seduction by the poet's own mistress. The poet refers to a relationship between the youth and another—apparently a rival poet, a "better spirit." The poet accepts the likelihood of his ultimate loss in this contest. However, he predicts that the youth will achieve immortality in "my gentle verse," and, despite the suggestion that the poet has also strayed, he assures the youth of his own fidelity.

Sonnets such as 17, 18, and 81, promising the youth immortality through the poet's words, and Sonnet 65, hoping that, despite the unconquerable ravages of time "in black ink my love shall still shine bright," suggest that at least some of the sonnets were intended for publication—sometime. That would seem the only way the poet's verses could provide the youth with immortality and the "black ink" recording his love could "shine bright."

Most of Sonnets 127 through 152 refer to the so-called "dark lady," apparently the poet's mistress and the person who seduced the lovely boy. The poet's feelings for this woman vary between lust and resentment.

In Sonnet 144, the poet tells us:

> Two loves I have of comfort and despair,
> Which like two spirits do suggest me still;
> The better angel is a man right fair,
> The worser spirit a woman coloured ill.
> To win me soon to hell, my female evil,
> Tempteth my better angel from my side,
> And would corrupt my saint to be a devil,
> Wooing his purity with her foul pride.

Whatever the poet meant by "coloured ill," he evidently found the lady's dark complexion physically attractive. In Sonnet 127, for example, he tells us that, even though "In the old age black was not counted fair . . . now is black beauty's successive heir" and that "my mistress' eyes are raven black" like "mourners" who though "not born fair, no beauty lack."

But the poet is certainly not pleased with her behavior. In Sonnet 131, he says, "Thy black is fairest in my judgment's place," but adds, "In nothing art thou black save in thy deeds."

Sonnets 135, 136, and 143 suggest that the author's name was "Will." These could, of course, refer to the Stratford man. But they could also refer to other candidates whose names or nicknames were "Will" or "Willy." Or, they could, at least in part, be a bawdy reference to a man's penis, known in England then (and even now) as his "Will" or "Willy."[2] This explanation might fit some of the punning uses of "Will" in Sonnet 135:

> Whoever hath her wish, thou hast thy 'Will,'
> And 'Will' to boot, and 'Will' in overplus;
> More than enough am I that vex thee still,
> To thy sweet will making addition thus.
> Wilt thou, whose will is large and spacious,
> Not once vouchsafe to hide my will in thine?
> Shall will in others seem right gracious,
> And in my will no fair acceptance shine?
> The sea, all water, yet receives rain still,
> And in abundance addeth to his store;
> So thou, being rich in 'Will,' add to thy 'Will'
> One will of mine, to make thy large 'Will' more.
>   Let no unkind, no fair beseechers kill;
>   Think all but one, and me in that one 'Will.'

It would be difficult, however, to make that case with reference to the last line of Sonnet 136:

> And then thou lov'st me, for my name is Will.

The "sugared" sonnets to the "beauteous and lovely fair youth" could well be taken as the expression of a homosexual relationship. That possibility is discussed more fully later on. In Sonnets 18 through 25, for example, the poet repeatedly expresses his amorous feelings for the "lovely youth." But men in the sixteenth century sometimes spoke in exaggerated terms of their "love" for each other when there was no homosexual relationship between them.

In Sonnet 20, Shakespeare calls the youth "the master-mistress of my passion," which seems to go beyond expressing courtly love. He also de-

---

2. The title of the American film, *Free Willy*, drew great laughs when it was first advertised in London.

scribes the youth as having "a woman's face, with Nature's own hand painted." But the poet goes on, in the same sonnet, to tell the youth, with humor, that God "pricked thee out" with something of no use to the poet, a statement strongly suggesting that the relationship was *not* homosexual, or, at least, not sexual. The last lines of this sonnet read as follows:

> *And for a woman wert thou first created;*
> *Till Nature, as she wrought thee, fell a-doting,*
> *And by addition me of thee defeated,*
> *By adding one thing to my purpose nothing.*
> *But since she prick'd thee out for women's pleasure,*
> *Mine be thy love, and thy love's use their treasure.*

Similarly, homosexuality would seem inconsistent with the dark lady sonnets, such as number 151, which seems explicitly to describe the poet's lust for his mistress, and sonnets such as 40 through 42, suggesting that the mistress has seduced the lovely youth.

Who *was* the lovely youth to whom these outpourings of affection were directed? If we can identify him, perhaps it will help us identify the poet. Sonnet 104 tells us that the poet has known the youth for three years, which might place their meeting around 1590 or 1591. But this is not particularly helpful in narrowing the field. As we have said, the young earl of Southampton is the most likely candidate. Southampton, a Cambridge graduate and patron of the arts, was reputedly a very attractive young man. In the miniature painting by Nicholas Hilliard and the recently revealed portrait at Hatchlands Park, we can see why Sonnet 20 describes the earl as having "a woman's face with Nature's own hand painted."

Unlike almost every male portrait of the time, the young earl has no beard, his hair is worn long, and his face seems soft and feminine in its beauty. Sonnet 3 speaks of the youth's mother and tells us that the boy's face recalls "the lovely April of her prime." This fits too. Southampton's mother was a renowned beauty. And, of course, *Venus and Adonis* and *The Rape of Lucrece* had been dedicated to him.

But it is difficult to accept that the proud and somewhat volatile young earl would not have responded with violence had a common actor written and published such highly intimate verses about him, such as allusions to his being "pricked out" and his being seduced by the poet's mistress, or that the earl would have shared the secrets of his private relationships and personal feelings with someone of such low standing, even if they knew each other.

I say "difficult" to accept, but not impossible. If the Stratford man wrote *Venus and Adonis* and *The Rape of Lucrece*, he had become a successful and well-known figure in the London literary scene. Even in his youth, Southampton was a patron of the arts. Conceivably, the two were introduced and some sort of relationship could have developed between them that, despite their enormous differences in class and background, led the poet to dedicate sonnets to the young earl.

Film fans might recall *Shakespeare in Love*, in which the poor playwright has a liaison with a rich and highborn young duchess. In the throes of love, both overlook their patent differences in status. Can we substitute a youthful earl for a young duchess? Is it possible? Yes. But is it probable? That is a more difficult issue we will explore later.

Of course, the sonnets may well have been written strictly for the poet's inner circle and published without his permission. That would square with the dedication's having been written by someone other than the poet himself and with the numerous typographical errors that poet would almost surely have caught.

The "fair youth" sonnets appear to be written by a much older man to one considerably younger. Examples are number 62 in which the poet refers to himself as "Beated and chapp'd with tann'd antiquity," and number 73 in which the poet says:

> That time of year thou mayst in me behold
> When yellow leaves, or none, or few, do hang
> Upon those boughs which shake against the cold,
> Bare ruin'd choirs, where late the sweet birds sang.
> In me thou see'st the twilight of such day
> As after sunset fadeth in the west;
> Which by and by black night doth take away,
> Death's second self, that seals up all in rest.

Yet these lines would have been written when the Stratford man was at most in his early thirties. Southampton, who was only nine years younger, would have been in his twenties. The Stratford man would not seem to have been nearly old enough to fit the sentiment, and the gap between his age and Southampton's (if the earl was the "lovely youth") would seem to have been far too small.

Conceivably, a romantic thirty-year-old writing for a lover or dear friend in his twenties could have felt himself quite ancient, and it is not unknown for young poets to adopt the conceit that they are old and sere. And, of course, there is always the possibility that the poet was writing from the point of view of an imaginary character, rather than his own.

On the other hand, in Sonnet 138, the poet admits lying to his mistress about his age, although "she knows my days are past the best." This seems to refer to a real situation and not a poetic conceit. It seems inconsistent with the conduct and attitudes of someone in his early thirties.

If Southampton was the "lovely youth," it is likely that Shakespeare wrote at least some of the sonnets no later than 1596. Sonnet 104 indicates that three years had elapsed since the poet first saw the youth. Shakespeare dedicated *Venus and Adonis* to Southampton in 1593, and it is reasonable to assume that he had seen the earl before that.

Stratfordians, unable to find people, relationships, or events in the life of the Stratford man that correspond to those described in the sonnets, tend to treat the poems as sheer fiction. It is difficult, however, to accept the view that the sonnets merely create imaginary characters and have nothing to do with the poet's life. The circumstances described seem too specific, too human, too personal to be fiction.

The poet expresses affection for a much younger man and ruefully laments that the youth is not female in form. Yet he urges the young man to marry and have children. The youth is seduced by the poet's mistress. The poet tries to accept this with equanimity, but cannot avoid a note of bitterness. As indicated in Sonnets 78 through 87, the youth turns his attention to a rival poet considered by the author of the sonnets to be more capable than he—possibly John Lyly or George Chapman. The poet describes his dark-visaged mistress with an odd mixture of obsession and disgust.

Can these very human and personal expressions be mere fiction? They do not have the feel and fabric of fiction. Shakespeare was a master dramatist, and the sonnets, while good poetry, are very bad dramatically. They are disjointed and have no "through line" or unifying theme. The characters are only vaguely defined. There is no informative beginning that "sets up" the plot, no challenge or problem to be resolved, and no ending that resolves it. Indeed, in the last two sonnets, the poet seems to have gone off to forget his problems by taking the curative waters at Bath.

The sonnets make sense as highly personal reflections meant to be kept in a drawer or given to the "lovely youth," who would understand all the allusions without the need for further exposition. They make little sense as dramatic fiction.

And if we are supposedly dealing with a set of fictional characters, it is odd that, in the middle, between the fair youth and the dark lady, we get what appears to be a reference in Sonnet 107 to a time of national crisis that has passed and ended well:

> *The mortal moon hath her eclipse endured,*
> *And the sad augurs mock their own presage;*
> *Incertainties now crown themselves assured,*
> *And peace proclaims olives of endless age.*

Isn't Elizabeth the "mortal moon"? And aren't we talking about the peace following the defeat of the armada? It seems to fit. What doesn't seem to fit is that this—and the rest of the sonnets—constitute the musings of a make-believe character.

It is even conceivable that the characters and situations of the sonnets bled over into the plays. Is unfaithful Cressida reminiscent of the dark lady of the sonnets? Did the older poet think of his relationship with the lovely youth in creating the shifting relationship between Falstaff, the aging knight, and young Prince Hal?

An alternative theory is that the sonnets were neither the mirror of Shakespeare's soul nor a deliberate attempt at fiction, but were merely random exercises in poetry, never meant to be taken as a whole and not necessarily intended to be in the order in which they were placed by Thomas Thorpe. The latter may well be correct. We have no way of knowing the order of presentation intended by the poet.

But the theory of random exercises seems unpersuasive. The people and relationships seem to carry over from one sonnet to another and the themes such as the poet's age, his self-perceived disgrace, and his reflection on immortality recur and suggest an intention to create a group of poems related to one another, rather than isolated exercises.

Sonnets 110, 111, and 112 might be taken to support the identification of

Shakespeare with the Stratford actor. In 110, the poet says, "I have gone here and there and made myself a motley to the view." Does this refer to acting on the public stage? In Sonnet 112, he refers to "the impression . . . that vulgar scandal stamped upon my brow." These ambiguous lines are, of course, too general to provide much of a clue to the author's identity.

Sonnet 111, however, must give us pause. Here, in what may be the most revealing sonnet of all, the poet indicates that his public life and work was forced on him by the unfortunate circumstances of his birth and that it has besmirched his name and altered his very nature:

> *The guilty goddess of my harmful deeds,*
> *That did not better for my life provide*
> *Than public means which public manners breeds.*
> *Thence comes it that my name receives a brand;*
> *And almost thence my nature is subdued*
> *To what it works in, like the dyer's hand.*

Ill fortune pressed him into "public means," which breeds "public manners," branding his name and almost subduing his nature "to what it works in"? On its face, it might seems unlikely that a highborn aristocrat like the earl of Oxford wrote these lines. But it would certainly fit a man who is forced by relative poverty to become a common actor and who feels he has been unfortunately and irrevocably shaped by his years in the public theatre, so that he has become what he does, just as the "dyer's hand" remains red.

Sonnet 111 would seem to provide a strong argument for the Stratfordians. Still, instead of focusing on these sonnets that might point to the poet as an actor, most Stratfordians tend to treat the sonnets as mere fiction or to shrug off any question as to what and who, if anyone, they describe, by saying, in effect, "Let's ignore these questions and just marvel at the poetry."

But the questions remain, and they may lie at the heart of the authorship question. As we have said, the events and relationships described in the sonnets do not correspond to anything we *know* in the life of the Stratford man, except that the "Will" sonnets could be a reference to his name, and Sonnet 111 could certainly refer to his being an actor.

If the sonnets are not sheer fiction, other questions about them remain naggingly unanswered. Who was the other poet to whom the fair youth turned his attention and to whom Shakespeare felt himself inferior?

And who was the "dark lady"? In Sonnets 127, 131, and 132, Shakespeare uses the word "black" in describing her, but it is commonly accepted that he meant "dark complexioned," with black hair and brows. A similar use of "black" as reflecting beauty in a woman can be seen in Biron's speech praising his beloved in *Love's Labour's Lost*, "No face is fair that is not full so black" . . . "she is born to make black fair." This suggests there really was a dark-visaged woman who, if not Shakespeare's lover, at least fascinated him with her raven hair, dark eyes, and olive skin.

One likely candidate for the "dark lady" is Emilia Lanier, the daughter of Battista Bassano, a half-Italian, half-Jewish musician. Emilia was married to another musician, Alphonse Lanier, but she was the longtime lover of Henry Carey, Lord Hunsdon, the patron of the Stratford man's company. Emilia, who was what we might today call a "liberated woman," wrote a volume of poetry of her own. She might well have been attractive to Shakespeare.

Another possibility is the wife of John Florio, who tutored Southampton in Italian and other languages. Florio expressed his idea of feminine beauty as "black eyes, black brows, black hairs"; and it is likely that his much younger wife fit that description. She would have been there in Southampton's household, possibly available to the sonneteer (if he were there), and also to the young earl. But we have no more evidence than that to infer that Mrs. Florio was, in fact, the "dark lady."

We cannot, with certainty, place anyone in the life of the Stratford man who quite fits what the sonnets tell us of the "dark lady." Nor can we do anything but speculate as to who in his life could be the "beauteous and lovely youth." Probably, he was Southampton; and the Stratford man could have had a relationship with the young earl, even though we have no evidence that they ever met.

Nor is there anything in the life of the Stratford man that fits with his having been "made lame by fortune's dearest spite," as the poet tells us in Sonnet 37 or his "lameness" to which he refers in Sonnet 89. With the possible exceptions we have discussed—including Sonnet 111 about the "dyer's hand"—nothing in the sonnets seems a reference to any event in his life. But then, we know so little of his life that we could be very wrong.

Curiously, as well known and successful as Shakespeare was by 1609, when the sonnets were first printed by Thomas Thorpe, they were not reprinted in his lifetime, or indeed, until thirty years after the appearance of Thorpe's version. Had persons with significant power suppressed any further publication? If so, why?

10.

BEHAVIOR AND OUTLOOK ON LIFE

Can we square what we know about the activities and attitudes of the Stratford man with what we can infer about Shakespeare from his writings? They seem quite different.

The Shakespeare of the poems and plays was a sensitive, highly intuitive man. His characters are rounded and complex, the product of a mature, perceptive mind. He displays keen understanding, if not sympathy, for his villains and an extraordinary comprehension of the flaws of his heroic characters and how they developed. He is capable of subtle irony as well as overt humor. He values right, order, honor, and love, although he can skewer those who are pretentious or hypocritical about such values. He shuns artificiality, meanness, and pomposity.

By contrast, the Stratford man appears to be acquisitive, selfish, petty, mean-spirited, litigious, and narrow. He walks out on his family, refuses to pay his wife's debt after deserting her, treats her dismissively if not insultingly in his will, sues his neighbors over a pittance, and hoards grain in time of scarcity, hoping to profit by the needs of his neighbors. And after first protecting his own property rights by private agreement, he acquiesces in an attempt to enclose common lands against the interests of his fellow townsmen.

Are these two men the same? It is difficult to accept. Yet there have been other men of genius, who lived selfish, even immoral lives or otherwise held despicable views or engaged in deplorable conduct. The selfish irresponsibility of Mozart comes to mind, as does that of Picasso. So does Beethoven's uncontrollable temper and yearning for public acceptance and financial advancement. Worse still was the virulent anti-Semitism of Wagner and T. S. Eliot and the murderous rages of Caravaggio. Marcel Proust, a probing, sensitive author, tended to be a frivolous (and bizarre) snob. But he wisely pointed out that "a book is the product of a different self from the one we display in our habits, in society, in our vices." Could that be true of Shakespeare as well?

Before we draw any conclusions from the incidents of the Stratford man's life, we should analyze some of those incidents to see the extent to which they really are inconsistent with his having been the great poet and playwright.

If there is any truth to the tale that he was forced to leave Stratford because he was caught poaching deer, that would hardly be significant evidence one way or the other. Great men often have youthful misadventures; for a young man in a rural area, poaching must have been a common kind of crime, not viewed as one involving moral turpitude—except perhaps to the lord whose deer were slain.

If, on the other hand, the Stratford man abandoned his family in 1585, as he appears to have done, it suggests a basic selfishness and lack of a moral compass. Still, he was very young when he left and perhaps was adventurous by nature. A wife and three children at that age may have seemed an oppressive burden, especially a wife eight years his senior and a marriage forced on him when she turned up pregnant.

Is it impossible to square that youthful conduct with the expressions of the more mature poet and playwright? Not at all. It does, however, create some doubt. That doubt is magnified if it is true that, years later, the mature Stratford man refused to repay forty-one shillings advanced for his wife after he left town.

Can we disqualify the Stratford man because, in 1596, William Wayte sought a bill of peace preventing him and others from causing Wayte harm? Not without knowing more of the facts, and we do not.

In 1596 and again in 1598, the Stratford man failed to pay his taxes assessed as a resident of St. Helen's Parish, Bishop's Gate. But he had moved from the parish, and may ultimately have paid the assessments. And, if we were to strike from the list of great men all those who were once delinquent in paying taxes, the list would, I suspect, be much shorter.

The same could be said for buying and selling real estate. It hardly disqualifies one from achieving greatness in some aesthetic field.

Nevertheless, there are things in the life of the Stratford man that do seem inconsistent with what we can infer about Shakespeare from his writings.

The Stratford man was litigious and apparently ready to sue or be sued over relatively small sums. We have already discussed his refusal to pay the debt of forty-one shillings incurred by his wife after he left home. Other examples are his 1604 suit against Phillip Rogers for one pound, fifteen shillings, ten pence, and his 1608 suit against John Addenbroke for six pounds. The readiness to take his neighbors to court over such petty claims does seem unlike the man we know from his writings as Shakespeare. And there are other such incidents.

In 1598 and the preceding year, there was a great shortage of grain in Stratford (and other places as well) caused primarily by very wet summers. Naturally, the shortage drove up the price. Having foreseen the shortage, some local businessmen sought to profit by hoarding large quantities of grain in advance. One such hoarder was William Shaksper, who had squirreled away ten quarters (eighty bushels). Some of his friends hoarded even more. Richard Quiney, for example, held a massive forty-seven quarters of barley and thirty-two quarters of malt.

Many of the townspeople were outraged. There was a shortage of bread, and significant malnutrition among the poorer citizens. Some even demanded that the hoarders be hanged "on gibbets at their own doors." Evidently, the matter was finally resolved without such draconian measures, but the incident does not reflect well on the attitudes and actions of the Stratford man.

In 1605, the Stratford man bought the right to receive one-half of the tithes paid by residents of the area for corn, grain, wool, lamb, and other natural products. The tithe was, in effect, a tax imposed on the products of the land. The Stratford man was collecting taxes on the fruit of his neighbors' work. This was neither illegal nor immoral; but does it sound like Shakespeare?

Some anti-Strats accuse the Stratford man of plotting to take away the ancient rights of local residents by enclosing common lands that were historically theirs to farm. This seems an overstatement. Enclosure was the highly controversial process of converting historically common farm lands into pasturage. It was despised by many because it reduced the employment of poor citizens in the common fields, eliminated income from selling the produce of those fields, reduced the tax base, and created shortages of grain that increased prices. On the other hand, it often created more profitable use of the land, since communal farming of small plots was neither scientific nor efficient.

In 1614, some well-to-do citizens of Stratford, including William Replingham and Arthur Mainwaring, sought to enclose hundreds of acres of common lands in the Stratford area. The town corporation and most of the citizens were strongly opposed to this scheme. There is no evidence that the Stratford man was part of the group seeking enclosure. Indeed, he held tithe interests on the produce of the affected land and stood to lose a considerable sum if that land was converted to pasturage.

What did he do? Did he fight for the rights of the poor whose livelihood would be destroyed? Not that we know of. What he did was to protect his own position. He entered into an agreement with Replingham in October 1614 under which he was indemnified against the loss of any tithing income caused by the enclosure. There is nothing in the agreement that required the Stratford man to support enclosure, but the obvious purpose of the agreement from Replingham's point of view was to prevent the Stratford man from opposing his unpopular scheme. And, so far as we know, he did not oppose it.

The Stratford Man's cousin Thomas Greene was town clerk and acted as solicitor for the town corporation in attempting to negotiate with Replingham and Mainwaring. He was unsuccessful in this, and the town corporation questioned his enthusiasm for their cause. Perhaps they had reason for doubt. Greene had a reversionary interest in the half of the local tithes not held by the Stratford man—giving him what, today, we would call a conflict of interest. In fact, Greene was included as a named beneficiary of Replingham's written promise to indemnify the Stratford man against loss.

On January 11, 1615, Greene's notes show that he even "supped" with Replingham, who "assured" Greene he would be "well dealt with" and confirmed "former promises by himself" and "his agreement for me with my cosen Shak-peare."

Despite his conflict of interest, Greene pledged his full support for the town's efforts to stop enclosure; and he appears to have kept this pledge. Greene was the author of another note that has led some Stratfordians to assert that Shakespeare was actually *against* enclosure. But the claim doesn't stand up to analysis. Here is what Greene wrote:

> Sept. W. Shakspeares tellyng J Greene that J was not able
> to beare the encloseinge of Welcombe.

Welcombe was the area to be affected by the enclosure. *Beare* probably means "endure" or "accept," although conceivably it could be an error and was meant to be "bar." The controversy concerns the meaning of *J*. There are two competing theories on this, neither of which is persuasive.

The first theory is that the second *J* is a mistake and was meant to be "he," so that the Stratford man was telling Greene that *he, the Stratford man*, was against enclosure. This seems unlikely. *J* was used twice only two words apart. It seems unlikely that the second use was different from the first. More probably they were intended to have the same meaning; and the first *J* can't be "he," because "Shakspeares tellyng he Greene" makes no sense.

The second theory is that both *J*s mean "I," so that the Stratford man is telling Greene that *Greene* can't bear enclosure. But Greene was an educated man and perfectly capable of referring to "Shakspeares tellyng *me*," rather than the nongrammatical "Shakspeares tellyng I Greene." Indeed on the same page, he refers to Mr. Replingham having "supped with *me*." He does not say that Replingham supped with "I Greene."

It could be argued that the first *J* is the true *J* but the second is an *I*. They are not formed in exactly the same way. But in his next note, Greene writes "James," forming the *J* exactly like the second *J* in the note about "W. Shakspeare."

The most likely explanation of the note is the simplest, even though neither side seems to have considered it. Thomas Greene, who made the note, had a brother, John Greene, who was also a solicitor for the Stratford corporation, as well as deputy town clerk. What the disputed note probably meant is that the Stratford man told *John* Greene ("J Greene") that John ("J") could not bear the enclosure. This could have been because any land *owned by John* would not be protected by Replingham's agreement protecting *Thomas* Greene and the Stratford man, or because, as the town's deputy clerk and solicitor, he could not afford to be seen as supporting enclosure.

In December 1614, William Combe, a large local landowner, joined the group pressing for enclosure. Combe was not a man for half measures. Pressing ahead without waiting for any kind of legal determination, Combe turned to self-help. In January 1615, Combe's men started digging a long ditch along the border of the area to be enclosed. Members of the town corporation tried to interfere, but they were attacked by Combe's men and roundly cursed by Combe himself.

But the townspeople were no shrinking violets either—especially the women. The next day, a band of women and children marched to the site and filled in the ditch. Even Combe was not up to assaulting his neighbors' wives and children.

A stalemate followed. If Combe's men redug the ditch, it was obvious the women and children would simply refill it the next day. Finally, the town succeeded in getting a court order against enclosure. In 1616, this order was affirmed on appeal. The famous jurist, Lord Edward Coke, then chief justice, ruled that Combe must "sett his heart at rest: he should neyther enclose nor laye downe any earrable nor plow any ancient greensward."

After losing the appeal, Combe tried unsuccessfully to negotiate a deal with the town corporation; the matter ended with the common lands still in the hands of the people.

Was the Stratford man a scheming proponent of enclosure? There is no evidence of it. Did he do anything to aid his neighbors in their plight? No. His sole interest seemed to be in protecting his own position. Once his interests were protected by Replingham's indemnity, he did nothing to help his fellow citizens. Perhaps we can't condemn him for his part in this drama, but we can hardly admire him.

In discussing the conduct of the Stratford man, we should recognize that even Shakespeare—the "great Bard"—sometimes acted in a way that might not be considered admirable today. Some of his story ideas were taken not just from ancient sources, but from other contemporary writers. For example, *As You Like It*, the subject of a "stay" registration in 1598, seems clearly based on Thomas Lodge's novel *Rosalynde*, first printed in 1590. *Two Gentlemen of Verona* mentioned by Francis Meres in 1598 is based on Jorge de Montemayor's *Diana Enamorada*, printed in English that same year. *Romeo and Juliet* seems primarily based on Arthur Broke's poem "The Tragicall Historye of Romeus and Juliet," published in 1562, which, in turn, was based on much earlier sources. *Hamlet*, although essentially based on Belleforest's *Histoires Tragiques*, published in 1576, has been said to owe some of its drama to Thomas Kyd's successful play *A Spanish Tragedy*. As discussed below, Shakespeare apparently copied numerous lines from Marlowe; *The Merchant of Venice* was certainly influenced by Marlowe's *The Jew of Malta*, although the plays are quite different and both are essentially based on Giovanni's *Il Pecorone*.

On the other hand, we have no indication that any of these other writers ever complained. Perhaps, as discussed in Chapter 15, their works were not considered protectable at law, and appropriating the ideas of other writers was so common that no one paid much attention.

We cannot infer from these instances of literary theft that Shakespeare was not acting in a manner consistent with the ethics of the time. But his overall conduct does not match the ideals inherent in his body of work. If it does not, can we disqualify the Stratford man because his conduct falls short of those high ideals?

On balance, the selfish and petty behavior of the Stratford man may not rule him out as the author of the Shakespeare canon. Still, it must be considered evidence tending to support the anti-Strat position.

II.

INTERNAL INCONSISTENCY

*J*ust as it is difficult to reconcile the crass actions and attitudes of the Stratford man with the sensitivity and humanity manifest in Shakespeare, it is sometimes difficult to reconcile the conflicting attitudes expressed within a single play.

A prime example is *The Merchant of Venice*. Shakespeare gives Shylock lines that movingly portray the feelings of a diasporic Jew living as a foreigner in a land of hostile Christians. Shylock asks rhetorically why Antonio curses and spits on him. He answers his own question. It's simple. Antonio treats him in this cruel and hostile way for only one reason: He's a Jew. But Shylock asks:

> Hath not a Jew eyes? Hath not a Jew hands, organs, dimensions, senses, affections, passions? Fed with the same food, hurt with the same weapons, subject to the same diseases, healed by the same means, warmed and cooled by the same winter and summer as a Christian is? If you prick us do we not bleed? If you tickle us do we not laugh? If you poison us do we not die? If you wrong us shall we not revenge?

What an extraordinary statement for the sixteenth century, when anti-Semitism was the accepted norm, and Jews were reviled and brutalized as the killers of Christ. Where did Shakespeare acquire this understanding of the inner feelings of a practicing Jew trying to survive in a hostile country? Probably not in England. The Jews had been expelled by Edward I in 1290. Some few had returned, but they were, at least ostensibly, converts to Christianity.

Some Stratfordians have pointed out that, in 1570, John Shakspere was fined forty shillings for charging twenty pounds on an eighty-pound loan, as if this could have created in the playwright a special empathy for the plight of the moneylender. That hardly accounts for the towering character of the Venetian Jew Shylock, or for the sensitivity and perception embodied in his great speech. It evokes understanding, if not sympathy for Jews, not for moneylenders.

We are moved again by Shylock when he learns that his amoral daughter Jessica, having run away with her Christian lover and Shylock's money, has also taken a ring given Shylock by his deceased wife. His friend Tubal tells him that Jessica traded the ring in Genoa for a monkey.

Distraught, Shylock responds, "Thou torturest me Tubal. It was my turquoise: I had it of Leah when I was a bachelor. I would not have given it for a wilderness of monkeys."

The loss of his ducats is upsetting, but it is the ring, the ring from Leah, that breaks his heart. And for that moment, in those few words, we see Shylock as a man who once had a love and a very different life. We see him as a human.

And these are not the only indications in *The Merchant of Venice* that Shakespeare had feelings and ideas that were unique in the sixteenth century. At the time, slavery was widely accepted throughout the world. Few paid attention to the plight of the slave, any more than to the plight of the Jew. Yet Shakespeare has Shylock make the following extraordinary argument to the duke of Venice, seeking permission to enforce his bond and take the famous pound of flesh from his defaulted debtor Antonio:

> *What judgment shall I dread, doing no wrong?*
> *You have among you many a purchased slave,*
> *which like your asses and your dogs and mules,*
> *you use in abject and in slavish parts*
> *Because you bought them. Shall I say to you*
> *'Let them be free! Marry them to your heirs!*
> *Why sweat they under burdens? Let their beds*

> Be made as soft as yours, and let their palates
> Be seasoned with such viands'? You will answer
> 'The slaves are ours!' So do I answer you:
> The pound of flesh which I demand of him
> Is dearly bought; 'tis mine and I will have it.
> If you deny me, fie upon your law;
> There is no force in the decree of Venice.
> I stand for judgment. Answer: Shall I have it?

Yes, Shylock is seeking to enforce a cruel pledge. But look at the understanding he is communicating at the same time of the plight of the slave and the hypocrisy of a law that permits human beings to be enslaved.

Other Shakespearean plays contain rather crude lines about Jews, but they are, for the most part, common slang expressions uttered by uneducated or rascally characters, that do not necessarily reflect the attitudes of the playwright himself.

Thus, in *Two Gentlemen of Verona*, the clown urges Speed to "go with me to the alehouse; if not thou art an Hebrew, a Jew" (act 2, scene 5, 53–55). And in *Henry IV*, Part 1, Falstaff bellows the false oath "they were bound, every man of them, or I am a Jew else, an Ebrew Jew" (act 2, scene 4, 178–179).

Of course, there are a number of anti-Semitic expressions by characters in *The Merchant of Venice*, but that is the very theme of the play, and, here again, they are emblematic of the characters themselves, not necessarily the views of Shakespeare, whose own feelings seem to come through in Shylock's great speech.

Shakespeare appears somehow, someplace, to have acquired an extraordinary view of the diasporic Jew, permitting him to feel for the unyielding, vengeful Shylock an understanding and perhaps even sympathy.

Yet the end of the same play gives us what is intended as joy and amusement at Shylock's humiliating comeuppance. The "heroine," Portia, disguised as a doctor of laws, convinces the duke that it is not punishment enough for Shylock to waive his harsh pledge and even waive recovery of his principal. He is subjected to a devastating sentence that delights everyone—not only loss of his property but, at Antonio's suggestion, forced conversion to Christianity, which costs him his livelihood as well (since a Christian was not supposed to lend money). And, of course, he has already lost his disloyal daughter, who has stolen his money and run off with a gentile playboy, who will now receive whatever property Shylock may have left on his death. The particular cruelty of the coerced conversion does not appear in any of Shakespeare's sources. It is an original feature of his own play.

And how does this stiff-necked, biblical character respond to all this humiliation, loss, and abandonment of his dearly held religion? "I am content," he says humbly, while the others rejoice at his downfall. Then the celebrants, including Shylock's daughter, go on to Portia's home in Belmont where love, music, happiness, and levity prevail.

There seems a striking inconsistency here, as if one man with extraordinary insight and sensitivity wrote the play and another—perhaps one with a sound commercial sense for what would appeal to the common London crowd—read it or heard it read and then made knowing suggestions as to how it should be revised in order to succeed commercially.

We can also see an inconsistency in the court scene between what Portia says and what she does. She tells Shylock he "must" be merciful. He responds, "On what compulsion must I? Tell me that." Realizing that one cannot be forced to be merciful, she makes her famous speech that "The quality of mercy is not strained. It dropeth as the gentle rain from the heaven."

But does Portia herself show mercy when, in the next moment, she turns the legal tables on Shylock? Absolutely not. Even the duke seems ready to be merciful. But not Portia. As an already defeated Shylock moves to leave the court, she cries "Tarry, Jew" and announces even more devastating punishments. And this is the lady who has just lectured us on the beauty and desirability of mercy.

Perhaps the original draft showed a merciful Portia joining with the duke and Antonio to impose a less draconian sentence on Shylock, one that would be more consistent with her speech advocating mercy and Shylock's pitiful "I am content." Such an ending, stressing the Christian mercy and goodness of Portia and Antonio, would fit much better with the lyric happiness and laughter of the play's end.

Perhaps the crowd-pleasing cruelty of the punishment was added at the last minute with no time to iron out the inconsistencies, leaving Portia to preach mercy but practice revenge, and Shylock to speak out so powerfully for his beloved religion and then cringingly to murmur "I am content" when forced to become a Christian.

If someone other than Shakespeare suggested the final humiliation of

Shylock as a sure crowd pleaser, it was perhaps that same person who added or suggested the gratuitously bigoted line when the dark-skinned prince of Morocco chooses the wrong casket, thus failing to win Portia's hand. When Morocco leaves, she says, "Let all of his complexion choose me so." In other words, "I hope no *black* suitor will choose the right casket and win my hand."

It's an ugly and unacceptable line in today's world. It probably got a great laugh in Shakespeare's time. But would a poet who so perceived and understood the plight of the Jew and the slave have gone out of his way to drop in such a racist line?

Was Shakespeare trying to diminish Portia in our eyes? She is the heroine of the piece, and it seems likely he wanted us to admire her. The line also seems unnecessary to the scene—almost as if it was tacked on separately, after the fact. Did someone else add it—someone who feared the play was a bit too soft on Jews and blacks, someone who knew the bigotry of his audience and knew they would relish the new line? Could it have been an experienced but relatively uneducated actor, co-owner of the theatre company, who had a keen eye for the box office and who was fronting for the actual poet and playwright?

Interestingly, W. H. Auden, in his famous lectures on Shakespeare, goes out of his way to emphasize that Portia "has no racial prejudice." He cites her telling Morocco that, were she not bound by the test of the caskets,

> *Yourself, renowned Prince, then stood as fair*
> *As any comer I have looked on yet*
> *For my affection.*

Either Auden was trying to make an unjustified point by ignoring Portia's clearly racist line after Morocco chooses the wrong casket, or he hadn't read the play for some time. Plainly, he is wrong.

There is an alternative explanation for the seeming inconsistencies in the play. Perhaps Shakespeare's very point was that all the principal characters but Shylock were shallow hypocrites. Perhaps that's why Portia says one thing to Morocco's face and another behind his back. Perhaps that's why she speaks out for mercy and acts in quite the opposite way.

We should remember that the goal of the handsome Bassanio is to get his hands on Portia's wealth (as well as her beauty) and that Antonio aids him in his fraudulent scheme by lending him the money to appear wealthier than he is.

And did Shakespeare want us to like Shylock's daughter, the disloyal thief Jessica, and Lorenzo, her stupid lover-accomplice? Perhaps we get a hint of how Shakespeare really felt about these two miscreants in their "On such a night as this" scene at the end of the play. In what appears to be a moment of high romance, Jessica is named along with Cressida, Thisbe, Dido, and Medea, suggesting from the tone and ambience of the scene that Jessica belonged among classical women who loved greatly. But, in fact, all of the listed women were evil, doomed, or both.

In the play Antonio reviles Shylock for charging interest on his loans. But Antonio makes a profit on the goods his ships transport. Portia inherited her money. Bassanio borrowed his for a deceitful purpose, and Jessica stole hers. Were these methods of obtaining money preferable to charging interest?

Did Shakespeare intend these inconsistencies to convey the utter hypocrisy of these characters and of the society in which they lived? Was that the "basic truth" Shakespeare had in mind and intentionally embedded in the subject matter of the play? It is an intriguing theory that could provide a reasonable explanation of the inconsistencies in the play. But it is certainly not the "accepted" view of the work and is probably not the correct view.

But can we accept the prevailing view that what seem patent inconsistencies were, nevertheless, the work of a single playwright? Could they have been the uneven result of the deliberate efforts of two contributors with very different sensibilities and goals?

Take another play. Did a revisor's suggestions alter the portrait of Joan of Arc in *Henry VI, Part 1*? In the earlier parts of that play, Joan is treated sympathetically as a sincerely religious, even heroic figure. Talbot, the great English commander, calls her a witch, but he doesn't appear to use the term literally, rather only to curse a skillful and deceptive opponent.

Later, however, Joan is portrayed as a demonic, deceitful witch and harlot. She calls on "fiends" for help against the English, and the fiends actually materialize on stage. When captured, she claims to be pregnant by one of several French nobles.

Of course, the audience consisted mainly of coarse, uneducated

Englishmen. Did a stage-wise collaborator point out to "Shakespeare" that it simply wouldn't do to present a sympathetic Joan to a bunch of slow-witted Francophobes? Was the play revised to pander to their prejudice?

One line Joan delivers is so blatantly inappropriate that it seems almost certainly inserted solely to please the groundlings. Perhaps Joan's most significant contribution to the French cause was to persuade England's powerful ally, the duke of Burgundy, to desert the English and come over to the French side—her side. Finally, she convinces the duke to take that momentous step, and he announces his new allegiance to the dauphin and to France—a decision that virtually assures a French victory. What is Joan's response? She cries out "Done like a Frenchman—turn, and turn again!"

Lest anyone think this is anything but a grave insult, virtually the same phrase is used in *Othello* to denote someone given to double dealing and betrayal. When the great Moorish general has been driven to a state of jealous fury by Iago's schemes, he snarls that the young wife he thinks has betrayed him is so devious "she can turn and turn, and yet go on and turn again."

The line, so full of outrage at Desdemona, fits the context in *Othello*. But as used in *Henry VI*, Part 1, the harsh and gratuitous insult is flatly irreconcilable with Joan, with the duke's decision, with French interests, with the situation, and with the play. Neither the real Joan nor Shakespeare's Joan could possibly have said that line in that circumstance, even as an aside. And it is not an aside. The nasty anti-French comment is hurled in the face of the duke and in the presence of the dauphin and other French nobles—immediately after the duke has made the pro-French choice Joan—a Frenchwoman—hoped for and worked so hard to achieve.

The groundlings must have loved the ultra-jingoist line. But it is so glaringly out of place I cannot believe its use was conceived by Shakespeare—not even by the young Shakespeare. Perhaps it was someone else.

Even *Hamlet*, considered by many to be Shakespeare's greatest play, has curiously uneven aspects. As printed in the First Folio, it would have run for four hours; and, through most of the play, the young prince remains thoughtful, introspective, and unable to carry out what he believes to be his sacred duty—to avenge the murder of his father.

Then, suddenly, in the latter parts of the play he becomes a veritable killing machine. All in all, he directly or indirectly causes eight deaths.

As Hamlet himself dies on stage, Horatio proclaims him noble ("Now cracks a noble heart") and the warrior Fortinbras, who will now be king, accords him a hero's military honors, although he was perhaps the least martial of Shakespeare's protagonists.

What has he done to earn those posthumous accolades? Although he says he dearly loved poor Ophelia, his gratuitous cruelty has driven her to madness and death. He has killed her father, Polonius, as well as her brother Laertes. He has devised the beheading of his old school chums, Rosencrantz and Guildenstern; and, of course, he has finally killed his uncle and brought about his mother's death and his own. And he's accomplished all this devastation in a fairly brief period, after devoting most of the play to a brilliant, but lengthy, exposition of his innermost thoughts—perhaps the first time any drama had given us that extensive a window into a character's psyche.

Did one man write a long and insightful study of an emotionally torn young man, and another, more practical man, with a trained eye on the box office, convince him that there was too much talk and not enough action to arouse and delight the groundlings?

Did that same stage-wise partner suggest a banal addition to Hamlet's death scene? As the scene may originally have been written, Hamlet lies dying, the victim of Laertes's poisoned sword. He strives weakly to give Horatio a message for the victorious Fortinbras, but death "o'er crows [his] spirit." He can only murmur, "The rest is silence." Then he dies. What has been added? In what purports to be the true and final version published in the First Folio, Hamlet's final line becomes, "The rest is silence. O, o, o, o." Were the four "o-groans" really the creation of the Bard himself? Or did another man with an actor's viewpoint say, "We've got to punch up the death scene, sir—maybe add some groans. Won't be a dry eye in the house."

Henry V is another play that seems to speak with two voices, one in the play itself, another in the chorus. The chorus consistently treats Henry as a great king and victorious warrior. But a good argument can be made that, in the play itself, Shakespeare intended even that great warrior king to be seen, at least by a thoughtful few, as an arch-hypocrite with an unpredictable, uneven temperament and a cruel streak that sometimes became visible beneath that veneer of nobility and glory.

A prime example is Henry's behavior toward Falstaff, first as young Prince Hal and later as the newly crowned Henry V. Falstaff, the fat and aging knight, disregards conventional wisdom and political correctness. Utterly dishonest in his conduct, he speaks with wit and disarming candor. He revels in his cowardice and corruption, unlike so many Shakespearean characters who mask vile motives behind socially acceptable verbiage. Although a liar through and through, he is, in a strange sense, the voice of truth.

In *Henry IV*, Part 1, Prince Hal and Falstaff drink, laugh, and carouse together. Hal seems to understand and even love Falstaff for his wit and candor. In Part 2, the prince slowly draws away from his old companion. Then, when he is crowned as Henry V, he cruelly rejects and humiliates Falstaff. Having committed that harsh act, the new king goes on to have a play of his own in which his vastly outnumbered army defeats the French at Agincourt and conquers France. Falstaff does not appear in *Henry V*, but his death, seemingly caused by his heartbreaking rejection, is movingly described. Captain Fluellen likens Henry to Alexander the Great, who killed his best friend Clytus in a drunken rage, while Henry "being in his right wits and his good judgments turned away the fat knight," killing his friend with far less excuse than Alexander.

Sixteenth-century audiences might never have accepted a portrayal of the great hero-king that did not illustrate his newfound sense of responsibility by having him flatly reject the lying, cowardly friend of his youth.

Yet no matter how often I turn it over in my mind, that cold rejection of "the fat knight" seems needlessly cruel. If Shakespeare was really portraying the ideal king, surely there was some middle ground, some putting aside of his past that would still let us attribute greater humanity to his hero—unless Shakespeare's intention was to show Henry as coldhearted and capable of hypocrisy and cruelty.

There are other examples that suggest this intention. Henry invades France because he is convinced by the archbishop of Canterbury that he is entitled to the French throne by descent from his great-great-grandmother. The French do not recognize Henry's claim on the ground that the Salic Law precludes inheritance through the female line. The archbishop assures him that the Salic Law applies only in Germany, and that, in any event, it is contrary to the Bible. Thus, he says, the French throne is rightfully Henry's.

The problem is that, if the Salic Law is limited to Germany and contravenes the Bible, then Edmund Mortimer, descended from a more senior female line than Henry, has a better claim to the *English* throne. The same argument that would give Henry the French crown would deprive him of the English.

Of course, no one mentions this. Certainly, Shakespeare must have seen the irony. Did he want us to think that Henry realized the hypocrisy that underlay his *causus belli*? Or did he want us to think the great warrior king was ignorant of comparatively recent English history? It is difficult to accept the latter.

Soon, three noblemen are summoned before Henry. The king knows they are guilty of treason, but they do not know he knows. Henry cleverly traps them into asserting the importance of denying mercy to malefactors. Then, he springs the charge of treason on them and has them quickly executed. What was their treason? They intended to do to Henry just what Henry's father, Bolingbroke, did to Richard II; and, most probably, they intended to replace Henry with Edmund Mortimer, who, if Henry's rationale for invading France was valid, was the rightful king.

During the campaign in France, Bardolph, another of Henry's old pals from his days of roistering and robbery, is charged with theft. Without hesitation, Henry orders his old friend hanged.

Then there is Henry's order to kill all the French prisoners, to slit their throats. Why? The French seemed to be reinforcing their depleted ranks, and also some French stragglers had plundered Henry's tent.

And there are other such examples. Did Shakespeare subtly paint Henry V as not quite the perfect, noble warrior of common opinion? It seems so. Yet the chorus unfailingly portrays Henry as the flawless hero-king. It seems quite inconsistent with the portrayal Shakespeare has given us in the play itself—at least if we examine that portrayal closely.

Did one man try to show us that even the greatest of English martial heroes could be flawed with hypocrisy and cruelty? Was that the "basic truth" he embedded in the "subject matter" of the play? And did another man tell him that approach would never work commercially, that, if they were going to suggest unfavorable aspects of the great warrior king, it had to be done subtly and that, at the very least, they needed a laudatory chorus to balance the presentation?

Perhaps what appear to be internal inconsistencies in some of the plays are emblematic of the broad social, legal, and political shifts gradually occurring in this period. England in the Elizabethan and Jacobean Ages experienced a slow change from the basically static and stratified feudal system to the more dynamic and individualistic forces of emerging capitalism. New ideas were developing among the educated aristocracy, ideas that questioned centuries of static beliefs. New ideas were arising among the lower class as well. But these were ideas about the possibilities of economic and social advancement.

Perhaps the original playwright came from the upper classes of a changing society, well educated, thoughtful, and ready to question traditional values and assumptions. Perhaps the tough-minded commoner who may have assisted the playwright with revisions based on a practical knowledge of the public theatre was a new-age man in a different sense, striving to improve his status and to reap the rewards of energetic capitalism and popular public taste.

If so, the irony is that the writings of the aristocrat display a sometimes cynical probing for truth and reality and a broad humanistic view, generally free of the strictures and prejudices of his class, while in the revisions we have posited, the stage-wise commoner exhibits a ready acceptance of conventional wisdom and, if not actual bigotry, then at least a willingness to pander to the bigotry of the crowd to the end of achieving commercial success.

12.

SEXUAL ORIENTATION

*H*omosexuality was certainly not uncommon in the sixteenth and seventeenth centuries. Bacon and Marlowe were homosexuals, as was James I, although he married and had children. But, at least in public, homosexuality was not considered acceptable. Indeed, a convicted "sodomite" could be subject to the death penalty.

Oscar Wilde was convinced that Shakespeare was homosexual, as Wilde himself was. Others have reached the same conclusion and have argued that, since the Stratford man was heterosexual, the two cannot have been the same.

It seems likely that the Stratford man was heterosexual. But, notwithstanding Wilde's strongly held view, there is no convincing evidence that Shakespeare was not.

In five separate plays, Shakespeare gave us heroines who dress and masquerade as males. They are Rosalind in *As You Like It*, Viola in *Twelfth Night*, Julia in *Two Gentlemen of Verona*, Imogen in *Cymbeline*, and Portia in *The Merchant of Venice*. Does this unusual pattern suggest that the Bard found sexual ambiguity appealing? Perhaps. But having females disguise themselves as males and exploiting the complications that flow from that situation may simply have proved effective theatre and a sure crowd pleaser, especially since the female roles were played by boys. Thus, Shakespeare could entertain his audience with a boy playing a girl masquerading as a boy. Evidently, the audience loved it; and if it worked, why not use it again—and again and again?

The sonnets are cited more than any other Shakespearean work as evidence of homosexuality. They do express the poet's fervent love for the fair youth, even referring to him as "the master-mistress of my passion." But, as we have seen, the same sonnet (number 20) goes on to tell the youth that nature "pricked thee out" with something of no use to the poet, which seems inconsistent with a homosexual relationship. Of course, this could have been a false clue designed to throw readers off the track. Or, the "love" repeatedly expressed by Shakespeare could have been homosexual but platonic.

There is another possibility: that the relationship was homosexual and erotic, but that the erotic contact was one-sided, the youth playing the passive role in sexual encounters and those roles not reversing. If so, the youth was "pricked out," but that was not something of interest to the older poet. It was there "for woman's pleasure," but not the poet's. But this seems inconsistent with the line in Sonnet 20 that, by her "addition," nature "me of thee defeated." If the poet was buggering the youth, and not vice versa, the fact that nature had "pricked" the boy "out" would not have "defeated" the poet. It would be irrelevant.

The recent disclosure of a portrait of the young Southampton—the likely fair youth of the sonnets—may shed some light on the issue. For centuries, the painting, now hanging at Hatchlands Park, a manor house south of London, was thought to be a portrait of Lady Norton, daughter of the Bishop of Winton. But patient research and a comparison with portraits of the mature Southampton make a convincing case for the proposition that the subject is not a woman at all, but the young earl.

The Hatchlands portrait is that of a very girlish young man in his late teens, unbearded, with highly arched eyebrows; a sensuous, cupid's bow mouth; and very long brown hair. He wears a large red-and-black earring, an extremely wide lace collar with matching cuffs, and a provocative expression. One hand seems to stroke his braided hair with long, tapering fingers.

The elongated heart-shaped face of the youth, while beardless and softer in its lines, seems the same as in portraits of the adult earl, even to the long chestnut hair and the choice of elegant, dandified clothing.

It is easy to see why the subject of the Hatchlands portrait was thought to be a young woman. Studying the pale, effeminate image evokes Shakespeare's lines from Sonnet 20:

> *A woman's face, with nature's own hand painted,*
> *Hast thou, the master-mistress of my passion.*

It also makes it conceivable that the poet felt a longing for the young earl that went beyond metaphoric love. But it is just as conceivable that he never allowed that longing to go beyond poetic expression.

Besides, if the fair youth was Southampton, which seems likely, he had at least one well-reported heterosexual affair in addition to his liaisons with the dark lady. That was his wooing, impregnating, and ultimately marrying the queen's maid of honor, Elizabeth Vernon. And either Southampton's girlish features hardened somewhat as he grew older or subsequent painters were careful to lessen the feminine aspects of his appearance. The portrait of Southampton in the Tower after Essex's rebellion shows him bearded and with a more angular and masculine visage.

The "dark lady" sonnets seem quite plainly to reveal that she had a sexual relationship with the poet and that he felt erotic desire for her. Sonnet 151, seemingly directed to the dark lady, reads as follows:

> *Love is too young to know what conscience is;*
> *Yet who knows not conscience is borne of love?*
> *Then, gentle cheater, urge not my amiss,*
> *Lest guilty of my faults thy sweet self prove:*
> *For, thou betraying me, I do betray*
> *My nobler part to my gross body's treason,*
> *My soul doth tell my body that he may,*
> *Triumph in love; flesh stays no further reason,*
> *But rising at thy name doth point out thee,*
> *As his triumphant prize. Proud of this pride,*
> *He is contented thy poor drudge to be,*
> *To stand in thy affairs, fall by thy side.*
> *No want of conscience hold it that I call*
> *Her 'love' for whose dear love I rise and fall.*

It seems clear that, with lines like "rising at thy name doth point out thee," "To stand in thy affairs, fall by thy side" and "for whose dear love I rise and fall," Shakespeare is making punning references to his being sexually aroused by the subject of the poem. If he's talking to the dark lady, this certainly indicates that he's heterosexual or at least bisexual.

But is he talking to her? The placement of the sonnets certainly indicates that. But Shakespeare may not have put the sonnets in this order. Others arranged them, beginning with the publisher, Thomas Thorpe. The present order may not be what the poet intended.

Could Sonnet 151 be meant for the fair youth and simply be out of order? There are phrases that could support that argument. For example, "gentle cheater" and "thy sweet self." Those seem more appropriate in addressing the fair youth than the dark lady. After all, in Sonnets 41 and 42, the fair youth is also accused of being unfaithful; and like "gentle cheater" in Sonnet 151, the poet calls the fair youth "gentle thief" in Sonnet 40.

But the last line of Sonnet 151 uses the pronoun *Her* in the phrase "I call Her 'love' for whose dear love I rise and fall." Does this mean the poem is addressed to a female? It would seem so—unless the *Her* was added as another false clue to throw a reader off the trail, if, somehow, this sonnet were publicly disclosed.

In Sonnet 135, the poet asks to "hide my will in thine . . . to make thy large will more," and adds "thou hast thy will and will to boot and will in overplus." This may have been bawdy double entendre, or he may have been using *will* in the sense of being willful.

The placement of the sonnet suggests that it is about the dark lady; and *will* was sometimes used to denote the female genitalia, as well as the male. But, here again, we cannot rely on the present order, which may not have been the same as Shakespeare intended.

If the poem was meant for the fair youth, the poet might have been referring to the fair youth using his capacious "will" in having sex with the dark lady and that the request "to hide my will in thine" and "to add to thy will one will of mine" may have been meant figuratively and poetically; that is, "think of me when you're with her and it will be as if we are enjoying her together."

The sonnets contain the theme of the youth feeling shamed by the relationship. That fate might not have been feared if the association were strictly platonic. But homosexuality is not necessarily the only potential source of that shame.

The fact is, we do not know for sure. But Sonnet 20, taken at face value, seems to suggest that the relationship between the two men was not sexual in nature. And, given Sonnet 151 as well, it would be only reasonable to infer that the poet either was bisexual and had romantic yearnings for the youth that were not acted out physically, or that he was strictly heterosexual and was simply expressing poetic love for the fair youth in the overblown terms sometimes used in the sixteenth century.

The balance of Shakespeare's writings provide no evidence of his being gay. In *The Merchant of Venice*, Antonio has strong feelings for Bassanio; and, despite the general mood of love and laughter at the end of the play, Antonio seems isolated and desolate at Bassanio's marriage. But, even if Antonio felt homosexual longings, he is simply a character in a play. His being portrayed as a homosexual would no more make Shakespeare gay than the portrayal of Shylock makes the Bard Jewish.

Venus and Adonis, which was dedicated to Southampton, is hardly a work one would share with, much less dedicate to, one's gay lover. It is an openly erotic tale of a lustful woman's seduction of a reluctant young man. She tells him, for example:

> *I'll be a park and thou shalt be my deer,*
> *Feed where thou wilt, on mountain or in dale;*
> *Graze on my lips; and if those hills be dry,*
> *Stray lower, where the pleasant fountains lie.*

While it is difficult to be certain about the matter, the evidence seems to weigh against the conclusion that Shakespeare was homosexual. More likely, in the sonnets, he was simply more than usually effusive in expressing his "love" for the fair youth—probably in the belief that his expressions were private. In addition, he had the unique capacity to understand and sympathize with a character's homosexual longings, whether or not he had experienced them himself.

Since it seems highly probable that the Stratford man was heterosexual, we can't rule him out as Shakespeare based on sexual orientation. Still, the threat of the public's *perceiving* Shakespeare and Southampton as gay lovers may have played a critical part in a concerted effort to identify Shakespeare with the Stratford man after the latter's death. This is a possibility we will explore later.

13

RELIGIOUS OUTLOOK

While we can reach no firm conclusion on the point, there are hints that the Stratford man may have been raised secretly as a Catholic. Indeed, he may have died one. Richard Davies, chaplain of Corpus Christi College, Oxford, in the seventeenth century, includes the following sentence in his writing about the Stratford man, whom he tells us was "a composer" of plays: "He dyed a Papist." Davies gives us no explanation and no supporting evidence.

We have already mentioned the handwritten Catholic testament found in 1757 hidden in the rafters of John Shakspere's house. The testament was a copy of a Jesuit document, thousands of which were smuggled into England by members of that militant order to distribute among those families who favored the old religion or might be induced to do so. We have only Edmund Malone's copy of the testament. The original, which Malone said he had received, was never found after his death.

It begins each section with "I John Shakspere." Probably the original was written out by someone else—likely a visiting missionary priest—and signed by John with his mark. Its authenticity has been doubted (even by Malone), but, if authentic, it certainly suggests that John was Catholic and remained loyal to the old church, albeit secretly.

To hold public offices as he did, John would necessarily have taken oaths to support the reformed Church of England and to recognize the queen as the head of that church. Even if he remained secretly a Catholic, it is doubtful that these oaths would have stopped him. He was hardly the only secret Catholic to take them.

If the Stratford man attended the local grammar school, he would have received a heavy dose of Protestant indoctrination. But, if John Shakspere wanted his son to have an education, he had little choice; and young William could have remained a secret Catholic while publicly observing the Protestant forms, just as his father may have done.

The two young men who would have been schoolmasters when William might have attended the Stratford school had Catholic connections, if not Catholic leanings. This is particularly true of Simon Hunt, who appears to have left Stratford for the University of Douai in France, which became a notorious training center for English missionary priests. Hunt apparently became a Jesuit, even serving at St. Peter's in Rome. Thomas Jenkins, Hunt's successor at the Stratford grammar school, was a fellow of St. John's College Oxford, a college known for tolerance of Catholics. Even the executed martyr-priest Edmund Campion had been a fellow there.

We cannot assume that these two schoolmasters softened the mandatory dose of Protestant teaching administered at the school, or even that the Stratford man went there. But, if he did attend, the two men may have made John's decision to enroll him an easier one.

There are other hints at the possibility that the Stratford man had Catholic leanings. Members of his mother's family, the Ardens, were Catholics; and the place of his marriage may suggest such leanings. The marriage license that permitted him to marry "Annum Whateley" describes the prospective bride as being from Temple Grafton, a small, nearby town. There is no entry for William's actual marriage in any Stratford record. Those records are no longer extant.

Assuming that "Annum Whateley" was a mistaken entry for "Anne Hathaway" (as seems likely), the bride did *not* reside at Temple Grafton. The couple may have listed that town because that is where they wanted to be married and possibly where they were, in fact, married. John Frith, the aged pastor of the tiny church at Temple Grafton was said to be a Catholic priest who had been allowed to retain his post because of his advanced age and the extremely small size of his congregation.

The Stratford man's twins, Hamnet and Judith, were named after his good friends Hamnet and Judith Sadler of Stratford, who were later included on a list of local recusants, those who did not attend Protestant services.

Do these facts tell us that the Stratford man himself was a secret Catholic? Not at all. They permit some fanciful speculation on the point, but no more than that.

And what of Shakespeare? He has his human characters like Macbeth and Joan of Arc interact with witches. Others speak with fairies and sprites, as in *A Midsummer Night's Dream* and *The Tempest*. He has characters pray, as in *Henry V*; but he never shows us, or even hints at, any intervention by the Judeo-Christian God. Did he not believe in that deity? That seems far too great a leap to be supportable. But Shakespeare's religious beliefs, if any, remain elusive.

In *King Lear*, Shakespeare shows an inclination to shun religious themes of any kind. The earlier *True Chronicle History of King Leir* was laden with religious motivation and divine intervention. But Shakespeare had none of it in his Lear play, and he even gives Gloucester the possibly blasphemous line, "As flies to wanton boys are we to the Gods—They kill us for their sport."

We can find insincere and selfish characters among the Catholic hierarchy in Shakespeare's plays. Examples are Cardinal Wolsey in *Henry VIII*, a man filled with ambition and greed, and the archbishop of Canterbury and the bishop of Ely in *Henry V*, who conceive a devious plan to retain the church's revenue and push the young king into a bloody war with France on what they must have known were specious grounds.

And there are extremely pejorative attacks on Catholic prelates in both *Henry VI*, Part 1, and *King John*, as well as on Joan of Arc in the former play. Nor are the leaders of the church the only Catholics skewered by the Bard. Friars and nuns are ridiculed as well. For example, in *All's Well That Ends Well*, the clown provides a list of things that naturally go together, like "ten groats" and "the hand of an attorney" and "a nail" and its "hole." Near the end of the list of usual matches, Shakespeare gives us "the nun's lips" and the "friar's mouth."

On the other hand, in both *Romeo and Juliet* and *Much Ado About Nothing*, Catholic friars are shown in a markedly favorable light. In *Measure for Measure*, friars are not only treated favorably, but Duke Vicentio disguises himself as one and cooperates with another in achieving a just and happy ending. Similarly, in *The Comedy of Errors*, the Abbess Aemilia is favorably portrayed and provides a turning point to the plot. But these are the lower Catholic orders. The church hierarchy generally gets rather negative treatment. That, of course, does not foreclose Shakespeare's having been a secret Catholic.

There are echoes of Catholic doctrine in *Hamlet*. Having succumbed quickly to poison administered by his envious brother, Hamlet's father dies "unanel'd" (i.e., denied the last rights of the church). Hamlet says he will pray to relieve his father from a term in purgatory, a notion inconsistent with Protestant belief. But, of course, *Hamlet* is set at a time before the Reformation, when the entire Christian world was Catholic.

Shakespeare gives us some other hints of sympathy for Catholic causes and feelings. The fat, bibulous hypocrite Sir John Falstaff in *Henry IV*, Part 1, was originally named Sir John Oldcastle. The actual Oldcastle held early anti-Catholic beliefs, which led to his execution in 1417, when England was, of course, thoroughly Catholic. Protestants came to consider Oldcastle a blessed martyr. Catholics considered him a rebellious outlaw.

When Shakespeare made Oldcastle the drunken rascal of *Henry IV*, Part 1, he was seemingly accepting the Catholic view of the man. Oldcastle's Elizabethan descendant, William Brooke, was Lord Chamberlain in the year between Henry Carey and his son George. Brooke strenuously objected to his ancestor's portrayal. Shakespeare simply changed the name of the character from Oldcastle to Falstaff. In an epilogue to *Henry IV*, Part 2, he added a unique disclaimer, probably to placate Brooke: "Falstaff shall die of a sweat, unless 'a be killed already with your hard opinions, for Oldcastle died a martyr, and this is not the man."

Apparently, the queen saw the play after the character was renamed. She was well pleased; and, according to Nicholas Rowe, she insisted that Shakespeare immediately write another play, showing Falstaff in love. He did. It was *The Merry Wives of Windsor*, but it presented a far less engaging Falstaff—indeed, a sort of bogus Falstaff.

Shakespeare gives us hints in the sonnets that he regretted the excesses of the Reformation. In Sonnet 64, he speaks of his sadness "When sometime lofty towers I see down-razed." In Sonnet 73, he refers to "Bare, ruin'd choirs where late the sweet birds sang." And in Sonnet 66, he protests against "purest faith unhappily forsworn."

Do these choices and references make Shakespeare a secret Catholic? I think not. But we cannot firmly conclude he was not. The same is true of the Stratford man.

We have already discussed what little we can infer about Shakespeare's attitude toward Jews. What about his attitude toward Islam?

Othello's final speech could be construed as providing some insight into the Bard's views on that subject. After he learns that Desdemona was innocent, that she had not been unfaithful, Othello refers to himself as "one that lov'd not wisely, but too well." Then, he speaks of an episode from his past involving a Muslim:

> in Allepo once where a malignant and turban'd Turk
> Beat a Venetian and traduc'd the state,
> I took by the throat the circumcised dog,
> And smote him thus.

At which point, Othello stabs himself and dies, falling upon the body of Desdemona for a final kiss.

Seemingly, Othello, a Moor who led the forces of Venice, saw the "turban'd" and "circumcised" Muslim as analogous to himself, one who had grievously violated the laws of nature and the state and whom he should strike dead. And, having been born a Muslim, wasn't Othello himself "circumcised," even if not "turban'd"?

Be that as it may, the views expressed by the great Moor seem to belong to the character and relate to the thoughts of that character in this specific and tragic situation. They are by no means Shakespeare's own views of Islam or of anything else.

In summary, we cannot draw any firm conclusion as to Shakespeare's religious beliefs except that he seems to have disapproved of hypocrisy and excess in the name of any faith. Nor do we know the religious attitudes of the Stratford man. Certainly, we cannot conclude that the two men had such different religious views that they were necessarily different men. Nor does any demonstrable similarity of religious belief convince us that they were the same.

14.

POLITICAL AND SOCIAL OUTLOOK

*D*o the political and social views of the Bard aid us in determining whether or not he was the Stratford man? Can we even draw reliable conclusions as to what those political or social views were? Can we really identify whatever "basic truths" the playwright may have intended to underlie the dialogue and action of the plays? In most cases, not with any degree of certainty. But many have tried. And the attempts have generated a vast and disparate panoply of claimed Shakespearean views.

Probably the first time Shakespeare's writings were employed to support a political agenda was when Essex's supporters used *Richard II* to foster the notion that there are times when it is proper and desirable to overthrow the reigning monarch.

Since then, virtually every segment of the political spectrum has claimed Shakespeare as its own. He has been described as the embodiment of German nationalism, eastern European Marxism, anti-Colonialism, as an advocate of class stratification and of the "white man's burden," and, of course, of British moral and political superiority.

Conservatives cite Ulysses's speech before Agamemnon's tent in act 1, scene 3 of *Troilus and Cressida* as Shakespeare's plea for a class-based society:

> *The heavens themselves, the planets and this centre,*
> *Observe degree, priority and place . . .*

> *but when the planets*
> *In evil mixture to disorder wander,*
> *What plagues and what portents! what mutiny! . . .*
> *O, when degree is shak'd,*
> *Which is the ladder to all high designs,*
> *Then enterprise is sick! How could communities,*
> *Degrees in schools and brotherhoods in cities,*
> *Peaceful commerce from dividable shores,*
> *The primogenitive and due of birth,*
> *Prerogative of age, crowns, sceptres, laurels,*
> *But by degree, stand in authentic place?*
> *Take but degree away, untune that string,*
> *And, hark, what discord follows! each thing meets*
> *In mere oppugnancy . . . right and wrong*
> *Between whose endless jar justice resides,*
> *Should lose their names, and so should justice too. . . .*
> *This chaos, when degree is suffocate,*
> *Follows the choking.*
> *And this neglection of degree . . .*

Certainly, Ulysses seems to be urging the importance of "priority and place" in a society organized along class lines or, as he puts it, by "degree." But *Troilus and Cressida* is a cynical play; and Ulysses's speech was probably not intended as a sincere exposition of his beliefs. He is speaking to two kings, Agamemnon and Menelaus, and to Nestor, prince of Pylos and the senior Greek commander. He has an agenda of his own and seems to be reciting principles cynically designed to appeal to his listeners and to achieve his purpose. Even if Shakespeare intended Ulysses to be completely sincere in espousing "degree" as indispensable to a peaceful and rational society, we cannot conclude that this was Shakespeare's own view, any more than we could conclude that Lady Macbeth's views on the advisability of murder were the Bard's own opinions on the subject.

There are those who contend that even Shakespeare's comedies are designed to instill audience satisfaction with the established order, by first altering, inverting, or disguising the relationships and then returning things to their proper order, sending the groundlings happily home, content with their lot. Was acceptance and appreciation of the status quo the "basic truth" the

Bard intended to embed in his comedies? It seems a considerable stretch and probably attributes to the Bard a political agenda he did not have.

If he intended to create that response in the common audience that saw a play once and reacted to it, a good argument can be made that he intended quite another, less optimistic response from thoughtful people who saw and read the plays more than once, and carefully.

Just as conservatives cite Ulysses, Marxists can cite blind Gloucester's speech to Edgar, whom he believes to be an impoverished beggar, in act 4, scene 1 of *King Lear*:

> Let the superfluous and lust-dieted man,
> That slaves your ordinance, that will not see
> Because he doth not feel, feel your power quickly;
> So distribution should undo excess,
> And each man have enough.

Is this not, they claim, both an early statement of what later became classic Marxist doctrine ("to each according to his needs"), as well as a call for the poor to rise and let the rich feel their "power quickly"? Perhaps, but it's an expression of Gloucester's view, not necessarily that of the playwright.

Similarly, in *All's Well That Ends Well*, when Bertram expresses reluctance to marry Helena because she is not of noble birth, the king rebukes him with a speech on the equality of man and the hollowness of inherited titles:

> Strange is it that our bloods,
> of color, weight, and heat, poured all together,
> would quite confound distinction . . .
> From the lowest place when virtuous things proceed,
> The place is dignified by the doer's deed:
> Where great additions swell, and virtue none,
> It is a dropseed honour: good alone
> Is good without a name, vileness is so:
> The property of what it should go,
> Not in the title . . . honors thrive,
> When rather from our acts we them derive
> Than our fore-gatherers: the mere word's a slave,
> Debouched on every tomb; on every grave
> A lying trophy; and as oft is dumb.

And those who assert that Shakespeare fostered the established "order" and "degree" might consider King Lear's rage against the hypocritical order and justice of his time, which would seem intended as a comment on the order and justice of Shakespeare's own era.

> LEAR: What, art mad? A man may see how this world goes with no
>   eyes. Look with thine ears; see how yond justice rails upon yond
>   simple thief. Hark in thine ear: change places, and handy dandy,
>   which is the justice, which is the thief? Thou hast seen a farmer's
>   dog bark at a beggar?
>
> GLOUCESTER: Ay, sir.
>
> LEAR: And the creature run from the cur? There thou mightst behold
>   the great image of authority: a dog'n obeyed in office.
>   Thou rascal beadle, hold they bloody hand!
>   Why dost thou lash that whore? Strip thy own back.
>   Thou hotly lusts to use her in that kind.
>   For which thou whipst her. The usurer hangs the cozener.
>   Through tatter'd clothes small vices do appear;
>   robes and fur'd gowns hide all. Plate sin with gold,
>   and the strong lance of justice hurtless breaks;
>   arm it in rags, a pigmy's straw does piece it.

This is hardly advocacy of the established, class-stratified order. But is it Shakespeare's own opinion or simply the argument he gives to the embittered Lear?

We see the same theme of the law's hypocrisy in other plays. In *Measure for Measure*, for example, Isabella pleads with Angelo to spare her brother's life by appealing to his sense of his own guilt:

> ISABELLA: If he had been as you, and you as he, you would have
>   slipped like him, but he, like you, would not have been so stern.
>
> ANGELO: Pray you be gone.
>
> ISABELLA: I would to heaven I had your potency, and you were Isabel!
>   Should it then be thus? No: I would tell what 'twere to be a judge,
>   and what a prisoner.

Later, she drives the point home. She says:

> *Go to your bosom, knock there, and ask your heart what it doth know.*
> *That's like my brothers' fault. If it confers*
> *A natural guiltiness such as is his,*
> *Let it not sound a thought upon your tongue*
> *Against my brother's life.*

Finally, Angelo seems to relent:

> *O, let her brother live!*
> *Thieves for their robbery have authority*
> *When judges steal themselves.*

Of course, the plot takes many twists and turns before Angelo really gets the point, but the potential hypocrisy of the law remains a principal theme.

The theme of legal hypocrisy recurs in the previously quoted scene from *The Merchant of Venice* when Shylock asks the Venetian officials how they can ask him to abandon his pledge of a pound of flesh when they maintain slaves whom they would not consider freeing or even treating fairly . . . Why? Because they "own them."

Even anarchists might find comfort in Jack Cade's rebellious cry in *Henry VI*, Part 2, "then are we in order when we are most out of order." But this revolutionary thought is that of the rabble-rousing Cade, certainly not that of Shakespeare, who recognized the obvious fact that different people hold and express differing points of view and speak in a way that reflects their beliefs and individual personalities and that is designed to achieve their own personal goals.

Perhaps the soliloquy of Phillip Falconberg in *King John* provides insight into Shakespeare's own cynical view of political discourse. Thus, the bastard son of Richard I speaks of "commodity" (i.e., unprincipled self-interest) and tells us:

> *Well, whiles I am a beggar, I will rail,*
> *And say, there is no sin but to be rich;*
> *And, being rich, my virtue then shall be,*
> *To say, there is no vice but beggary;*

Still, this may represent only the credo of the character, not the outlook of the Bard.

One attitude, however, does seem clearly to be that of Shakespeare himself. Although he can be cynical about men in power, as he seems to be in *Henry V* and certainly is in *King Lear, Troilus and Cressida*, and *King John*, he seems always to mistrust common mobs and their leaders. It is a safe bet that he preferred King John and even Richard III to Jack Cade and to the Roman mob in *Julius Caesar*. Sometimes, Shakespeare exhibits an understanding of the deprivations that motivate an angry crowd of commoners. But he invariably despises the violence of the mob and the demagogic leaders who foment that violence and seek to profit by it.

We can see an example in the lines he gives the rebel leader Jack Cade, in addressing the crowd and encouraging an uprising:

CADE: Be brave then; for your captain is brave, and vows reformation. There shall be in England seven half penny loaves sold for a penny; the three-hoop pot shall have ten hoops; and I will make it a felony to drink small beer. All the realm shall be in common, and in Cheapside shall my palfry go to grass. And when I am king, as king I will be,—

ALL: God save your Majesty!

CADE: I think you good people—there shall be no money; all shall eat and drink on my score, and I will apparel them all in one livery, that they may agree like brothers, and worship me their lord.

BUT: The first thing we do, let's kill all the lawyers.

CADE: Ay, that I mean to do. Is not this a lamentable thing, that of the skin of an innocent lamb, should be made parchment? That parchment, being scribbled o'er, should undo a man? Some say the bee stings; but I say, 'tis the bee's wax, for I did but seal once to a thing, and I was never mine own man since.

Cade orders the mob's execution of a clerk, because he is found to have "a book in his pocket with red letters i'nt" and because he writes his name, rather than just making a mark, "like an honest, plain-dealing man."

"Hang him with his pen and ink-horn about his neck," cries Cade to the enraged crowd.

He executes poor, palsied Lord Say for similarly inane reasons. Among them, "he can speak French; and therefore he is a traitor." He has "corrupted the youth of the realm in building a grammar school." He "hast caused printing to be used"; and perhaps worse, he "hast men about [him] that usually talk of a noun and a verb."

Later, when his army of rabble has entered London, Cade begins to reveal his personal goals. "The proudest peer in the realm shall not wear a head on his shoulders, unless he pay me tribute; there shall not a maid be married, but she shall pay to me her maidenhead ere they have it."

But the mob, like all mobs in Shakespeare, is easily persuaded to switch allegiance. They desert Cade, swayed by Lord Clifford's patriotic invocation of Henry V.

Perhaps Shakespeare shows a bit of sympathy for the starving fugitive Cade, as he is finally killed by an honest country squire whose garden he has invaded. But it seems clear that Cade is meant to be deplored along with the absurdly motivated butchery of his rebellion.

We see the mob in action again in *Julius Caesar*. Shakespeare never explicitly takes a position on whether Brutus and his co-conspirators were justified in killing Caesar, or Antony was justified in acting with Octavius to take revenge. He probably felt that neither side acted admirably. But he does not tell us so.

There is no question, however, about the Bard's attitude toward the Roman mob. First, Brutus sways them to approve Caesar's murder and to praise the conspirators. Then, only minutes later, Antony works them into a frenzy of hatred for Brutus and the conspirators. They rush through the streets with firebrands, screaming their rage at those who, shortly before, they were praising to the sky. They come upon poor Cinna the poet, who has the misfortune to have the same name as one of the conspirators:

3 CIT: Your name, sir, truly?

CIN: Truly my name is Cinna.

1 CIT: Tear him to pieces; he's a conspirator.

CIN: I am Cinna the poet, I am Cinna the poet.

4 CIT: Tear him for his bad verses, tear him for his bad verses.

CIN: I am not Cinna the conspirator.

4 CIT: It is no matter, his name's Cinna; pluck but his name out of his heart, and turn him going.

3 CIT: Tear him, tear him!

In *Coriolanus*, Shakespeare adopts a somewhat more balanced approach to the anger of the common crowd. At least, he presents their point of view. As the play begins, a hungry citizen cries out to the mob of his fellows:

> We are accounted poor citizens; the patricians good. What authority surfeits on would relieve us: if they would yield us but the superfluity, while it were wholesome, we might guess they relieved us humanely; but they think we are too dear: the leanness that afflicts us, the object of our misery, is as an inventory to particularise their abundance; our sufferance is a gain to them—Let us revenge this with our pikes, ere we become rakes: for the gods know I speak this in hunger for bread, not in thirst for revenge.

Coriolanus, a heroic but stubborn and plainspoken general, arrives and berates the crowd. He will not "flatter" them with "good words." To him they have never been loyal or reliable. He tells them just what he thinks:

> What's the matter, you dissentious rogues. That, rubbing the poor itch of your opinion, make yourselves scabs?
> . . . .
> He that trusts to you, where he should find you lions finds you hares; where foxes, geese: you are no surer, no, than is the coal of fire upon the ice . . . who deserves greatness, Deserves your hate; and your affections are a sick man's appetite, who desires most that which would increase his evil. He that depends upon your favours swims with fins of lead, and hews down oaks with rushes . . . With every minute you do change a mind, And call him noble that was now your hate, Him vile that was your garland.

Later, Coriolanus is urged to speak to the common people and attain their approval of his becoming consul. Reluctantly and bitterly, he does; but corrupt politicians turn the crowd against him. As he told them to their faces in the earlier scene, the crowd is fickle, easily swayed. Outraged, they demand his death or banishment. Despite the seeming merit of their earlier plea for bread, they are portrayed just as Coriolanus described them—brutal, venal, unthinking.

But Coriolanus is stiff-necked and basically without the ability to understand, much less sympathize with, the needs and desires of the people or even to make sound judgments as to his own conduct. Instead of bending or seeking a peaceful exile, he goes over to the Volscians, Rome's bitter enemy.

Which side does the Bard favor? Probably he prefers Coriolanus to the mob, and, certainly, he deplores the politicians who incite its passion. But he does present the weaknesses of Coriolanus and the human needs that motivate the crowd.

Another view Shakespeare seems to have held was an opposition to killing, even when motivated by what appear to be high principles or what might seem justifiable revenge—perhaps even in battle.

Brutus kills Caesar for what he tells himself is the public good. But Brutus suffers for making that choice, as does Rome.

Nor does any good come when Romeo kills Tybalt or when Richard II is slain at the ambiguous request of Bolingbroke. And when, after failing to take an honest stand on anything, the weak and wordy Richard II lashes out to kill two servants, did Shakespeare mean us to approve? I think not.

Certainly, no one profits from Macbeth's murders or from those Shakespeare attributes to Richard III.

And even Henry V—what good came from the executions he ordered, from his slaughter of the French, from his command to cut the throats of all French prisoners? Henry died young, and, on his death, England began the agonizing process of losing everything he had gained.

Is Hamlet an exception? Are we meant to applaud the eight deaths he causes in the process of avenging his father's murder? Maybe. But maybe not. I have not yet seen it asserted that Shakespeare was advocating abolition of the death penalty. But, even that claim may come. The notion is not so farfetched. In *Timon of Athens*, Alcebiades makes a plea to save the life of a friend who has killed a man. The senators hear his plea, but reject it, announcing gravely, "We are for law—he dies" and "He forfeits his own blood that spills another." Sadly, Alcebiades replies, "Must it be so? It must not be."

In *Measure for Measure*, the basic "jeopardy" created by the plot is the potential imposition of the death penalty on Claudio and the attempts by his sister and others to save him from that fatal sentence. In the same play, an executioner is said to be no better than a common pimp. The provost offers to release a prisoner if he will serve as assistant to the executioner Abhorson. The provost tells Abhorson, the prisoner "hath been a bawd."

The executioner is shocked. "A bawd, sir? Fie upon him; he will discredit our mystery" (i.e., our profession).

The provost's reply may suggest Shakespeare's view:

> Go to, sir; you weigh equally;
> a feather will turn the scale.

Perhaps the play that is currently the subject of the most political debate is *The Tempest*. The magus, Prospero, is the rightful duke of Milan. But he has been exiled to a small island, where he adopts as a servant and educates the semihuman Caliban, teaching him language and other civilized skills. Therein lies the issue. Is Prospero the beneficent guide to Caliban's enlightenment or the quintessential colonial power enslaving Caliban, the innocent native who, before Prospero arrived on the island, was ignorant but free? Today, we often see Caliban played as black or Native American to dramatize his plight and his attempt to end his exploitation by the colonizing white man. Did Shakespeare have that in mind? I think not; but there are those who would disagree.

And so it goes, play after play. What really were Shakespeare's political and social views? What were the "basic truths" he intended? Aside from his dislike of mobs and hypocrisy, we can't be certain. While the question allows for interesting speculation and stimulating argument, the Bard's political and social views do not tell us whether he was the Stratford man or someone else.

Other than what we might infer from some relatively unattractive examples of his behavior, such as his hoarding grain, suing his neighbors, and protecting only his own interests in the enclosure dispute, we have no clear idea of the political or social views of the Stratford man. Having succeeded in acquiring substantial property and raising his status to that of "gentleman," he may well have had stronger feelings about the need to preserve order and less sympathy for those not so fortunate, than would an educated, free-thinking aristocrat, who, despite his wealth and position, perceived the brutal inequities of the prevailing order.

While Shakespeare's political and social outlook remains a matter that can be, and has been, debated, there are two opinions he expressed that might seem inconsistent with what the Stratford man was likely to have voiced.

The Stratford man was heavily involved in the acquisition of real estate, including the second largest house in town, evidently a source of great pride. His interests in land and its yield were quite substantial.

Now consider Shakespeare. Hamlet despised Osric, whom he calls a "water-fly" to his face. It seems Osric is a significant land owner. Hamlet treats this with derision. Turning to Horatio, he says that Osric "hath much land," he is "spacious in the possession of dirt." Is this insult something penned by the Stratford real estate dealer? It may seem unlikely, but it can't be ruled out. This is not a major or repeated theme in Shakespeare; and since it is doubtful that the Stratford man felt embarrassed or at all defensive about his real estate holdings, he could well have had a sufficiently playful sense of humor to have given Hamlet the amusing line without concern that it would degrade his own position.

But his attitudes on being a gentleman may have been quite another matter. As we have seen, the Stratford man strove—possibly even to the point of bribing officials—to establish himself as a "gentleman," by obtaining a coat of arms in his father's name (along with the motto "not without right"). His eagerness to attain this improved social status was evidently so obvious and extreme that it served as the basis of a biting public send-up by Ben Jonson ("not without mustard"). It would be surprising if the Stratford man did not have considerable sensitivity on the subject, as well as a proclivity to resist any attack on gentlemen as a class.

Yet Shakespeare had a tendency to portray those who fancied themselves gentlemen as fools, louts, cowards, liars, or all of these. Examples are Parolles in *All's Well That Ends Well*; Osric, Rosencrantz, and Guildenstern in *Hamlet*; Cloten and Iachimo in *Cymbeline*; Tybalt in *Romeo and Juliet*; Don Armado in *Love's Labour's Lost*; Roderigo in *Othello*; Lorenzo and even Bassanio in *The Merchant of Venice*; and, of course, those two "gentlemen" of Verona, whose ridiculous "happy" outcome was probably meant by the Bard as a satire on the class as a whole.

In act 1, scene 2 of *Love's Labour's Lost*, Don Armado refers to being a gentleman as "the varnish of a complete man"; but Armado is a verbose fool, and the fatuous remark is meant to make that clear.

Is this repeated theme in Shakespeare consistent with views that would have been expressed by the Stratford man either before or after he managed to become "William Shaksper, gent."? It seems unlikely.

Isn't it more consistent with the attitudes of a highborn nobleman, who could look on lowly commoners with tolerance and humor, so long as they acted as individuals and not as a mob, but who was inclined to view social climbing "gentlemen" with skepticism and even disgust?

15.

THE WILL

We have already mentioned the Stratford man's will. It describes him as "William Shackspere of Stratford-upon-Avon in the county of Warwick gentleman." It was prepared by Francis Collins, a lawyer who had replaced Thomas Greene as town clerk. The will consists of three pages, probably handwritten by Collins's clerk, although possibly by Collins himself. It has a number of corrections and interlineations, which apparently was not unusual.

It has been contended that the Stratford man wrote the will himself, proving that he could write quite well. This seems wishful thinking. The testator's signatures are totally different from the writing of the will itself, not only in the formation of the letters, but in the shakiness of the signatures, as opposed to the relatively smooth, flowing hand of the text.

Some have found even the style and organization of the will hard to reconcile with the work of the Bard. The Reverend Joseph Greene, who, in 1747, as vicar of Stratford's Holy Trinity Church and master of the town's grammar school, wrote that the will "appears to me so dull and irregular, so absolutely void of the least particle of that spirit which animated our great poet; that it must lessen his character as a writer to imagine any sentence of it his production." It did not, of course, occur to Reverend Greene that the Stratford man might not have been the "great poet." But Greene's remarks may be unfair to the Stratford man. He was no doubt extremely ill at the time; and, in any event, the style of expression would seem attributable to Collins, rather than to his client.

Even aside from questions of style, this seems a strange will for a famous poet and playwright. It seems the narrow testament of a petty (and possibly spiteful), small-town trader. It deals with his "barnes, stables, orchardes, gardens, landes, tenementes and heredimentes." It specifies bequests of individual items of personal property such as his "wearing Apparrell," his "plate," his "broad silver gilt bole," and his "sword." By interlineation, it leaves to his wife his "second best bed with the furniture" (i.e., the sheets and pillows). It does not refer to her as "his beloved wife" as was commonly done. Nor does it leave her anything else or even name her.

Although the Stratford man was concerned and careful about matters of property, his will mentions no books, no manuscripts, no unfinished works, no literary property of any kind, and no interest in any theatre.

Do these omissions prove the anti-Stratfordian case? Not necessarily. But they raise significant questions. Take books, for example. A number of men active in the theatre left specific bequests of books. Even the widow of fellow actor Henry Condell left such a bequest. William Cartwright, an actor who died in 1586, left a specific bequest of books in his will; and the inventory of his estate lists what appears to be over 1,000 volumes. But the will of the Stratford man, who, if he was "Shakespeare," used a myriad of source works in his poems and plays, mentions not one book.

Still, many people today who have large libraries sign wills in which books are not singled out, but are simply included in a residuary bequest, such as one disposing of "all my remaining property of every kind and character." Perhaps the Stratford man followed the same course.

He did provide for a residual gift to his daughter Susanna and his "sonne in Lawe John Hall," leaving them "all the Rest of my goodes chattels Leases plate Jewels & household stuffe whatsoever." This could certainly be meant to include books which would be both "goodes" and "chattels."

Anti-Strats argue that, even aside from the will, there is no record of the Stratford man or any of his descendants ever possessing any books. This is not correct. In 1627, his daughter Susanna reported the theft from her home of personal property including "books." Her husband John Hall, in his 1635 will, left his "study of bookes" to Thomas Nash. It is possible that the Stratford man had a substantial number of books, which were included in his residuary bequest and were either stolen from his daughter's house or were received by John Hall and passed on to Nash by Hall's will.

Unfortunately, the inventory, which was attached to the will and would have been presented in the probate proceedings, has never been found. Possibly, it was destroyed in the great fire of London.

But what of literary property? What about his rights in plays? Where are they in the will? They are not covered in his residual bequest. One would not describe intangible rights in literary property as "goods" or "chattels." Yet, if the Stratford man owned such intangible rights in 1616, why were they not disposed of on his death?

The answer may be that he was not the owner. Anti-Strats argue that the will shows that someone else was the true author and owner of the plays—someone like Oxford, Marlowe, or Bacon. Stratfordians respond, "Yes, there was another owner, but not some pseudonymous, playwriting aristocrat. The plays were owned by the theatre company."

They could be correct. Typically, playwrights had contracts providing that they were paid specified sums and that, in return, the company owned all rights in the play. Customarily, the playwright was given an earnest payment on signing, with further advances on delivery of a specified number of sheets, and a final payment when the completed work was handed in. No such contract with Shakespeare has been found. Possibly, he assigned all rights in the plays to the theatre company by such a contract or in some subsequent transaction. If so, the company would have been owner of the plays at the time of his death, and the plays would not appear in his will.

Most performances of Shakespeare's plays were by the Lord Chamberlain's Men—later the King's Men. Unfortunately, the records of that company have not been preserved. Probably, those that were not destroyed in the Globe fire were lost or destroyed during the period in which Cromwell's "roundheads" outlawed the theatre. This period, from 1642 until 1660, ended when the monarchy was restored with the coronation of Charles II.

Probably because of his great stature, Ben Jonson was able to retain ownership of his plays. But Shakespeare was of great stature as well. Why would he not have reserved ownership, as Jonson did? One answer may be that Jonson freelanced, writing for various companies, while, after the formation of the Lord Chamberlain's Men, Shakespeare wrote exclusively for that company and may have assigned his plays to them.

Moreover, if Shakespeare was the Stratford man, he may have acquired his sharer's interest in the Lord Chamberlain's Men, and his housekeeper's interest in the Globe and the Blackfriars Theatre by assigning the rights to his past and future plays, rather than paying cash. There are no extant records of any such transaction. But there are also no records that show any cash payment by him for his ownership share. He might have traded the right in his plays to Burbage and the Lord Chamberlain's Men in exchange for his ownership interest.

But he had no interest in any company or theatre run by Phillip Henslowe, which leads to another puzzling fact. Henslowe and his son-in-law Edward Alleyn kept careful records of their payments to playwrights. Since they performed some of Shakespeare's plays in the early years, we would expect his name to appear as being paid for them. Curiously, it does not. Why did he receive no payments for these early performances of his plays?

If the plays were written by the Stratford man, he may have retained ownership in them when they were performed by Henslowe, but transferred his rights to the Lord Chamberlain's Men when he became a sharer or when he acquired his interest in the Globe. This seems unlikely, since the Henslowe performances were early in Shakespeare's career, when it is doubtful that he had the bargaining power to retain ownership in his work. Whether or not he retained ownership, why was he not paid for writing the plays? If the author was the Stratford man, wouldn't he have insisted on payment? If the true author was a titled nobleman, might he not have waived payment?

Putting aside the curious absence of any payment by Henslowe for Shakespeare's early works, what of the later plays—particularly the manuscripts unpublished at the Stratford man's death? Why are they not mentioned in his will?

Protection for published works was typically enjoyed by the printer, rather than the playwright or theatre company. This protection was found in the rules of the Company of Stationers, an organization of booksellers and printers supervised jointly by the Privy Council and the Court of High Commission, an ecclesiastical court. The Stationers' Company maintained a register. When a bookseller or printer listed a work in the register, he was granted the exclusive right to publish and sell it—a right that could be transferred. If that occurred, the transfer could be recorded in the register.

Severe penalties were imposed by the Court of Star Chamber on those who violated this publishing right.

In the latter part of the eighteenth century, the leading copyright cases of *Millar v. Taylor* and *Donaldson v. Beckett* held, by a divided court, that the common law protected an author's copyright, even after publication of his work—at least until the Statute of Anne created statutory copyright in 1735, giving protection for published works, but only for a limited term. The great William Blackstone successfully argued *Millar* for the plaintiff and later rendered an opinion as one of the judges in *Donaldson*. Lord Mansfield, along with the majority in both cases agreed with Blackstone that such protection existed.

But these cases came more than a century after the Stratford man died. Possibly, the law on this point was unclear when he made his will in 1616. And, again, it is probable that the theatre company or its assignees owned at least the published plays.

Eighteen of Shakespeare's plays were registered and published before the First Folio in 1623, beginning with *Titus Andronicus* in 1594 and continuing through *Othello*, which was registered in 1621 and published in 1622. Eighteen plays were added by the First Folio registered in 1623. All the plays were registered by printers, publishers, or booksellers, who presumably acquired the publishing right by purchase from the theatre company.

For example, Park Honan reports that, in 1597 and 1598, the Lord Chamberlain's company sold four plays by Shakespeare to Andrew Wise "as a cash raising device." Actually, Wise registered only three plays in those years: *Richard II, Richard III,* and *Henry IV*, Part 1. In 1600, he registered two more: *Henry IV*, Part 2, and *Much Ado About Nothing*. Honan gives no supporting citation, so we cannot ascertain the source of his statement; but it seems to have been the theatre company, rather than Shakespeare himself, that sold the plays to Wise. If so, it is a reasonable inference that the company, rather than Shakespeare, owned them, and that they would have been acquired from the author by prior contract, by later purchase, or as the price of his ownership share in the company or the playhouse. This was probably true of his other plays as well.

This might explain why the *published* plays were omitted from the Stratford man's will. But what about the unpublished manuscripts? Of the thirty-six plays included in the First Folio, published in 1623, eighteen had not been published by 1616, when the Stratford man died, including such great works as *King Lear, Hamlet, Macbeth,* and *Othello.* There seems little doubt that the common law protected works that had not yet been published, and performance of a play was not considered publication. Considering Shakespeare's glowing reputation, the unpublished plays would have had significant value. Why did this property-conscious, careful man not mention and dispose of such valuable property along with his "silver gilt bowl" and "second best bed"?

Possibly, the plays that had been performed were also owned by the theatre company, even though they had not yet been published. But there are unpublished plays for which there is no clear record of performance by 1616. If they had never been performed, had Shakespeare agreed that anything he wrote at any time was owned by the theatre company *even before it was performed*? Possibly; but, again, we have no record of any such transaction.

While certainly not determinative, the failure of the Stratford man's will to deal at least with the unpublished plays lends some support to the anti-Strat cause. And, aside from the intangible literary property, where are the physical manuscripts? They are not mentioned in the will, and they have never been found—not one.

Perhaps the foul papers were discarded when the fair copies were made. Perhaps the fair copies of published plays might have been retained by the printer, or discarded as no longer useful. Even the theatre company would not need them once the printed copies were available.

But what happened to the unpublished manuscripts? If they were not in the playwright's possession at the time of his death, where were they? If they had been performed or even delivered to the theatre company, but not yet published, the company would probably have carefully guarded them.

Possibly, some of the manuscripts were destroyed in the Globe fire of 1613. However, there are numerous accounts of the fire, but not one mentions the loss of any manuscripts or play books. They might have been saved from the flames or they might, more logically, have been stored at Blackfriars, rather than at the open and vulnerable Globe.

Perhaps all of the manuscripts were discarded after the printing of the First Folio. Since all of Shakespeare's plays were now available in printed form, there may have seemed no need to save any of the manuscripts. But why are they not referred to in the will?

One possibility is that the physical manuscripts were "goodes" and "chattels," and might have been included in the residuary bequest. William

THE WILL ✠ 171

Cartwright mentioned no manuscripts in his will, but his probate inventory showed that he had 100 of them. If the Stratford man's inventory had been found, it might have had a similar entry.

The will raises other difficult questions. It makes no mention of the decedent's interests in any theatre or acting company. These interests would have been valuable assets, which would not be included as "goodes" or "chattels." The Stratford man held an interest in the playhouse itself at both the Globe and Blackfriars. These were tenancies in common, not joint tenancies, so that they could pass by will, rather than going automatically to the other co-tenants. At the Globe, his housekeeper's interest was in a ground lease and could have been included in the term *Leases*, as used in the will. This seems to have been true of his interest in Blackfriars as well.

But what of his interest as an actor-sharer in the company? These men shared in company profits after deduction of a portion paid to the housekeepers as rent. Apparently, a sharer made a contribution when he was admitted and received a payout of some kind on retirement or death. The will says nothing about any such interest or payment right. Conceivably, that interest could also be included in "Leases," since the actor-sharers did bear a charge for rent to the housekeepers.

Possibly, the Stratford man sold or transferred his interest as a sharer and as a housekeeper before his death. Co-owners of the house had to contribute to its maintenance. As we have seen, the Globe was virtually destroyed by fire in 1613, and the cost of rebuilding would have required a significant capital contribution from the co-owners of the ground lease, with only sixteen years left to go on the lease term. It is possible that, at that time, the Stratford man sold or relinquished all of his interest in the Globe, as a housekeeper and actor-sharer, to avoid making the contribution. Perhaps his Blackfriars interests were sold or exchanged for the same reason at the same time. We have no evidence of such a transaction.

Stratfordians tend to reason that their man *must* have sold his theatre interests, because they do *not* appear in his will. But that is more of the circular, bootstrap reasoning that tends to plague this field of inquiry. Perhaps the Stratford man never really owned those interests, but held them for someone else—the true playwright. That would also explain why they are not mentioned in his will.

Leaving his wife his "second best bed" has been taken as an indication that the Stratford man was a mean and petty fellow, far different from the understanding, humanitarian author of the plays. This may be unfair. We do not know the relationship between the Stratford man and his wife, except that they lived apart for many years. She was older than he, and perhaps the marriage was forced on him by reason of her pregnancy, or, if it was romantic at its inception, perhaps it had deteriorated before he left home around 1585.

And Anne was not left penniless. Under the English law then applicable, she would have been entitled to a dower right regardless of what his will provided. This would have given her a life interest in all of her husband's real property, including the right, during her lifetime, to dwell in the family residence. She may have been entitled to one-third of his personal property as well; but, at this time, that depended on the custom in the particular county, and it's not clear what the custom was in Warwickshire at this time.

In acquiring his property near the Blackfriars Theatre, the Stratford man appears to have entered into a mortgage transaction evidently designed to preclude Anne's acquiring a dower interest in that property. But he appeared to be the outright and unencumbered owner of the balance of his real estate, which, accordingly, would have been subject to Anne's dower claim.

Possibly, Anne Hathway requested this particular bed, since it had come from her old family home. The Stratford man may have felt that she would remain in the family home and receive a dower interest in his property, but that this would not necessarily include her family bed and made the interlineation to ensure that she would have it.

Another, more romantic possibility is that the "best" bed was reserved for guests, so that the "second best bed" was the one the Stratford man had shared with Anne.

The fact that the will does not call Anne "beloved" or "loving," while perhaps a departure from the norm, may simply reflect the style of the lawyer, rather than any resentful feelings on the part of the Stratford man. He was reputed to be very fond of his daughter Susanna, who is the principal beneficiary of his will. Yet the will uses no affectionate term for her either.

The will left money to buy commemorative rings for three actors, "my ffellowes John Hemynge, Richard Burbage and Henry Cundell." There is no recognition of a relationship with any *writer*, an odd omission in the will of a playwright who supposedly had lived for many years in the London theatrical world, sometimes working with other playwrights. Did he make no friends among them? If he was Shakespeare, where were the "private friends" to whom he read his "sugared sonnets"? Were they all dead?

In sum, a good case can be made for the proposition that the will of the Stratford man seems inconsistent with his having been the author of the Shakespeare canon. Is that argument unassailable? By no means. But, here again, the will may permit us to draw reasonable inferences that may help us in forming an opinion.

16.

THE MONUMENT

*M*uch of the Stratfordian case hinges on two things: the First Folio and the monument in Stratford's Holy Trinity Church. The monument can be seen there today. With its quiet churchyard and weatherworn headstones, its soft beige stone, stained-glass panels, and carved white marble bearing the patina of centuries, Holy Trinity seems a typical English country church.

There is one exception. Set high in the wall of the North Chancel, with its base seven feet above the floor, is an elaborate monument containing a life-size, painted, poly-chrome bust of "Shakespeare." He is wearing a red shirt, white collar and cuffs, and a shiny black vest. His rotund face bears a rather vacant expression and is a brightly lacquered brown, as if he has just returned from a vacation in Spain. Perhaps this was meant to conform to Shakespeare's own description of himself in Sonnet 62 as "beated and chapped with tanned antiquity." The figure's left hand rests on a piece of paper. His right holds a large quill, as if he had just looked up from writing. The paper is carved marble. The pen is an actual goose-feather quill. Oddly, the paper on which he is writing rests on a black and red pillow with gold tassels.

The bust appears before a white marble background and is framed by black marble columns. Above the bust are two small cherubs, one holding a spade, the other holding a torch, with its hand on a skull. Between them is the Stratford man's coat of arms and, above that, another skull.

The monument was erected between 1616 and 1622. As it presently appears, it would seem squarely to connect the famous author with the Stratford man.

The problem for the Stratfordians is that the monument, as originally constructed, may have been quite different. It was pictured, along with other monuments, in an engraving made from a drawing by Sir William Dugdale in his comprehensive book *Antiquities of Warwickshire*, published in 1656. It was pictured again in an engraving made in 1709 for Nicholas Rowe's biography of Shakespeare. Both Dugdale and Rowe considered the bust to be a likeness of Shakespeare, the poet and playwright. Yet both engravings are very different from the image now in the Stratford church. *Most significantly, they show "Shakespeare" without a quill pen or writing paper. Instead, he is depicted with both hands clutching what appears to be a sack of grain.* Was this a reference to the Stratford man's reputation as a grain hoarder or at least as a successful commodities trader?

And what of the inscription? Today, it contains lavish praise in Latin comparing Shakespeare to great men of the classical age. It reads as follows:

> *Iudicio Pylium, genio Socratem, arte Maronem*
> *Terra tegit, populus maeret Olympus habet*
>
> *(A Nestor in judgment, a Socrates in intelligence, a Virgil in art.*
> *The earth buries him, the people mourn him, Olympus has him.)*

It has been argued that the Latin references to Nestor, Socrates, and Virgil do not fit a famous poet and playwright. This criticism may be apt as to Nestor. He was the son of the king of Pylos (thus, "Pylium") and was the oldest of the Greek commanders at the siege of Troy. He was not a poet or playwright. It may also be true as to Socrates, who was a philosopher and teacher, but also not a poet or playwright. But it is not true of Virgil ("Maronem"), who was not only a poet, but the author of *The Aeneid*.

The inscription might fit Shakespeare (at least the Virgil part), but it would hardly have been understood by the common folk of Stratford. Even if they had understood the Latin, they would probably not have grasped the cryptic references to "Pylium" (Pylos was the county of Nestor's origin) or "Maronem" (Maro was the last name of the poet Virgil). Why did the creators of the monument choose those seemingly obscure references rather than using the more common names Nestor and Virgil? Was it to reduce the likelihood that the townspeople would think their neighbor was being compared to great men of the classical age? Perhaps, even if the local residents grasped those references, they would probably have taken them for typical funereal excess for a deceased man of wealth, rather than a factual statement that the deceased was a poet.

The present inscription also contains a second paragraph in English:

> *Stay passenger, why goest thou by so fast*
> *Read if thou canst, whom envious death hath plast*
> *With in this monument Shakspeare; with whom*
>
>   *s*
>
> *Quick nature dide. Whose name doth deck y tomb,*
>   *t*
> *Far more then cost. Sieh all y he hath writt*
> *Leaves living art, but page, to serve his witt.*

Does "all y he hath writt leaves living art, but page, to serve his witt" tell the reader that this is a poet? Perhaps, but not without ambiguity. "All y he hath writt" could even be understood as all the legal documents and business correspondence of a skillful trader. Even the word *art* was sometimes used in a pejorative sense to mean "cunning," and *witt* is more suggestive of mental quickness than of poetic ability.

The 1656 engraving by Dugdale shows only the first words of the Latin inscription. As portrayed by Rowe in 1709, the inscription contains only the Latin paragraph, not the English.

Interestingly, the monument spells the name "Shakspeare," rather than "Shakespeare," a name that was by then famous.

We have no independent evidence that, at the time of the Stratford man's death in 1616, the citizens of Stratford considered him a renowned author or anything other than a retired actor, real estate dealer, and grain speculator. Perhaps, in 1616, they would have laughed at a monument depicting their rich and contentious neighbor as a great poet and playwright. Probably, all of that changed in 1623, with the publication of the First Folio, linking the playwright to Stratford and fellow actors. At that point, the townspeople, like the rest of England, must have come to believe that the Stratford man was, in fact, the great Bard. After the First Folio, the Stratford monument was probably believed to honor the famous poet and playwright, not just a local tycoon.

As time passed, Stratford began to thrive as a tourist destination. Vast sums were generated from the public's belief that this is where Shakespeare was born, lived, and died. One could visit what is supposed to be his birthplace and his wife's cottage. Plays were performed. Souvenirs were sold. Inns and pubs were filled.

Stratfordians have argued that Sir William Dugdale's work was sloppy and that his engraver, Wenceslaus Hollar, was often inaccurate. But Dugdale was a highly respected expert in the field. He was from Warwickshire and reportedly knew the family of the Stratford man. His original sketch still exists and shows that his engraver copied it faithfully.

Moreover, *Antiquities of Warwickshire* was corrected and revised in a second edition published in 1730 and edited by Dr. William Thomas. Apparently, all of the monuments were rechecked by Dr. Thomas, who lived near Stratford and took great pride in Shakespeare. He found errors in Dugdale's work, blaming this on persons Dugdale hired.

Yet, even though Shakespeare was a very famous man by 1730, and even though Thomas made corrections to the depiction of other monuments in the book, the engraving of "Shakspeare's" monument in Stratford remained unaltered. The quill is not there. Nor is the paper. It seems unlikely that Dr. Thomas would not have corrected such a glaring error in the most important monument in the book, had such an error existed in Dugdale's original engraving.

What is the explanation? By 1746, the original monument had become "much impaired and decayed." In 1748, "Mr. John Hall, Limner" was hired to "repair and beautify" it. A document was prepared setting out just what Hall was to do. Unfortunately, the document has not been found. One inference is that, in "repairing and beautifying" the monument, the city fathers decided to substitute the conventional depiction of an author, quill pen in hand, for the one that seemed to portray a rich grain trader and possibly to add to the inscription an English paragraph referring to what he "hath writt."

The problem with that theory is that George Vertue made a vague sketch of the monument in 1737 *showing the Bard with a quill pen in his hand even before John Hall made his "repairs."* This leaves at least four possibilities: (1) Dugdale, Rowe, and Thomas were all inaccurate, and the quill was there from the start; (2) the quill was originally there, but had been removed or broken off before Dugdale's work in 1656; (3) the quill was not originally there, but was added not in 1748, when the monument was "repaired," but between 1730, when Thomas made his check on Dugdale's work, and 1737, when Vertue did his sketch; or (4) the quill was not originally there, Vertue made a fanciful sketch in 1737, adding the quill from his own imagination, and his sketch was used as a model for the repair work done in 1748.

The monument depicted by Dugdale in 1656, again by Rowe in 1709, and once again in Thomas's 1730 revision of Dugdale's work is so different from the one now in Stratford that it seems difficult to attribute the difference to mere sloppiness, haste, or clerical error. Perhaps the piece of paper could have been overlooked, but not the quill. The long white feather is just off the center of the bust as it now appears. It extends from the subject's hand on the pillow all the way to his right shoulder. Its glaring white stands out against the black of the vest and the red of the shirt. Apart from the brown balding head, it is the focal point of the portrayal.

If the quill was there when Dugdale, Rowe, and Thomas inspected the monument, they could not have missed it. It cannot have simply been overlooked by any of them, much less all three of them.

Did some seventeenth-century visitor to the church steal the quill before Dugdale sketched the monument in the 1650s? Not likely—not with the quill a good ten feet above the floor of the church. The quill has been replaced many times over the centuries, probably whenever it became worn and dusty. Could it have been in the process of being replaced when it was sketched? Again, not likely. There would have been an abundant supply of goose-feather quills in a town like Stratford; and, almost certainly, a new quill would have been obtained before the old one was removed. Moreover, it is impossible to believe that such a temporary absence occurred just when Dugdale visited the monument in the 1650s and, again, when Rowe was there in 1709, and, once again, in 1730, when Thomas made his check.

It seems reasonable to conclude that there was no quill in the monument at or before the time in 1730 when Thomas checked on Dugdale's sketch, and that it was either added between 1730 and 1737 or Vertue added it from his own imagination, setting a precedent followed when the monument was restored in 1748.

If, rather than an actual goose feather, the original quill had been carved stone, it could have been broken off before Dugdale's sketch. Given its position high above the church floor, this seems unlikely, although not impossible.

On the other hand, there may have been no quill until the eighteenth century. Perhaps the original monument was designed with deliberate ambiguity, to satisfy a need for a monument that would be recognized by the people of Stratford as the acquisitive grain and real estate trader of their town (even to the local spelling, "Shakspeare"), while, at the same time, it could be understood, at least by those with knowledge of Latin (as well as of Nestor's homeland and Virgil's family name), as identifying the Stratford man with great classical thinkers and thus with the famous author.

But, if the objective was to identify the Stratford man with the poet and playwright, why the need for such ambiguity? Why not put the pen and paper there from the start? Was the potential disbelief of the townspeople such a formidable danger?

Of course, even if the quill had been there from the beginning, the anti-Strats would remain unconvinced. Since we have no record of who erected or paid for this monument, it could have been placed in the church by influential persons who sought to preserve the illusion that Shakespeare was the Stratford man. It seems clear that the monument was not commissioned by the Stratford man's family or the town council *or anyone in Stratford*—at least that the English inscription was not. It explicitly states that Shakespeare is buried "with in this monument." Anyone in Stratford would have known that the Stratford man was not buried *within* the monument, but under the floor of the church, beneath the crude exhortation not to move his bones.

What outsider would finance an expensive monument to be placed in Stratford's church? Some friend or admirer of Shakespeare's work who believed he was the Stratford man? If so, where was the friend or admirer when the Stratford man died? So far as we know, no one said a word about his death. So who paid for the monument? And why? Who would have been motivated to connect the Stratford man with the famous poet and playwright if it was not so?

Did that same person, or group of persons, arrange for the Stratford man to be buried beneath the church floor, rather than in the churchyard with his fellow citizens?

Like so many aspects of the Shakespeare mystery, the monument raises intriguing questions. Later, we will explore one possible answer to all of them.

17.

THE FIRST FOLIO

By far, the strongest of the Stratfordian arguments lies in the First Folio, the complete collection of Shakespeare's plays published in 1623, seven years after the Stratford man's death. If the First Folio had never been published, the world might never have connected the author of the plays with the Stratford man.

The frontispiece to this critical volume describes its contents as follows:

> *Mr. William*
> *SHAKESPEARE'S*
> *Comedies,*
> *Histories &*
> *Tragedies.*
> *Published according to the True Original Copies*

Following this is a controversial engraving by Martin Droeshout, who was only twenty-two when the engraving was done. It purports to depict the author of the plays. But some anti-Strats have argued that it does not really do so—that, instead, it depicts a stupid "pudding-faced" individual who is not the poet at all. They argue that, if closely examined, the image can be seen to be a mask worn by someone else entirely and to contain other signals that it is not really Shakespeare.

Maybe so. But it is difficult to see these things in the engraving itself. It does appear to have one side of the subject's coat backwards, but this may simply be poor draftsmanship, rather than an attempt to convey a subtle message. As to the "mask," it appears more likely to be a line separating the subject's jaw from his neck.

After the controversial frontispiece, there are two letters signed by the noted actors, John Heminge and Henry Condell, who are announced as the First Folio's editors. Some scholars have concluded that the letters were actually written by Ben Jonson, rather than the two actors, and that the real editor of the First Folio was Jonson himself.

One letter is addressed to the earls of Pembroke and Montgomery. The other is to the readers in general. The first oozes insincere adulation. The second is simply a sales pitch for the book. It claims that the First Folio is based on "the true original copies" of Shakespeare's work and that its editors have eliminated the many errors contained in the "Stolne and Surreptitious" editions previously published. The fact is, the First Folio is riddled with errors.

The letter goes on to make the famous assertion that, in receiving Shakespeare's manuscripts, "we have scarce received from him a blot in his papers." In notes found later, Jonson himself wrote of hearing that Shakespeare "never blotted out a line."

The letters of Heminge and Condell also claim "our Shakespeare" to have been "a friend and ffellow" of theirs. Stratfordians argue from this that the author and the actor were clearly one and the same. A "ffellow" appears to have been a term actors commonly used in reference to another member of their company. If Heminge and Condell really made the statement that Shakespeare was their "ffellow" (a conclusion with which the anti-Strats disagree), it certainly tends to support the Stratfordian case. After writing numerous plays in which the two actors performed, a playwright might possibly have been considered a "friend and ffellow," even if he was not a fellow *actor*. But it seems unlikely.

Moreover, Heminge and Condell are clearly referring to the author of the plays as their "friend and ffellow." Most of the anti-Strat candidates for that authorship are high-ranking and important persons. It is most improbable that two common actors like Heminge and Condell would have referred to exalted men like the earl of Oxford or Sir Francis Bacon as their "friend and ffellow."

The words would fit the two actors' relationship with the Stratford man quite well. He was a fellow actor, and his will left Heminge and Condell money to buy memorial rings, referring to them as "my ffellows." Unless this provision of the will was a part of an elaborate plot, it shows that, not surprisingly, the Stratford man did consider them each a "friend and ffellow."

Considering these factors, it seems highly probable that Heminge and Condell, if they wrote the letters, were telling us that the playwright Shakespeare was the Stratford man. At least four possibilities flow from this. Either (1) the Stratford man did write the plays, (2) Heminge and Condell were unaware of the true author and assumed it was their fellow actor, (3) they knew he was not the real playwright and were part of a plot to continue the impression that he was, or (4) they didn't write the letters at all. Certainly, however, their letters must be considered evidence supporting the Stratfordian position.

That position is further strengthened by what follows the Heminge and Condell letters. This is a poem of forty couplets by Ben Jonson himself, extolling Shakespeare. It contains two passages seized upon by the Stratfordians as clinching their case. The first is as follows:

> *And though thou hadst small Latine, and lesse Greeke,*
> *From thence to honour thee, I would not seeke*
> *For names; but call forth thund'ring Aeschilus,*
> *Euripides, and Sophocles to us,*
> *Paccuvius, Accius, him of Cordova dead,*
> *To life againe, to heare thy Buskin tread,*
> *And shake a stage . . .*

This passage is frequently cited by Stratfordians as absolute proof that, having "small Latine and lesse Greeke," Shakespeare must have been the relatively uneducated Stratford man.

Here again, as in the case of Francis Beaumont's reference to the "dim light of Nature," we encounter a fundamental inconsistency. As we have seen, a basic element of the Stratfordian position is that Shakespeare "must have" attended the Stratford grammar school and that it "would have" afforded him a thorough knowledge of Latin and Latin authors—a classical education that Anthony Holden and others contend was virtually the equivalent of that provided university graduates. But he cannot have had both a thorough classical education and, at the same time, "small Latine and lesse Greeke."

Charlton Ogburn, a leading anti-Stratfordian, gives Jonson's "small Latine and lesse Greeke" line a different reading. He points out that, according to the *Oxford Universal Dictionary*, *though* can mean "even if" or "even supposing that," as well as "notwithstanding." He argues that this was necessarily Jonson's meaning, because *hadst* is subjunctive, and the balance of the lines use the conditional "I *would* not seeke," rather than "I *do* not seeke."

Thus, Ogburn contends, the correct interpretation is *"Even if* you had small Latin and less Greek (which you do not), I would call on the classical authors of the past to hear you shake a stage." Ogburn's grammatical analysis may be technically correct. But was Jonson that careful about his syntax, and were the rules of grammar the same in 1623 as today?

Besides, Jonson says he would have the great classical authors come to life "to heare thy Buskin tread, And shake a stage." That almost certainly means to hear you *act*, not just to see plays you have written. A buskin was a type of boot worn by actors on stage. A playwright might "shake" a stage with his words, but he wouldn't "tread" the stage wearing a "Buskin." Only an actor would do that. Jonson was clearly saying that Shakespeare was an actor as well as a playwright. And who could that be other than the Stratford man?

The second passage cited by Stratfordians as proving their case appears to tie Shakespeare to Stratford. Jonson refers to Shakespeare as "Sweet Swan of Avon." This has been taken as a clear reference to Shakespeare's being from Stratford-upon-Avon. It certainly seems to be. The Avon also flows through Rugby, where Edward de Vere, the earl of Oxford, once maintained a home. And Oxford is a prime candidate to have been the true author, if the Stratford man was not. But construing the line as a reference to Oxford seems unpersuasive. Oxford had sold his place in Rugby more than forty years earlier.

Another interpretation of this poetic reference is to Mary, countess of Pembroke, who lived on the other bank of the Avon opposite Stratford. The countess, a poet in her own right, has also been advanced as a candidate for the Shakespeare authorship. She was depicted in a well-known portrait with lace swans embroidered on her collar. Nevertheless, construing the "Sweet Swan of Avon" as a reference to the countess, or to anyone other than the Stratford man, seems too much of a stretch, particularly when taken with Jonson's reference to Shakespeare's buskin treading a stage.

Do these statements by Jonson nail the case for the Stratford actor? It would seem so—*if Jonson knew the facts and was telling the truth.* While not a certainty, it is a reasonable assumption that Jonson knew the identity of the playwright—knew whether he was the actor from Stratford or someone else for whom the actor was fronting. But whether Jonson was telling the truth is a far more serious and complex issue.

The fact that Jonson praises Shakespeare so lavishly in his introduction to the First Folio does seem inconsistent with some of Jonson's other comments on the Bard. If Jonson was equating Shakespeare with the Stratford man, we cannot forget his sardonic parody of the latter's attempt to become a gentleman by acquiring a coat of arms. It was hardly a friendly act when Jonson had a silly character adopt the motto "not without mustard," making fun of the Stratford man's pompous "not without right."

In about 1602, Jonson wrote *The Poetaster,* another play that satirized writers. One pretentious author, Crispinis, sometimes hyphenates his name as "Cri-spinis" (like "Shake-speare") and boasts of a new coat of arms that makes him a "gent'man." This too seems to lampoon the Stratford man. Jonson's poem in the First Folio refers to Shakespeare as the "Starre of Poets." As John Michell has pointed out, the Greek word for star is *aster.* Was "Starre of Poets" meant as a cryptic reference to Shakespeare's being the "Poetaster" satirized in Jonson's earlier play?

In the same period, Jonson wrote a series of verses about his fellow writers. One, called the "Poet-ape," used other people's material as his own. It is generally thought that this was also a cutting reference to Shakespeare.

According to his fellow poet, William Drummond, Jonson said that "Shakspeer wanted arte." And, according to Shakespeare's eighteenth-century biographer, Nicholas Rowe, Jonson frequently reproached Shakespeare for "want of learning and ignorance of the ancients." John Dryden wrote an essay on "Dramatique Poetry of the Last Age." According to Dryden, Jonson described certain "bombast speeches of Macbeth" as "horrour." And Jonson was quoted as describing *Pericles,* then attributed to Shakespeare, as a "mouldy tale."

Finally, in 1620, just three years before the First Folio, Jonson compiled a list of distinguished persons he had known. Shakespeare did not even make the list. To Jonson, he was not even a distinguished person. Yet, in the First Folio, he refers to Shakespeare by such laudatory phrases as "Soul of the Age" and "Starre of Poets."

Did Jonson change his mind about Shakespeare between 1620 and 1623? Or was he paid to strike this new pose? Sometime after 1623, Jonson made an entry in one of his notebooks to the effect that "players" had claimed that Shakespeare "never blotted out a line." Jonson's recorded answer was "would he had blotted out a thousand." Although he goes on to say that "[t]here was ever more in him to be praised than to be pardoned," it is hard to square this very mixed review with the lavish and unqualified praise in the First Folio.

In writing as he did for the First Folio, was Jonson going along with (and perhaps profiting by) a charade organized by some highly placed persons?

The introductory material in the First Folio continues, giving the Stratfordians even more ammunition. It includes a poem by Leonard Digges, which also supports the view that Shakespeare was the Stratford man:

> Shake-speare, at length thy pious fellowes give
> The world thy Workes: thy Workes, by which, out-live
> Thy Tombe, thy name must when that stone is rent,
> And Time dissolves thy Stratford Moniment,
> Here we alive shall view thee still.

Certainly, say the Stratfordians, this shows that, whether or not he was originally shown with pen in hand, the great poet and playwright William Shakespeare was the man depicted in the Stratford monument, and, therefore, he must have been the Stratford man.

But in this battle neither side will surrender an inch. "No," say the Oxfordians, Digges's reference is not to Stratford-upon-Avon, but to another, more prominent town called Stratford, which was northeast of London, adjoining Hackney, where the earl of Oxford was buried. It is, they claim, a reference to Shakespeare's being Oxford. The Stratfordians seem to have the better position on this issue. If the reference was really to a monument marking Oxford's burial place, why would it not have spoken of "thy Hackney moniment," rather than to a monument in the next town?

Following Digges's poem in the First Folio is a list of the twenty-six "Principall Actors in all these playes." This has been called unique. It is not.

Similar lists were included in the First Folio of Ben Jonson's works published in 1616.

In the First Folio of Shakespeare's works, his own name heads the list of "Principal Actors," preceding even the famous actor Richard Burbage, who managed the company. Yet, we have no record of Shakespeare's having played lead roles, such as Hamlet, Macbeth, or Lear. Nicolas Rowe reported that "tho' I have inquired I could never meet with any further account of him this way, than that the top of his performance was the Ghost in his own Hamlet." The Ghost is, of course, a rather small part; and, unless Rowe was joking, it would seem unlikely that Shakespeare the actor had anywhere near the stature of Burbage. Why, then, would he precede Burbage in the list of players?

Some anti-Strats have argued that the true Shakespeare was a nobleman and, for that reason, was given priority. This seems to make no sense, unless the pseudonymous nobleman was an actor on the public stage, as well as the playwright, a hypothesis for which there seems no evidentiary support. It is possible that Shakespeare is listed first among the actors, simply because, in addition to acting in the plays, he wrote them or, at least, was being held out as the person who wrote them. It was, after all, the First Folio of Shakespeare's plays, so that listing him first among the actors does not seem surprising.

But, in the First Folio of Jonson's own works, published in 1616, following the text of *Every Man in His Humour*, there is a list of the "principall comoedians" who appeared in the play when it was first performed in 1598. Shakespeare heads that list too, and, there, he was *not* the playwright—Jonson was. We have no indication that the actor from Stratford was known for comedic roles. Yet, he is listed first in that group. Why? We do not know. Perhaps it was a special tribute in light of his death in the year Jonson's First Folio was published. But there is no evidence supporting that hypothesis.

Even in the Royal Wardrobe Account for March 15, 1604, listing nine actors to be issued red cloth to wear in King James's procession through London, Shakespeare was listed first. Perhaps he was not such a minor actor after all—or, perhaps, he was (whether correctly or erroneously) perceived as a poet and playwright, as well as an actor, and, for that reason, headed these lists.

Considering Heminge and Condell's "friend and ffellow," plus Jonson's "small Latine and lesse Greeke," his references to Shakespeare's "Buskin" treading "a stage" and to the "Sweet Swan of Avon," plus Shakespeare's leading the list of actors and Digges's reference to "thy Stratford Moniment" all together, it is difficult not to conclude that they were squarely intended to tie the playwright of the First Folio to the Stratford man. Yes, Heminge and Condell could have referred to a writer as their "ffellow" even if he was not an actor; Jonson could have been using the subjunctive; the Avon does run elsewhere than Stratford; and, yes, there was even another town called Stratford; and the editors could have placed Shakespeare at the head of the actors' list because he was a nobleman. Taking all of these references together, however, it seems overwhelmingly probable that Shakespeare and Shakspere were intentionally being identified in the Folio as the same person.

If we were to assign percentages of probability to each of these lines, the combined result would be an extremely low probability that the First Folio was intended to convey anything else. Even if we were to assign a 50 percent probability that Jonson did not mean that Shakespeare actually *had* small Latin and less Greek and the same chance to his not meaning that Shakespeare was an actor when he said the Bard trod the stage in a buskin, and the same 50 percent probability that he didn't mean Stratford-upon-Avon when he referred to "Sweet Swan of Avon," and the same odds to the possibility that Heminge and Condell were talking about someone other than the Stratford man when they called Shakespeare their "friend and ffellow" and to the possibility that the "Shakespeare" who led the list of actors was meant to be someone other than the actor from Stratford or someone other than the "Shakespeare" who wrote the plays; and, even if we considered it a fifty–fifty proposition that Digges's "Stratford Moniment" referred to a monument near Hackney, then, taking all these assertions together, the probability that the authors of the prefatory material intended anything but to create the impression that Shakespeare was the Stratford man would be about 1.5 percent, or an enormous longshot. And assigning a fifty–fifty probability in each such instance is extremely generous to the anti-Strats.

In summary, the First Folio provides very significant support for the Stratfordian case. It is not, however, dispositive of the issue—that is, not a "smoking gun." Still, to avoid concluding that Shakespeare was the Stratford man, we have to assume that Jonson was either ignorant of the true facts or lying, and that the same is true of Heminge, Condell, and Digges.

Even if Jonson and Digges were unaware that the actor was fronting for someone else, it seems impossible that Heminge and Condell would not have known the truth about the source of the plays in which they appeared over all those years.

This leaves the possibility of a deliberate lie, that Jonson, Heminge, Condell, and Digges were all in on the game, deliberately creating the false impression that the Stratford actor and grain dealer was the author of the plays. But why would they do this seven years after the Stratford man's death? If the Stratford man had been fronting for such a well-known personage, what reason was there to keep up the pretense in 1623? Somehow, someone would have to have wanted to perpetrate the charade even well after the Stratford man's death.

Is it *possible* that the statements preceding the First Folio are a hoax? Certainly. But why? Later, we will explore a possible answer.

18.

WHAT'S IN A NAME?

A point often made by the anti-Strats is the difference in spelling between "Shakespeare" or "Shake-speare," as used on the poems and plays, and "Shaksper" or "Shakspere," as used by the Stratford man, even after poems and plays had been performed and published under the name *Shakespeare*.

But the point cuts two ways. If someone wanted a common actor to pose falsely as the author of the poems and plays, why use a different spelling for the pseudonym? Why not enhance the chances of successful concealment by announcing the poems and plays as the work of William Sh*ak*spere, rather than William Sha*ke*speare? Perhaps the actor had already adopted the grander-sounding "Shakespeare" as his stage name, even before he was asked to pose as the playwright.

Or perhaps the true author asked the actor who was to be paid to front for him to use "Shakespeare," rather than the less dramatic "Shakspeare." If so, it's probable that the actor would have been glad to make the slight spelling change to a name that possibly sounded better as well.

Of course, Elizabethan spelling was often inconsistent. On at least one occasion, the earl of Oxford, a prime candidate for the Shakespeare authorship, signed his name "Oxeford." This could simply have been a slip of the pen, the earl meaning to sign "Oxenford," the Latin version of Oxford. On the other hand, it may indicate that *e*'s could be added to or dropped from a name with little concern. Shakespeare, or one of its variants, was not an uncommon name. E. K. Chambers lists eighty-three different spellings of that name in the records of various English cities, towns, and persons.

The poet and playwright first became well known under the name *Shakespeare* with the highly successful publication of *Venus and Adonis* in 1593 and *The Rape of Lucrece* in 1594. Then quarto editions of *Titus Andronicus* and *Romeo and Juliet* were published anonymously in 1594 and 1597, a puzzling choice since Shakespeare had become a well-known author. But quarto editions of *Richard II* and *Richard III* were published under the name *Shake-speare*.

It has been argued that the use of the hyphen indicates a pseudonym. Not necessarily. And the hyphen was not consistently used. More likely, it was simply careless spelling or typesetting.

In 1598 *Love's Labour's Lost* was published under the name *Shakespere*, and *Henry IV,* Part 1, was, here again, published anonymously. The quarto edition of *The Merchant of Venice* appeared in 1600 attributed to "Shakespeare," while, in the same year, *Henry V* was published anonymously.

From that point forward, all of the plays (as well as the sonnets in 1609) were published under the name *Shakespeare* except the second quarto edition of *Henry IV*, Part 1, which was attributed to "Shake-speare" and, oddly, the quarto edition of *King Lear*, which bore the name *Shak-speare*.

Putting aside this last, the poet and playwright was obviously known in London as "Shakespeare" or "Shake-speare." In London this was generally true of the Stratford man as well, both in his acting career and otherwise. In 1602, the angry official of the College of Arms in London, who complained that the Stratford man's family was unworthy of being awarded a coat of arms, referred to him as "Shakespear ye Player."

Yet, for the most part, even after Shakespeare became famous, the Stratford man continued to be called "Shakspere," "Shaxper," "Shacksper" or the like in Stratford; and, more significantly, he continued to sign his name as "Shaksper," "Shaksp____," or something similar, even in London. Seemingly, his signature on legal documents would be the best reflection of his true name. Yet, on each occasion, it was "Shak," rather than "Shake."

In *Belott v. Mountjoy*, the Stratford man is referred to in the various court papers as "William Shakespeare gent." (i.e., gentleman). More important, however, is his own signature on a 1612 deposition in the *Mountjoy* case. Although the deposition was signed long after "Shakespeare" had become well known as a poet and playwright, the signature, in a childish, almost illegible hand, appears to be "Willm Shaksp." But the *k* is blotted and the *p* at the end is crossed, which has been interpreted as meaning "per." If so, the signature would be "Willm Shaksper." And this is considered his *best* signature.

In the Stratford man's 1613 purchase of the old gatehouse of the Blackfriars Theatre, the body of the deed refers to the new owner as "William Shakespeare of Stratford-upon-Avon," as does a mortgage, securing the unpaid balance of the purchase price. The Stratford man signed both the deed and the mortgage. His signature is even more childish and illegible than on the *Belott v. Mountjoy* deposition. On the deed, the "William" can be made out, but the last name is far more difficult to decipher. It appears to be either "Shaksp____" or "Shaksper." On the mortgage, the first name is abbreviated "Wm" and the last name appears to be "Shaksp____." The first syllable in the last name on both documents is "Shak" and neither *k* appears to be followed by an *e*.

In 1616, first in January and ultimately on March 25th, the Stratford man made his famous will. It refers to him as "William Shackspeare." It is signed, presumably by the Stratford man himself, three times, once on each page. The signatures are, to a great extent, illegible, perhaps the result of illness and a shaky hand. The first is totally illegible. The second resembles his earlier signatures but is far shakier. It seems to be "Shakspere," but the letters after the *k* could be almost anything. The third signature begins with the words *By me* which, along with the "William" that follows them, seem to be in a more precise hand, possibly written by someone else. The last name, which resembles other, earlier signatures appears to be "Shakp" followed by a separate squiggle that is probably "ere" or even "eare."

Equally significant with the Stratford man's own signatures are the entries of Thomas Greene, the Stratford town clerk. Greene was a solicitor and later a successful London barrister. He was also the Stratford man's cousin. Between September 1614 and September 1615, he made notes about the enclosure controversy. The notes are at the Shakespeare Birthplace Museum in Stratford. In the entries of September 5, 1614; November 17, 1614; December 23, 1614; January 9, 1615; January 11, 1615; and September 1615, Greene refers to the Stratford man as "Mr. Shakspeare," "Mr. Shakspear," "Cousin Shakspeare," "Cousin Shakspear," and, finally, "W. Shackespeare." Although Greene's spellings vary somewhat, they all seem to use "Shak" or

"Shack," rather than "Shake." And this too was long after the poet and playwright had become famous as "Shakespeare"—with an *e* and a long *a*.

Since Greene was an attorney and eventually a successful barrister, it is certain he could read. He also knew his cousin very well and had spoken and written his name many times. If the Stratford man was the great poet and playwright, Greene must have known it. Yet Greene resisted the famous name, Shakespeare, and stuck to the more usual Stratford spelling of his cousin's name.

Based on the spelling in all of the relevant documents, what can we conclude?

1. Elizabethan and Jacobean spelling of names was frequently varied. We have seen not only the variation in the spelling of the Stratford man's name, such as "Shackspere," and "Shaxpere," "Shagspere," and "Shackesespere," but also in the spelling of Hemminge, Condell, and Phillips in the same documents. There are many other examples. Evidently, sixteenth-century writers and printers had no concern about consistency in spelling names.

2. Nevertheless, the overwhelming majority of references that are clearly to the poet and playwright are spelled "Shakespeare" or "Shake-speare." The very few deviations include one reference in the 1600 version of "The Return from Parnassus" at Cambridge ("Shakspeare"), a bizarre spelling ("Shaxberd") in the record of the Office of Revels in 1604, and the 1608 quarto edition of *King Lear* ("Shak-speare"). Probably these are simply misspellings; and it seems fair to conclude that the name of the person widely recognized as the author of the poems and plays was spelled "Shakespeare" or "Shake-speare," and pronounced with a long *a*.

3. The majority of documents concerning the Stratford man's activities in London refer to him as "Shakespeare" or some long *a* variant. They do so even during his lifetime. Among them are the March 15, 1595, record of performances of actors before the queen; the documents pertaining to the family coat of arms; the October 1, 1598, tax assessment; the inventory of the Brend estate listing the occupants of the Globe Theatre; the Manningham diary in 1602 reporting the bawdy tale of the two actors; the

1603 order from James I authorizing actors to perform publicly; the 1604 grant of red cloth to various actors; the Phillips will in 1605; younger brother Edmund's burial near London in 1607; the text (but not the signature) of the documents in the *Belott v. Mountjoy* case; the text (but not the signatures) of the Blackfriars purchase and mortgage in 1613, and a 1615 complaint in Chancery by the Blackfriars landowners.

4. The vast majority of Stratford records use "Shackspere," "Shaxpere" or some other variant that seems to call for a short *a*, although the pronunciation is not a matter about which we can be certain. These records include family birth and death records and various deeds. Even more telling are the Stratford man's own signatures and the records made by Thomas Greene, since Greene was a solicitor, the Stratford town clerk, and the Stratford man's cousin.

   There are two documents, one in 1556 and the other in 1557, referring to the Stratford man's father as "Johannem Shakyspere" and "John Shakyspeyr." This might have called for a long *a* pronunciation (as "Shakey-spear"). But the *y* between *k* and *s* appears to have been silent. For example, a fifteenth-century poem refers to "alle werkys of this worlde that ever were wrought." It seems apparent that "werkys" was pronounced "works" and not "workeys." So, probably, "Shakyspere" was also pronounced without sounding the *y*.

   However, quite a few Stratford records use "Shakespeare" or some variant. These include the deed to New Place in 1597, the 1602 deed to the 107 acres of land, the 1602 conveyance confirming the purchase of New Place, the 1602 purchase of property opposite New Place, the purchase of local tithes in 1605, the 1610 deed confirming the purchase of the 107 acres, and John Combe's 1614 will.

5. Arguably, aside from Greene's notes and the spelling of his own solicitor, the best evidence would be the signatures of the Stratford man himself. They would certainly seem to represent the "correct" spelling of his name. Yet they *all* appear to be some variant of "Shakspe" or "Shakpe," even when they refer to activities in

London and were made after the poet and playwright became famous as "Shakespeare."

Does this evidence support the conclusion that "Shaksper," the actor from Stratford, and "Shakespeare," the eminent poet and playwright, were two different men? Hardly. It does not follow that, by signing himself "Shaksper," he was telling the world that he was not the great Bard. True, he continued to sign himself in that original manner even when he was obviously aware that, in London, and especially in the theatrical world, he was known as "Shakespeare." But the use of "Shakespeare" on stage, and for general purposes in London, was surely with his consent; and his seeming comfort with the use of different spellings (or possibly even different pronunciations) in different places and for different purposes could be as consistent with his being the author of the poems and plays as with his fronting for someone else who was the real author. Indeed, the disparate forms of his name appear to have little significance in dealing with that fundamental issue.

19.

WHAT'S IN A FACE?

Many of the readers and playgoers who admire or even idolize Shakespeare are disappointed in the most famous likenesses of the great Bard. These are the Droeshout engraving in the First Folio and the bust in the Shakespeare monument at Stratford. Both show a bald, bland-looking man that Mark Twain called "bladder faced." The face reflects none of the intelligence or humor one would expect of Shakespeare.

Supposedly, Anne Hathaway approved both images, but we have no way of knowing if that is true. If it is true, does it suggest that the subject of these likenesses was not really the witty, brilliant author of the poems and plays, but only a retired actor living out his days in rural Stratford, collecting taxes and dealing in real estate?

Now, however, we have what may be another and totally different portrait that raises new and different issues. A gentleman in Canada has brought forth a small painting of a young man wearing an Elizabethan collar. It is done in tempera on an oak panel. In the upper left-hand corner it is dated 1603. Stuck on the reverse side is a faded linen label. It states "Shakspeare. Born April 23, 1564, Died April 23, 1616, Aged 52, This likeness taken 1603, Age at that time 39 yrs."

The report of the Canadian Conservation Institute states that the oak panel has been carbon dated to the late sixteenth or early seventeenth century and that the "materials and techniques" are consistent with that period. The linen label has been carbon dated to that period as well.

The owner, who has, to this point, remained anonymous, claims that the portrait has been in his family 400 years and that, according to his family legend, it was painted by an ancestor named John Sanders, who was an actor and painter of scenery with Shakespeare's theatre company. The face portrayed is that of an auburn-haired man with blue-green eyes, whose expression indicates curiosity and wit, as well as what some viewers have called "sex appeal." It's a face that might fit Manningham's bawdy tale, in which "William the Conqueror" bested "Richard the Third" in the attempt to bed a theatre groupie.

The hair and eye color match a description of Shakespeare attributed to Marlowe. While this is a younger and leaner man than the one in the Droeshout engraving, the features are not so dissimilar as to preclude their being the same person. The hair is already receding, leaving a high forehead. The eyebrows, nose, lips, mustache, and jawline are not unlike those portrayed by Droeshout. The eyes have a different shape, but that could be attributed to artistic license or incompetence—or both.

Was this the Stratford man? We don't know. The family legend squares with that, as does the spelling of the name on the label. It could, of course, be an elaborate hoax designed to fetch a high price at auction. One could take an old painting, find an old piece of linen, even reproduce ink used in the period, write the inscription, use one of several processes to fade the ink, and then affix the label to the back of the painting.

Even if the label was written in the seventeenth century, it might not be Shakespeare at all. By then—and certainly after the First Folio in 1623— Shakespeare had become a well-known literary figure. Undoubtedly, his portraits commanded a higher price than those of lesser-known subjects. Thus, the seventeenth-century owner of the portrait of an undistinguished relative might have been motivated to claim it as a likeness of Shakespeare before trying to sell it. Given a willingness to press his deceit somewhat further, he might even have attached a fictional label identifying the sitter as the Bard.

Of course, this portrait may really be the actor from Stratford, as the label indicates. But does that tell us he was also the great poet and playwright? Not at all. It does, however, make his appearance seem far more consistent with the way we would like to picture Shakespeare than the Droeshout engraving or the Stratford monument.

There are a number of other portraits of "Shakespeare." They bear a vague resemblance to each other, and they all show a face suggesting greater intellect and character than the bland images of Droeshout and the monument. The problem is that, with the possible exception of the newly revealed Canadian portrait, none of these works appears to have been made by an artist who ever met his subject. How do we know these are really likenesses of the Bard, or, for that matter, of the Stratford man? The fact is, we don't. They may simply be imaginative guesses by the artist, influenced by prior "likenesses" or wishful thinking.

There is a portrait hanging in the Folger Library in Washington, D.C., that has been claimed to be a likeness of the Bard painted over a portrait of the earl of Oxford. But, as we will discuss in considering Oxford's candidacy, the claim may well be false and, if it is true, may lack evidentiary significance.

In short, there seems to be nothing in any of the portraits that tells us whether the Stratford man wrote the Shakespeare canon or, if he did not, who did.

Part III

THE OTHER CANDIDATES

✠

Having considered the facts we know concerning the Stratford man and those we know concerning Shakespeare the poet and playwright, can we come to a firm conclusion as to whether or not they were the same person? No, not if we are to be objective and fair in our analysis. Too many documents are ambiguous. Too many facts are susceptible to differing interpretations. Given all we know about the two men—and we know precious little—the most realistic conclusion is that the Stratford man may or may not have been the author of the Shakespeare canon.

To contend that there is simply no issue here, that it is clear beyond any doubt that the Stratford man was the sole author of the poems and plays, is to blind oneself to the evidence that does create significant doubt. That evidence may not prove the anti-Strat case, but it certainly creates a legitimate issue. Again, the issue is *not* the merit of the Shakespeare canon. It is unquestionably great and probably the greatest such body of work, regardless of the identity of its creator.

BUT IF THE STRATFORD MAN WAS NOT SHAKESPEARE OR THE AUTHOR OF HIS WORKS, WHO WAS? OR IF HE WAS NOT THE *SOLE* AUTHOR, WHO WORKED WITH HIM IN CREATING THOSE WORKS? BEFORE WE CAN COME TO A REASONED CONCLUSION, WE MUST CONSIDER NOT JUST THE EVIDENCE INDICATING THAT THE STRATFORD MAN WAS OR WAS NOT SHAKESPEARE, BUT ALSO THE EVIDENCE TENDING TO SHOW THAT SOMEONE ELSE WAS. OBVIOUSLY, IF IT WAS *IMPOSSIBLE* FOR ANY OTHER PERSON TO HAVE WRITTEN THE POEMS AND PLAYS, WE WOULD PUT ASIDE OUR DOUBTS ABOUT THE STRATFORD MAN'S AUTHORSHIP AND RESOLVE THE MATTER IN HIS FAVOR.

UNFORTUNATELY, IT'S NOT THAT EASY. THERE ARE OTHER CANDIDATES WHO CANNOT BE RULED OUT AND WHO COULD HAVE BEEN THE TRUE AUTHOR. WHAT WE FACE THEN IS A QUESTION OF COMPARATIVE PROBABILITY. WE MUST CONSIDER EACH OF THE MAJOR CANDIDATES IN TURN, IN ORDER TO COMPARE THE LIKELIHOOD THAT ONE OF THEM WAS THE TRUE BARD WITH THE LIKELIHOOD THAT THE GREAT POET AND PLAYWRIGHT WAS, IN FACT, THE STRATFORD MAN.

20

EDWARD DE VERE, EARL OF OXFORD

*T*oday, the principal anti-Stratfordian candidate is Edward de Vere, the seventeenth earl of Oxford. Virtually every factor that argues against the Stratford man's having authored the Shakespeare canon is consistent with Oxford having done so. The Oxfordian movement has had many well-known advocates. Sigmund Freud, for example, was a staunch Oxfordian, convinced that *Hamlet* was based on Oxford's own story. One of my favorite professors at Harvard Law School, W. Barton Leach, was also a leading and articulate Oxfordian.

Oxford was born in 1550, a descendant of probably the oldest and most distinguished of English families. Oxford's forebear, the thirteenth earl, was one of England's great military leaders. In 1485, he led the victorious Tudor army at the Battle of Bosworth Field, putting Elizabeth's grandfather, Henry VII, on the throne. Oxford's father, also known for his valor, kept a company of actors, as his son would later do.

Oxford attained a bachelor's degree from Cambridge and a master's degree from Oxford. He studied law at Gray's Inn, although he never practiced as a barrister or solicitor. He traveled extensively in Europe, including France and Italy, where he spent considerable time in Venice and visited Mantua, Padua, Siena, Verona, and probably Naples and Rome. He was classically educated. His tutor was his uncle, Arthur Golding, a noted translator of Ovid, a poet widely used by Shakespeare. Oxford read and spoke fluent French and Italian. By the time he was thirteen, he was writing letters in courtly, elegant French. He loved literature and bought books in various languages when he was still very young.

Oxford had both military and naval experience. Even in his twenties, he distinguished himself as an officer in fighting against the Scots. He was sent as second in command of an English expeditionary force to defend the low countries against a Spanish invasion. The military terms used by Shakespeare would have come easily to him. He also commanded a warship against the armada, having fitted it out at his own expense. He would have known such naval terms as *raise your fights*, *give fire*, and *yare*. Highly skilled in the use of weapons, he was victorious in many tournaments against the best opponents England and Europe had to offer.

Oxford was also familiar with the aristocratic sports found in Shakespeare's writings, such as falconry, tennis, and lawn bowling. His writings, like Shakespeare's plays, even contained metaphorical references to falconry. Being a Cambridge graduate and having studied law, he would have been reasonably familiar with "inside" Cambridge phrases, as well as legal terminology.

Clearly, Oxford had the diverse knowledge and fluency in foreign and classical languages required to have written the poems and plays.

Oxford became the hereditary Lord Great Chamberlain and companion to the monarch. He also became a great favorite at court. The queen referred to him affectionately as "my Turk." There was even gossip that Elizabeth and Oxford were lovers. But Oxford married Anne Cecil, daughter of Lord Burghley, the queen's closest advisor.

The earl's subsidiary title, Viscount Bolebec, carried with it arms comprised of a rampant lion shaking a spear ("Shake-speare"?). Gabriel Harvey wrote of Oxford, "Thine eyes flash fire, thy countenance shakes a spear." Was this a punning reference to his coat of arms? To his pseudonym?

Oxford was a patron of acting companies. He took over the earl of Warwick's company and maintained a boys company that played at Blackfriars Theatre. He was also a prominent patron of writers. Edmund Spenser, John Lyly, Anthony Munday, and others dedicated works to him.

But Oxford was more than just a patron of the arts. He also wrote poetry and plays himself. In *Palladis Tamia*, written in 1598, Francis Meres called Oxford "the best for comedy among us." But Meres also lauded "Shakespeare" and referred to a number of his plays. This suggests that

Meres thought Oxford and Shakespeare were two different men or at least pretended that's what he thought. And, of course, if the Stratford man was fronting for Oxford, that is just what Meres was supposed to think.

If Oxford was *known* for writing plays, why would he bother to pretend that the Stratford man was writing them? Is this inconsistent with the reason given for Oxford's using a front—that is, that it would be unseemly for a nobleman to write plays for the public theatre? Not necessarily. Probably, the plays known to be written by the earl were performed only privately for friends or at court, while, of course, Shakespeare's plays were public, commercial ventures. Meres does not tell us. But there is no record of the public performance of any play attributed to Oxford. This could, of course, be because there were none, or it could have been because his authorship of the publicly performed plays was concealed.

Oxford was also described as a skilled poet. He used iambic pentameter as did Shakespeare, and some of his poetry is similar in theme and outlook to that of Shakespeare. In 1622, well after the deaths of both Oxford and the Stratford man, Henry Peacham listed those Elizabethan poets "who honored Poesie with their pens and practice." First on the list was Oxford. Ironically, Shakespeare was not mentioned.

Sir Sidney Lee said that Oxford "wrote verses of much lyric beauty" and expressed agreement with the comment that he "was the best of the courtier poets in the early days of Queen Elizabeth."

Thomas Macaulay wrote that Oxford "won for himself an honorable place among the early masters of English poetry."

An anonymous sixteenth-century book, *The Art of English Poesie*, reported that "many notable gentlemen in the court" have written well, but either suppressed their work or published it without using their names. Oxford is given as the prime example.

The 1609 dedication of the sonnets to "our ever-living poet" strongly suggests that the "poet" was someone already dead. The Stratford man was still alive at the time. Oxford had died in 1604.

As discussed above, however, the dedications to *Venus and Adonis* and *The Rape of Lucrece* seem difficult to reconcile with the manner in which Oxford would have addressed his fellow aristocrat Southampton. Of course, Oxford may have been trying to create the false impression that, since the poems were being published, rather than merely read to friends, the poet was someone of lower status.

It has been argued that Oxford's poetry is of lesser quality than Shakespeare's. Given Shakespeare's towering reputation and iconic status, it would be difficult to quarrel with the idea that the world has given Shakespeare's poetry far greater attention and acceptance than that of Oxford. But the quality of poetry, like the quality of art, is, to a considerable extent, a subjective matter that varies over time. In Oxford's day, his poems appear to have commanded as much praise as Shakespeare's, if not more. Unfortunately, we do not have any of Oxford's plays—unless they are the ones attributed to Shakespeare.

No Shakespearean character appears to embody the characteristics of the Stratford man; and what we know of his life and relationships does not seem to fit most of the sonnets or to be reflected in any of the plays. By contrast, both the sonnets and other parts of the Shakespeare canon fit Oxford's life reasonably well.

If Oxford wrote the sonnets, the "lovely youth" was probably Southampton, and the "dark lady" was probably Anne Vavasor, Oxford's longtime mistress.

If, as seems likely, Southampton was the "lovely youth," there was a sound reason for Oxford to have written the initial sonnets urging him to marry and procreate. Oxford's father-in-law Lord Burghley was Southampton's guardian, as well as master of the wards. Having the power to arrange marriages for his wards, Burghley arranged a match between the highborn Southampton and his own granddaughter Elizabeth Vere. The prospective bride was Oxford's daughter. But Southampton refused the match and was severely criticized for his recalcitrance. It would seem only natural for Oxford, as the rebuffed girl's father, to have written sonnets designed to convince the stubborn young earl to change his mind. If so, the effort failed. When Southampton would not marry the girl, Burghley fined him £5,000.

The sonnets refer to the poet as "beated and chapp'd with tanned antiquity" (62), describe his days as "past the best" (138) and place him in "that time of year . . . when yellow leaves, or none, or few, do hang" (73). They stress a marked difference in age between the poet and the lovely youth. It is a winter–spring relationship. The age difference between Oxford and Southampton (if he was the "lovely youth") fits the sonnets far better than that between the young earl and the Stratford man. When the sonnets were written, Southampton would have been in his twenties, while the Stratford man would still be in his early thirties. Their difference in age was a mere nine years. Oxford, on the other hand, would have been approaching fifty, already exceeding a normal life expectancy at the time. He would have been twenty-three years older than Southampton, an age gap that fits the sonnets quite well.

Similarly, the relationship between the writer of the sonnets and Southampton would fit a relationship between Oxford and Southampton far better than one between Southampton and Will Shakspere of Stratford. Some of the poet's words would have seemed highly presumptuous, if not grotesquely offensive, if said to the highborn earl by the common actor from Stratford, but they might not have been considered inappropriate if directed to Southampton by a fellow nobleman.

There is no substantial evidence that Oxford, who fathered children by both his wife and his mistress, was homosexual. He was once accused by his cousin, Lord Henry Howard, of "buggering a boy that is his cook and many other boys." But Oxford had first accused Howard (it seems justifiably) of treason. Howard responded by launching a vitriolic barrage of disparate charges against Oxford, most of which were patently untrue or at least grossly exaggerated. The charge of buggery was one such charge.

Howard's charge might appear consistent with the love expressed in the "lovely youth" sonnets. But, as we have said, Sonnet 20 (the "pricked thee out" one) suggests a relationship between two males that was nonsexual. And the "dark lady" sonnets indicate the poet's having had a physical relationship with a mysterious woman. Of course, nothing precludes Oxford's having been bisexual and having romantic feelings for the fair youth, even if he did not act on them physically.

Is there an inconsistency between Oxford having romantic feelings for Southampton and, at the same time, urging him to marry Oxford's own daughter? Not necessarily. Marriage, especially an arranged, noble marriage, was not to be confused with romance.

Oxford injured his leg on his European trip and, later in life, described himself as "lame." This could account for the poet's "lameness" referred to in Sonnet 89.

The "Will" sonnets might seem a problem for the Oxfordians, since their candidate's given name was Edward. "Not so," they say. It seems Oxford was called "Willy" by his friends.

If Oxford was the poet, what was the "shame," "disgrace," and "outcast state" to which he refers in the sonnets? Could it be the charge of buggery? That charge and the resultant public gossip could have caused Oxford to have feelings of shame and disgrace.

But there are other matters to which Oxford might have referred. The earl's reputation had been severely tarnished by scandal, quarrels, and financial ruin. In writing to an intimate friend of the same social class, references to his "shame" and "disgrace" may have related to these matters.

In Sonnet 36, the poet also warns the youth that his "bewailed guilt" might "do thee shame" and, in Sonnet 71, he warns that the world may "mock you with me after I am gone." Oxford's decline in reputation among the courtiers could conceivably have tarnished someone like Southampton, if the two earls were closely associated. At least Oxford may have thought so.

Of course, if Oxford was concerned about the charge of homosexuality, it would only be realistic to fear that even a nonsexual but seemingly romantic relationship with Southampton could severely damage the younger man's reputation. And if the warmth and love suggested by the sonnets were found to exist between the two men, others might doubt that their relationship was merely platonic.

But if that was Oxford's fear, why allow anyone but the fair youth himself to see the sonnets that expressed the poet's feelings? Perhaps he didn't. He probably read a few "sugared sonnets" to his friends, but they may not have been the ones that could prove embarrassing. With the exception of a few sonnets published by Jaggard without permission, the sonnets were not published until 1609. Oxford had died five years earlier.

Oxfordians encounter serious difficulty with Sonnet 111. Why would Oxford refer to "the guilty goddess of my harmful deeds, that did not better for my life provide than public means which public manners breeds"?

Oxford did encounter severe financial problems, so that he may have felt himself ill provided for. But did this lead him to "public means" that tend to create "public manners," so that he "almost" took on the characteristics of what he worked in, "like the dyer's hand"? It doesn't seem to fit.

Perhaps, if Oxford wrote these lines, he was referring to his poems and plays being publicly performed—albeit under a pseudonym. But was he led to these pursuits by not being well provided for? We do not even know that he was paid for his works. Nor would the public hawking of his poems and plays have given his name "a brand," as the sonnet also indicates, except among those few who may have known he was "Shakespeare."

And could Oxford have believed that his concealed relationship with the poems and plays to have "almost" changed his character to become what he works in "like the dyer's hand"? Even with the "almost," it does not sound like something the proud earl would say—unless this sonnet was a form of apology to the lovely youth for a display of anger or rudeness by Oxford. In that context, while the literal meaning of the words would certainly be an exaggeration, they could have been intended as a self-deprecatory poetic conceit.

The balance of the sonnet is consistent with this possibility. The poet offers to drink vinegar ("eysell") and asks the lovely youth's pity, which he says is enough to "cure" him.

There may have been a posthumous connection between Oxford and the publication of the sonnets. William Hall, who brought the manuscript to the publisher, appears to have lived in Hackney, where Oxford spent his last years and owned a home. That home was sold shortly before the sonnets appeared. Did Hall somehow get access to one or more manuscripts left in the house by the deceased earl?

In a 1640 version of the sonnets, published under the name "John Benson" (probably a reversal of "Ben Jonson"), the preface states that the sonnets did not attain the "glory" of the author's other works "by reason of their Infancie in his death." Probably, the sonnets were written in the mid-1590s. If "Benson" was referring to the date they were written, they would hardly have been in "their Infancie" some twenty years later when the Stratford man died, in 1616. On the other hand, they could have been considered in their "Infancie" when Oxford died in 1604.

But the sonnets were published only seven years before the Stratford man's death. "John Benson," whoever he was, may have meant that the sonnets were not *published* until shortly before the poet's death, which would have been consistent with the Stratford man, but not with Oxford, who died before their publication. Of course, "Benson" may simply have made up the entire "Infancie" claim.

Like some of the sonnets, there are Shakespearean plays that seem to fit Oxford and events of his life. Freud argued that Hamlet *was* Oxford, that, in creating that play, Oxford was acting out his own oedipal feelings. There certainly are considerable similarities between Hamlet and Oxford. As in the case of the Danish prince, Oxford's father died when Oxford was young, and his mother soon remarried. Oxford was sent to London where he became a royal ward in the home of Sir William Cecil (later, Lord Burghley). Freud saw Oxford's mother in Hamlet's mother, Queen Gertrude, and saw Oxford's stepfather in Gertrude's new husband, King Claudius.

And there are other similarities. The rather pompous Burghley may have been the model for Polonius (also principal minister to the crown). Oxford's relationship with his father-in-law Burghley was generally confrontational, and Oxford was considered a supporter of Burghley's rival Essex (but not the latter's rebellion). Oxford was certainly more motivated and better placed than the Stratford man to mock the powerful Burghley.

Burghley wrote a list of guiding principles for his son Thomas, much like Polonius's "neither a borrower nor a lender be" speech to *his* son Laertes, setting out the principles that he should live by. The Parisian gambling of his son was a matter of great concern to Burghley, just as Laertes's dissolute life in Paris distressed Polonius.

Stratfordians resist the idea of a relationship between Burghley's "principles" and Polonius's advice to Laertes. *Hamlet* was published in 1603 and was probably written before that. Burghley's principles for his son were not published until 1618. But these were the dates of publication, not creation. Burghley obviously wrote his guiding principles before 1598, when he died. It is quite likely that they were seen or heard by his son-in-law, Oxford, before Burghley died and before *Hamlet* was written.

Oxfordians see Burghley's daughter Anne as Polonius's daughter Ophelia. Oxford married Anne when he was twenty-one and she but fifteen. Four years later, he left her to travel extensively in Europe. On his return, he heard that she had borne a daughter in his absence and that this was another man's child (a rumor almost surely false). Oxford refused to return to her, cruelly rejecting her, as Hamlet rejects Ophelia. Oxford raged at Burghley, just as Hamlet confronts Polonius, "Conception is a blessing, but not as your daughter may conceive." For years, Anne begged Oxford to return, but was rebuffed. Ultimately, he reconciled with the poor girl, but, like Ophelia, she died.

Oxford kept a company of players like those coached by Hamlet. Both

Oxford and Hamlet were captured by pirates while traveling to England by sea. Oxford fought a duel, as did Hamlet, and stabbed one of Burghley's servants, as Hamlet stabbed Polonius.

The characters Horatio and Francisco in *Hamlet* could have been drawn from Oxford's cousins Horatio and Francis Vere. And, just as Hamlet soliloquized, "To die, to sleep, perchance to dream," Oxford wrote, "What should we account of death to be resembled to anything better than sleep." Of course, the comparison of death to sleep was hardly unique, even in Elizabethan times.

There are lines that could be references to Burghley, but do not necessarily point to Oxford as the playwright. For example, Joseph Sobran points out Hamlet's reference to Polonius as a "fishmonger," when Hamlet is feigning madness. Sobran sees this as an allusion to Burghley's repeated attempts to increase the consumption of fish in order to support the English fishing industry. It may well be. But any well-informed Englishman— possibly even the Stratford man—would have been likely to know of Burghley's pro-fish campaign (he fostered a bill requiring two compulsory fish-eating days per week) and might have inserted the inside joke in *Hamlet*.

Others have considered Hamlet to depict not Oxford, but the earl of Essex—young, indecisive, yet hopelessly impulsive. They consider Hamlet's father, King Claudius, to have been Elizabeth's longtime favorite Robin Dudley, the earl of Leicester. They point out that Essex's father, Walter Devereaux, died under suspicious circumstances after a quarrel with Leicester. It was a common rumor that Leicester had poisoned Devereaux. Soon thereafter, he married Devereaux's widow, Essex's mother. Sound familiar?

But Elizabeth was vehement in her defense of Leicester and in her belief that the suspicion bruited about was a vicious slander. It would have been very dangerous to have repeated that "slander." It is therefore difficult to imagine that even the most well-placed nobleman/poet would have intended a publicly performed play to dramatize this accusation against Leicester that so enraged the queen.

Like Hamlet, the character Bertram in *All's Well That Ends Well* bears some similarities to Oxford. Thomas Looney described Bertram and the storyline as follows:

A young lord of ancient lineage, of which he is himself proud, having lost a father for whom he entertained a strong affection, is brought to court by his mother and left there as a royal ward, to be brought up under royal supervision. As he grows up, he asks for military service and to be allowed to travel, but is repeatedly refused or put off. At last he goes away without permission. Before leaving, he had been married to a young woman with whom he had been brought up, and who had herself been most active in bringing about the marriage. Matrimonial troubles, of which the outstanding feature is a refusal of cohabitation, are associated with both his stay abroad and his return home.

Looney was a committed Oxfordian. But his description of what happens to Bertram in *All's Well That Ends Well*, while vague and incomplete, is not unfair, and does bear some resemblance to events in the life of Oxford. And there is more. Bertram, who has rejected his wife, is fooled into sleeping with her, believing she is another woman.[3] The same story—probably apocryphal—was told about Oxford and his wife. Of course, similarity between Oxford and Bertram does not mean that Oxford was Shakespeare. The playwright may have simply known Oxford or even known of him and based the character on that knowledge. Or it could be mere coincidence.

A significant piece of Oxfordian evidence is the earl's personal copy of the Geneva Bible, which can be seen at the splendid Folger Library in Washington, D.C. In it, Oxford has used underlining and tick marks to denote numerous biblical passages. These passages arguably appear in Shakespeare's works or represent themes present in those works. Oxford appears to have noted those particular passages as ones that interested him and possibly ones to be used later in his own writings. Perhaps he was simply interested in the same biblical references as Shakespeare. Perhaps it was more than that. In fairness, however, it should be noted that Oxford marked many passages that do not appear in Shakespeare's works

---

3. This is the famous "bed trick" Shakespeare evidently liked. He used it again in *Measure For Measure*, although the woman in bed there was not the wife of the duped male.

and that Shakespeare, who quoted frequently (but not always accurately) from the Bible, used biblical references that are not marked in Oxford's Bible.

Roger Strittmatter has written a comprehensive 515-page dissertation, analyzing in detail the underlined and tick-marked passages in Oxford's Bible and relating them to the Shakespeare canon. But not many of Strittmatter's examples are instances in which Shakespeare has quoted directly from a biblical passage marked by Oxford. Most are, at best, passages using some similar term or phrase or expressing an interest in the same theme or subject matter.

It has been asserted that Oxford marked the phrase from 2 Samuel 21:19 ". . . the brother of Goliath the Gittite, the staff of whose spear was like a weaver's beam." In act 5, scene 5 of *The Merry Wives of Windsor*, Falstaff says, "I fear not Goliath with a weaver's beam." This certainly seems a direct allusion to the biblical passage. Having peered at length at 2 Samuel 21:19 in Oxford's Bible, however, I was unable to see any kind of mark indicating the earl's interest in that passage.

Strittmatter does make a compelling case for the proposition that the passages noted in Oxford's Bible show that, in many areas, his interests and views paralleled Shakespeare's and are certainly closer to the Bard's than were the interests and views of Bacon or Marlowe—or what we know of the interests and views of the Stratford man.

While Oxford's Geneva Bible may be considered evidence somewhat supportive of the Oxfordian cause, it is, by no means, a "smoking gun."

In 1586, the notoriously frugal Elizabeth awarded Oxford the enormous allowance of £1,000 per year. Was this for writing the plays? It could have been for many things. If, for example, Oxford was in financial difficulty, the allowance could have been given in recognition of the heroic part played by Oxford's forebear in establishing the Tudor dynasty, and to permit the earl, as one of the nation's greatest peers, to continue living like one.

If Oxford wrote the plays, that might tell us why the queen took no action against the playwright despite her fierce resentment of the deposition scene in *Richard II*. She appears to have been genuinely fond of the earl, and, especially if he consented to write under a pseudonym, she may have turned a blind eye toward his expression of ideas that would have landed another writer—especially a commoner—in prison, or worse—much worse. Moreover, on reflection, she may have considered that the totality of his works tended to show that everyone suffered from the overthrow of a reigning monarch.

For those who fancy clues in literary works, Shakespeare may have left us some that could point to Oxford. For example, in Sonnet 76, he employs some ambiguous and strange lines that could be construed as a clue to his identity:

> Why write I still all one, ever the same,
> And keep invention in a noted weed,
> That every word doth almost tell my name,
> Showing their birth and where thy did proceed?

Now, substitute "E. Vere" (Oxford's name, Edward Vere) for "ever" and recognize that "weed" means a garment, and we get what Oxfordians see as a clear statement that Oxford was the sonneteer. With that substitution, they construe the sonnet as reading:

> Why write I still all one, E. Vere the same,
> And keep my writings clothed,
> That the word "every" doth almost tell my name (i.e., E. Vere),
> Showing who created these works.

Other Oxfordians reach the same conclusion by treating "ever" as an anagram and rearranging the letters to spell "Vere."

In Sonnet 125, Shakespeare wrote, "Were't aught to me I bore the canopy?" Oxford, the hereditary lord chancellor, bore the royal canopy at least twice that we know of: once at the celebration of the armada's defeat in 1588, and again at Elizabeth's funeral in 1603. The first occasion would fit the timing of the sonnets. The second would probably not. Did the Stratford man ever carry the royal canopy? Certainly not, unless it was a prop in some play.

If the fair youth was Southampton, Oxfordians need to deal with Sonnet 104, which indicates that it has been only three years since the poet first saw him. Given the relatively limited number of Elizabethan noble families, wouldn't Oxford have known his fellow peer for more than three years when the sonnet was written?

Not necessarily. It is not at all improbable that Oxford would not have met Southampton until the younger man was in his teens. Yet Southampton, who was born in 1573, was not fourteen until 1587. If, for example, Oxford wrote Sonnet 104 in 1593, when Southampton was twenty, he could well have met him only three years before that, when the young earl was seventeen. And, of course, Oxford could have started the sonnets well before 1593.

Another place to find clues to historical mysteries is in contemporary portraits. Some have been repainted in ways that suggest that a discernable message lies in the alteration. Portraits of Richard III, for example, were repainted after his defeat in 1485 to add a hump, since the false story had been circulated that he was a hunchback. Humorously enough, the hump was sometimes added on the right side and sometimes on the left.

Some Oxfordians have argued that the same phenomenon occurred with respect to the earl of Oxford. In the late 1930s, Charles Wisner Barrell, working with a team of assistants, used x-ray and infrared technology to examine what he asserted were three portraits of Shakespeare that had long hung in the homes of distinguished English families. Barrell claimed that each of the three was actually a portrait of the earl of Oxford that had been painted over centuries before to appear as "Shakespeare."

Barrell wrote an article in the January 1940 issue of *Scientific American* describing his findings. Unfortunately, the article discussed only one of the three portraits: the Ashbourne portrait, which now hangs in the Folger Library in Washington, D.C.

The present portrait bears a painted inscription indicating that it was done in 1611 and that the subject of the painting was then forty-seven. That would fit the Stratford man, who was born in 1564. But x-ray examination showed the painting had originally borne a different inscription. Barrell reported that the canvas had been rubbed so hard to remove the original inscription that small holes had been worked through its surface. A faint shadow of a family crest could also be discerned. Barrell said it appeared to be the arms of Oxford's second wife. Also apparent were the initials "CK," which Barrell assumed was Cornelius Ketel, a leading Dutch portraitist of the time.

Barrell opined that the present inscription was added in an orange-gold paint, different from the yellow-gold tones found elsewhere in the painting. But that was not all he said was added in the newer orange-gold paint. According to Barrell, an odd signet ring on the sitter's long thumb had been repainted and had once borne the likeness of a wild boar, an emblem of Oxford's family. Barrell said that the orange-gold paint had been used to cover it over. Oxfordians, relying on Barrell's findings, point out that Oxford's correspondence indicates that he had such a signet ring and that the Stratford man apparently did not have such a ring, since none is mentioned in his will.

And Barrell's report raises even more questions. The man portrayed was in dress that would be worn only by a person of considerable status—a black velvet doublet and black hose, with inserts of gray satin and a black leather belt of French design worked with gold filigree. An actor–grain dealer from Stratford would not wear such garments to pose for his portrait. They do not have the appearance of costumes for the stage, and other actors and writers of the period, such as Richard Burbage, Edward Alleyne, William Sly, and even Ben Jonson were portrayed in plain, unadorned outfits.

Barrell's report says that the neck ruff has also been repainted and that much of the original ruff was painted out. Barbara Burris, writing in the Winter 2002 issue of *Shakespeare Matters,* points out that the large circular ruff in the original version was very much the French style in the late 1570s and early 1580s, when Ketel was painting in England. And Oxford was noted for adopting French and Italian styles in appearance. Burris adds that the wrist ruffs worn in the Ashbourne portrait went out of style by 1583, and would not have been worn in 1611.

Burris is a committed Oxfordian, even describing Oxford as "the same man whom J. Thomas Looney discovered to be the real Shakespeare in 1920." That assertion may suggest a bias; but it does not make her findings invalid.

Oxfordians also argue that, although the hairline has been raised, the features of the sitter are not unlike those of the noted Portland portrait of Oxford; that the earl had long, tapering thumb and fingers like the Ashbourne figure; and that, according to Barrell, x-ray analysis shows beneath the altered hair the large and distinctive "Oxford ear."

Barrell points out some links between the descendants of Oxford and his second wife and the Ashbourne portrait that might be consistent with its having been in the possession of one or more family members for centuries.

Unfortunately, Barrell's article did not provide his analysis of the other two Oxford portraits he examined. He concluded, however, that, like the Ashbourne portrait, they were originally images of the earl of Oxford that were reworked centuries ago to fit a conception of Shakespeare.

But the entire Oxfordian argument based on the Ashbourne portrait may well be founded on unsupportable assumptions in Barrell's 1940 report. The documentation available at the Folger Library seems to make a good case for the proposition that the figure originally portrayed was not Oxford at all, but rather Sir Hugh Hamersly, at one time lord mayor of London.

According to the Folger documents, the coat of arms that was painted over—three rams' heads on a shield topped by a griffin perched on a helmet—was that of Hamersly. All that is legible of the scrolled motto beneath the shield are the letters *MORE*, which fits with Hamersly's motto "HONORE ET AMORE."

The Folger commissioned a recent chemical, physical, and radiological analysis of the Ashbourne portrait by the Canadian Conservation Institute. This detailed analysis, using modern scientific technology, casts very serious doubt on Barrell's assertions. It reveals that the legend bearing the date of the painting that now says "1611" was originally "1612," and that the change made by scraping and repainting was to remove the *2* in "1612" and to add over it, in pale yellow paint, a *1* making the date of the painting "1611."

It is noteworthy that the original painting also bore the legend that the subject of the painting was "47" and that this has not been changed. The fact that the painting states that the subject was forty-seven may tell us why the "1612" was changed to "1611."

According to the Folger documents, what occurred was this: A teacher and sometime painter named Clement Kingston owned the portrait of Sir Hugh Hamersly. Probably seeking to boost the sale value of the work, Kingston converted the portrait from one of Hamersly to one of Shakespeare, a far better-known and more saleable image.

Kingston painted over the front of Hamersly's hair with skin-colored paint to create Shakespeare's well-known bald pate. He repainted the date of the portrait, changing it from "1612" to "1611." Why? Because the legend said the subject was "47." Born in 1565, Hamersly was forty-seven in 1612, the original date on the portrait. The Stratford man, who, after the First Folio, was certainly believed to have been the poet and playwright, was a year older and was forty-seven in 1611, the new date on the portrait. Kingston could have changed the age of the sitter from "47" to "48," but evidently decided instead to change "1612" to "1611." There was no need to change both in order to make the timing fit the Stratford man.

Changing "1612" to "1611" would have made no sense at all if the original subject had been Oxford, as claimed by Barrell. Oxford was forty-seven in 1597 and sixty-one in 1611.

Kingston painted over Hamersly's coat of arms, which would have been a dead giveaway. One thing that was *not* painted over, according to the Canadian Conservation Institute, was the thumb ring, the very object Barrell asserted *was* painted over and had originally been a wild boar signet, like Oxford's. No wild boar, said the Canadian report, the ring is just as originally painted.

Possibly, when he had finished converting Hamersly into Shakespeare, Kingston decided to add his own initials and then changed his mind and deleted them, since they might have led to exposure of what he had done. If so, perhaps the "CK" shown in the x-rays stood not for the Dutch master Cornelius Ketel, but for the English teacher/painter Clement Kingston.

Ketel was in England from 1573 to 1581. There is no indication of a date in that period having been on the original painting; and why would Ketel put "1612" on a portrait that was really done in the 1570s? Besides, Ketel typically painted on wood panels, while the Ashbourne portrait was done on canvas.

Of course, the conclusion that the subject of the original portrait was Hamersly conflicts with Burris's view that the costume pictured is not consistent with a date after 1580. At that time, Hamersly was only fifteen, Oxford was thirty, and Ketel was painting in England, where he was reported to have done a portrait of Oxford. If Burris is correct about the dating of the costume, it would seem unlikely that the artist would have posed Hamersly in attire thirty years out of date.

And other questions remain. Why would Hamersly, who was a haberdasher and civic official, be dressed as a nobleman? Why would he be holding a book, hardly a symbol of his occupation or position? Don't the costume and the book better suit Oxford, who was, of course, a high-ranking nobleman and one known to write poetry?

Still, the originally painted date "1612" can be seen in the x-ray photos, and that date, taken with the unchanged age of the sitter, "47," fits Hamersly and cannot be squared with Oxford, who would have been sixty-two at the time, and had died eight years earlier.

Even assuming that the original Ashbourne image was that of Oxford, rather than Hamersly, what does that prove? Despite the arguments of some Oxfordians, it is extremely difficult to believe that Oxford's descendants or anyone else converted Oxford's likeness to that of Shakespeare in order to convey the message that Oxford *was* Shakespeare.

How could they have known that, centuries later, x-ray technology would be invented and would reveal the original figure beneath the repainting and the original inscription almost rubbed out and covered over with new paint? Indeed, the assertions in Barrell's report suggest that those responsible for the repainting tried very hard to *prevent* any discovery that the portrait was originally of Oxford, rather than that they wanted to make that clear to the world in later centuries.

What, then, can we conclude about the Ashbourne portrait? Even if the original figure was not Hamersly, it may not have been Oxford either. And, even if it was Oxford, painting the Bard's likeness over the earl's would not be evidence that the two were the same. Perhaps they were, but the Ashbourne portrait doesn't prove it or even support that conclusion.

As for the mysterious other paintings asserted by Barrell to be likenesses of Shakespeare painted over portraits of Oxford, it is unfortunate that Barrell's article tells us nothing about them. Assuming, however, that Barrell saw other portraits of the Bard painted over the images of someone else and that he believed the original image was Oxford, the explanation may lie in the same commercial motivation attributable to Kingston. Shakespeare had become quite famous and his portraits were rare and highly prized—possibly even more than portraits of Oxford. Perhaps others, like Kingston, converted portraits of various subjects into portraits of the Bard in order to enhance their sale value. It is unlikely that Oxford's wealthy descendants would have done this. But portraits of Oxford may well have fallen into other hands. And, of course, the original images may not have been Oxford at all.

In 1591, Oxford remarried. His new bride was one of the queen's maids of honor. Her substantial wealth, together with the queen's generous stipend, lessened considerably the financial pressure Oxford had felt most of his life. He had a son by his new wife, who became the eighteenth earl on Oxford's death, but died childless in 1625.

The 1591 reference to the playwright "Willy" in Edmund Spenser's *The Teares of the Muses* seems to refer to someone who had previously written comedies and perhaps other plays, but who had chosen to suspend or abandon that work, at least for a time—probably in 1590 or earlier. That pattern does not seem to fit the Stratford man and probably does not even refer to Shakespeare. However, it could possibly fit Oxford (remember, his nickname was "Willy"). Oxford probably wrote comedies that were privately performed before 1590. He may have stopped his playwriting activities following the death of his first wife and in the period preceding his remarriage in 1591.

In the last phase of his life, Oxford and his wife lived quietly away from London and the court. Less is known of his activities in this period. We know that he continued to support a company of actors. There is some confusion in that regard. Shakespeare's plays in this period were performed by the Lord Chamberlain's Men. Oxford's hereditary title was "Lord Great Chamberlain," not "Lord Chamberlain," an office which had a totally different function.

From 1594 to his death in 1596, Lord Hunsdon, the Lord Chamberlain, was the patron of Shakespeare's company. From 1596 on, Hunsdon's son, appointed Lord Chamberlain in 1597, was the company's patron. Whether the company was ever sponsored by Oxford is a matter of some debate. It probably was not.

Willowbie His Avisa, written in 1594, involves the Lady Avisa, generally thought to be Queen Elizabeth, and the lady's various suitors, one of whom is called H. W., a young man aided by an "old player" called "W. S." H. W. may well be Southampton (Henry Wriothesley), and a number of scholars have taken the "old player" to be Shakespeare. The Stratford man was only thirty at the time, hardly an "old player." Oxford was forty-four, which was nearing the end of normal life expectancy in the sixteenth century. Certainly, Oxford's age is a closer fit than that of the Stratford man. But, while Oxford appeared in privately performed dramas, we have no evidence of his ever being a professional "player" in the public theatre, which seems to be suggested by the term *old player*.

By reason of his position, Oxford sat on the jury of peers that convicted Essex and Southampton of treason in 1601. If Oxford wrote the sonnets and meant them for Southampton, he must have felt considerable pain on condemning his young friend to what seemed his likely execution. As it turned out, while Essex was quickly beheaded, Elizabeth allowed Southampton to languish in the Tower. On her death in 1603, James I pardoned him and restored his lands and titles. James also seemed to honor Oxford, even appointing him to the Privy Council. By then, however, Oxford was in ill health, and it is doubtful that he played any significant role in the new government.

Oxford died on June 24, 1604, apparently of the plague. A bizarre set of circumstances followed his death. That very day, a number of Oxford's associates were arrested and held in the Tower, while their homes were searched and their documents examined. Meanwhile, the king and his son were closely guarded. The following day, the arrested men were released, and the entire matter seems to have been hushed up.

Some anti-Strats believe that Oxford had been acting for the government, leading a group that wrote plays on patriotic and moral themes under the name "Shakespeare." They suggest that the government feared Oxford may have left written evidence of this scheme that would be revealed on his death. Why the potential disclosure of such a playwriting group would create this evident panic is not made clear. Nor would the possibility of such a relatively benign disclosure create a physical risk to the king and his heir, requiring a reinforced guard. If these curious events were related to Oxford's death, as seems likely, it is probable that the government's concern was something more serious than the disclosure of a playwriting group. Sadly, there seems to be no evidence of what that something could have been.

As in the case of the Stratford man, no one spoke of Shakespeare's having died at the time of Oxford's passing. But, as we will discuss below, there may have been good reason to avoid referring to Oxford as Shakespeare, even after the earl's death. In the case of the Stratford man, there was no such reason.

It has been reported that, following Oxford's death, King James had eight Shakespearean plays performed at court. Oxfordians argue that this was a "final tribute" to their candidate. There seems to be no record indicating that these performances were any kind of "tribute." It may have simply been that the king liked the plays. On a number of occasions, James had a different play performed at court each night for several nights.

Other events occurred in the years just after 1604 that might be taken to support the Oxfordian case. In 1605, 1608, and 1611, inferior plays written by others were published under Shakespeare's name, a name which by then would certainly have enhanced sales. This had not occurred before 1604. Yet Shakespeare made no protest or attempt to stop the misuse of his name or even to correct the record. Was he dead?

Certainly, the reference to "our ever-living poet" in the 1609 dedication to the sonnets suggests that the poet was, by then, dead, as does the fact that the dedication was written by someone other than the poet himself. The apparent failure of Shakespeare to speak out, like his fellow writers, on the death of the prince of Wales in 1612 provides some support for the contention that he was no longer alive, although there could have been other reasons for that silence.

Between 1598 and Oxford's death in 1604, thirteen plays by Shakespeare had been published in quarto form—one after another. But between 1604 and 1608, no new Shakespearean plays were published. In 1608 and 1609, three new plays were published: *King Lear* and *Troilus and Cressida*, as well as *Pericles*, which may or may not have been by Shakespeare. *Othello* was published in 1622. Then, in 1623, the First Folio included all the previously published plays, plus eighteen never-before-published plays.

The contrast between the publishing activity in the period 1598 to 1604 (thirteen plays in six years, or about two per year) and between 1604 and 1623 (four plays in nineteen years or one every five years) is rather striking. Did the author go into semiretirement? Did he die and did others finish work he had started earlier or publish work he had finished earlier, but publish it only sporadically until 1623? Of course, publication dates are not necessarily good indications of the dates of creation or even performance. A slowdown in publication does not tell us that Shakespeare was no longer writing. Nor do late publication dates tell us that the plays were not written or even performed years before they were published.

The main difficulty for the Oxfordians is that they must explain why so many plays were performed and published for the first time only after Oxford's death in June 1604. Were they all written at an earlier time and held back? Were they left incomplete and finished by someone else?

Traditional dating places the creation of some nine of Shakespeare's plays after 1604. These plays are *King Lear, Macbeth, Timon of Athens, Antony and Cleopatra, Coriolanus, Cymbeline, The Winter's Tale, The Tempest,* and *Henry VIII. Pericles, Prince of Tyre,* is often added to the list as a tenth play.

Oxfordians argue that this traditional dating often arises from attempts to fit the creation of the plays to events in the life of the Stratford man, rather than from any evidence of when the plays were actually written. It is true that some Stratfordians assume that such events as the death of his son

Hamnet in 1596, the death of his father in 1601, or the onset of his fortieth birthday in 1604 had significant impact on the Stratford man's work and, since they also assume he was Shakespeare, they tend to infer the dates of creation of certain plays from the occurrence of such events.

These attempts sometimes run afoul of the Stratfordians' own dating. For example, the assertion that Shakespeare's plays became darker and more brooding following Hamnet's death in 1596 cannot be squared with what most scholars list as Shakespeare's next four plays. The two parts of *Henry IV* are no darker than the earlier history plays and, indeed, introduce comedy into the histories in the person of Falstaff and his companions. Of course, Falstaff is cruelly rejected by the newly crowned Henry V, but that hardly justifies characterizing the two *Henry IV* plays as "dark" or "brooding." *The Merry Wives of Windsor* may not be the Bard's best comedy, but comedy it is. So, of course, is *Much Ado About Nothing*. And these are the remaining two plays usually assigned to this period.

The same is true of the death of the Stratford man's father. According to most traditional dating, the Bard's next plays were *Troilus and Cressida* and *All's Well That Ends Well*. *Troilus* is certainly cynical; but it cannot fairly be called "dark and brooding." Nor can *All's Well That Ends Well*, even though, as a comedy, it too is tinged with cynicism. And while some great tragedies, such as *Othello, Macbeth,* and *King Lear*, were first noted after the Stratford man's fortieth birthday, the contention that this birthday caused a sea change in Shakespeare's writing seems nothing but rampant speculation.

The Stratfordians have a more objective and perhaps more persuasive standard to go by in looking at dates of publication, performance, and mention of the particular plays. Certainly, the dates of a play's first publication and its first performance or mention are *some* evidence of the date of its creation. The fact that twenty-two plays were published for the first time after Oxford's death in 1604, ten of the twenty-two plays had apparently not been *performed* by that year, and eleven were apparently not even mentioned in writing until after Oxford's death certainly tends to support the argument that at least some of these plays were written after 1604. And if even one of Shakespeare's plays was written after that year, Oxford was obviously not the author—or at least not the sole author.

Dates of publication or performance are not, however, conclusive. If they were, we could reason that, since nineteen of the plays had not been published by 1616, when the Stratford man died, *he* could not have been the playwright either.

In 1598, Francis Meres, in his *Palladis Tamia*, listed *Two Gentlemen of Verona* among Shakespeare's comedies. We know, therefore, that it was written no later than that year. Yet it was not published until the First Folio in 1623, and there is no record of its performance until even later. If *Two Gentlemen* could lie completed, but unpublished and unperformed for twenty-five years, so could other Shakespearean plays.

Yet, but for Meres, we might conclude falsely that *Two Gentlemen*, having been neither published nor performed before 1623, *must* have been written after 1604.

The plays commonly said to have been neither published nor performed nor even mentioned until after Oxford's death include *Measure for Measure, Othello, King Lear, Macbeth, Timon of Athens, Antony and Cleopatra, Coriolanus, Cymbeline, The Winter's Tale, The Tempest,* and *Henry VIII.* There are twelve if we count *Pericles.* Is it possible that all of these plays like *Two Gentlemen* were written in or before 1604 and were neither printed nor performed nor even written about until later?

Certainly, it's possible. But is it likely? Performances of *Measure for Measure* and *Othello* were reported within a few months of Oxford's death, and so are not a problem. They could easily have been written before he died. But *Timon of Athens* would have to have been laid aside without publication or apparent mention for at least nineteen years from 1604 to 1623. Others, such as *Henry VIII, The Tempest, The Winter's Tale,* and *Macbeth* would have to have been left in apparent obscurity for substantial but shorter periods. While perhaps not definitive, the fact that so many plays were neither published nor mentioned for extensive periods after 1604 gives the Oxfordians much to explain.

A similar but much less forceful argument could be made about the Stratford man himself. *Timon of Athens* was neither printed nor mentioned in writing until 1623, seven years after his death. Traditional dating tends to place its composition in 1606 or 1607. If so, it lay in obscurity for sixteen or seventeen years before it was first published or even written about. Of course, to accept the Oxfordian position, we must accept the fact that, since the earl died twelve years before the Stratford man, more plays lay in obscurity for a substantially longer time.

One other thing can be said in defense of the Oxfordians. While publication dates can be reliably traced, dates of performance or "mention" are a different matter. Records of plays performed before 1590 are relatively scarce. We do have records kept by Henslowe and Alleyn; but, after 1594, Shakespeare's plays were performed by the Lord Chamberlain's Men, and the records of that company have not been preserved.

Records of some performances at court have been maintained, but we have no complete and accurate record of performances at the Globe or Blackfriars, and we must rely on scattered and fragmentary "mentions" in letters, diaries, and the like. Such mentions may give us the *latest* date on which a play was first performed. They do not give us the *earliest* date, except in those rare instances in which a play is described as "new."

Given these facts, we cannot conclusively assume that a particular play was not performed just because no written mention of it has been found. Nor can we even assume that there was no mention of a play, simply because no such writing has been preserved.

Moreover, plays written by aristocrats were often performed privately. Typically, there would be no record or mention of such performances. We simply cannot conclude with finality that a Shakespearean play that was unpublished by 1604, and for which we have no record of performance or even mention by that year, was, in fact, not written and even performed before then—possibly even before 1590.

A. S. Cairncross, certainly a traditionalist, assigns an earlier date of composition to some of the supposedly "late" plays. For example, he places *Macbeth* and *King Lear* prior to 1591, and assigns *Taming of the Shrew* to (approximately) 1591 and *The Tempest* to 1603. Yet, these plays, like *Two Gentlemen of Verona*, were not published until 1623.

Similarly, the creation of *All's Well That Ends Well*, which was also not published until 1623, is usually placed in 1602. But Sir Sidney Lee puts it in 1595, and the Henry Irving *Shakespeare* lists it in 1590 to 1592.

Indeed, where some of Shakespeare's plays are thought to have been copied from "older" works by other sixteenth-century playwrights, this may, in fact, not have been the case. The "older" plays may also have been written by Shakespeare.

Some Stratfordians try to determine composition dates by the use of detailed metric charts, which seem unpersuasive. Others look to what they assert is the degree of maturity and assuredness in the writing. But that necessarily requires intensely subjective judgments as to what is more and what is less "mature" and which style shows increased self-assurance. A writer's style does not progress as a smooth, consistent line. It may move in a general direction but is more likely to do so in fits and starts. It may also vary with the genre and subject matter. The argument may also overlook plays written earlier in Shakespeare's career and revised at a time of greater maturity.

In many instances, Stratfordians point to events outside the plays to which they argue Shakespeare makes reference and which can be assigned specific dates. But most of these instances are ambiguous and do not necessarily support the firm conclusions Stratfordians would draw from them. Moreover, the plays may have been revised at a later time to add crowd-pleasing current references or, for that matter, to delete references that might prove embarrassing.

An example of the latter is the glowing and optimistic reference to Essex's Irish campaign in *Henry V.* The reference appears to place the writing of that play between March 1599, when Essex left for Ireland, and September 1599, when his campaign ended in humiliating failure. These lines have been deleted in the quarto version of the play published in 1600. This makes sense. They would have proved a significant embarrassment had they been left in, and the queen would not have been pleased. Peculiarly, the lines were reinstated in 1623 when the play was included in the First Folio. Elizabeth was no longer on the throne, and presumably it was thought that memories of the failed campaign had grown dim.

Turning to those plays often claimed to have been written after Oxford's death, we begin with *Othello*. We know the play was performed at court on November 1, 1604. Even if that was its *first* performance, it is highly probable that the play was written before Oxford's death in June of that year. At least one eminent Stratfordian finds indications that *Othello* was written around the same time as *Hamlet*, if not earlier, which would place it years before Oxford died.

Measure for Measure was performed at court on December 26, 1604, and, as in the case of *Othello*, was probably written before June of that year.

The first *recorded* performance of *King Lear* was at court on December 26, 1606. As we have seen, an earlier but *unrecorded* performance cannot be ruled out. Nor can we assume that, even if it was not performed until 1606, it was not written before Oxford's death in 1604.

An older play entitled *The True Chronicle History of Kinge Leir* was registered with the Stationers' Company on May 14, 1594. The story told in *Leir* is similar, but different in a number of aspects, from that related by Shakespeare in *Lear*. And *Leir* may have been based on the play *King Leare*, which was registered a month earlier, in April 1594 and, according to Henslowe's diary, was performed at Easter 1594. This earlier *Leare* may have been Shakespeare's original version of *King Lear*. That would coincide with Cairncross's composition date of 1591. But *may* is the operative word here. We do not know.

Others have argued that Shakespeare's *Lear* could not have been completed before March 1603, when a work by Samuel Harsnett was registered with the Stationers' Company, since devils appearing in *Lear* have names used by Harsnett. But, of course, Harsnett could have taken the names from the *Leare* registered in 1594. More likely, however, both Shakespeare and Harsnett found the names in the *Miracle Book*, which Harsnett concedes in his preface was a source. Harsnett's work may have been available before it was registered; and, even if Oxford only saw it in March 1603, he could have easily added the devils' names before his death in June 1604.

There are other clues in *Lear*, but none is determinative. As Professor Chambers puts it with reference to the composition of *Lear*, it is "difficult to fix the date with precision." The play uses "British," rather than "English," as in the earlier plays. This suggests it was written after James I, already king of Scotland, took the throne, becoming now the king of "Great Britain." But that was in March 1603; here again, it does not necessarily place completion of the play after Oxford's death in June 1604. That word could easily have been changed between March 1603 and June 1604 or at any time before the play was published in 1623.

More difficult for the Oxfordians is Gloucester's reference to "these late eclipses" in act 1, scene 1. This is generally taken as a reference to the double eclipse of both the sun and moon that occurred in 1605. Of course, an eclipse was not that unusual an event; but Gloucester uses the plural, *eclipses*, and double eclipses are quite rare. The eclipses were anticipated and written about as early as 1588. But Gloucester refers to the *late* eclipses, that is, eclipses that have recently occurred, not that are anticipated in the future. Shakespeare might not have been referring to the double eclipses as opposed to two separate eclipses of the moon or the sun. And even if it was a reference to the double eclipses of 1605, it could have been added in that year or later by someone other than the playwright, in order to give an older play a more current feel. Of course, there is always the possibility that the playwright did not have any actual eclipses in mind.

Macbeth provides similar referential clues that, as in the case of *Lear*, cannot give us conclusive proof of the date of its creation. The play includes a song that is also sung in a play by Thomas Middleton. Middleton's play was evidently not written until after 1609. Did Shakespeare simply lift this song from Middleton—in which case, he probably did so after 1609—or did Middleton copy it from *Macbeth*? Another possibility is that Middleton was brought in at an earlier time to write a song for an incomplete *Macbeth*, thought to be unready for presentation, and later felt free to use the song in his own play.

Another reference claimed to fix the composition date of *Macbeth* after 1604 is the play's reference to "equivocation." To the Jesuits, equivocation meant concealing the truth under interrogation. They argued that this was morally and religiously justified. King James and the Protestant authorities disagreed, believing that such equivocation was a mortal sin. It has been contended that the lines in *Macbeth* about "equivocation" are a reference to the Jesuits' involvement with the gunpowder plot of 1605. If so, the argument goes, the play could not have been written, or at least completed, before Oxford's death in 1604.

In act 2, scene 1 of *Macbeth*, a drunken porter hears a loud and repeated knocking. The porter cries out "Knock, knock! Who's there i' the other devil's name? Faith here's an equivocator, that could swear in both scales against either scale; who committed treason enough for God's sake, yet could not equivocate to heaven: O, come in Equivocator."

He explains that he had been "carousing till the second cock," and he speaks of the invidious effect of drink: "[d]rink may be said to be an equivocator with lechery: it makes him, and it mars him; it sets him on, and it takes him off; it persuades him and disheartens him; makes him stand to, and not stand to: in conclusion, equivocates him in a sleep, and, giving him the lie, leaves him."

Another reference appears in Macbeth's speech in act 5, scene 5. He has felt invulnerable since a witch told him he has nothing to fear until Burnam Wood comes to his Castle Dunsinane, something that should be impossible. Later, Malcolm's forces, about to attack the castle from Birnam Wood, cut branches to hold before them, concealing their numbers as they advance. To Macbeth, Birnam Wood seems to be coming to Dunsinane, the very situation to which the "fiend" referred. He cries out that he begins "to doubt the equivocation of the fiend that lies like the truth."

On one hand, Shakespeare does repeatedly play with the words *equivocator* and *equivocation*, as if his audience would recognize those terms as the subject of some well-known public occurrence. On the other, the use of these terms in the play are certainly not an explicit reference to the gunpowder plot and may not have had anything to do with it.

The words *equivocation* and *equivocal* were used well before 1604 other than in the context of the Jesuits. For example, Shakespeare himself used *equivocation* in act 5, scene 1 of *Hamlet*, which was probably written in 1601 or earlier and is certainly not a reference to the 1605 plot. Similarly, he used *equivocal* in act 5, scene 3 of *All's Well That Ends Well* to describe the coward Parolles. And that play was probably written in 1602 or 1603. Moreover, even the Jesuits' beliefs about equivocation were known and debated long before both the gunpowder plot and Oxford's death.

A tragedy of *The Kinge of the Scottes* was performed at court in 1567. Could it have been a much earlier version of *Macbeth*? If so, it was almost surely not by Shakespeare. None of the candidates would seem to have been old enough. Bacon would have been six. Marlowe and the Stratford man would have been three. Even Oxford would have been only seventeen. Henslowe's company bought a play called *Malcolm King of Scots* in 1602. In 1600, William Kempe, in his *Nine Daies Wonder*, wrote about "a penny poet, whose first making was the miserable stolne story of Macdoel, or Macdobeth, or Macsomewhat, for I am sure a Mac it was, though I never had the maw to see it." Was the "penny poet" Shakespeare and the play *Macbeth*? Or was it some other playwright who had "stolne" the story from Shakespeare or some other source? Either way, it suggests that *Macbeth* might have existed in some form before 1604.

Macbeth is also shorter than most Shakespearean plays and has elements that are seemingly unresolved. Possibly, the play was started but not considered finished at the author's death.

The *Tempest* is commonly assigned a creation date of 1611, when it was performed at court. But, here again, there may have been unrecorded performances long before then; and, of course, the play could have been written years before it was finally performed. Oxfordians point to what might have been intended as a satire of *The Tempest* in Ben Jonson's *Volpone*, written in 1605, suggesting that *The Tempest*, too, may have been written before Oxford's death.

Stratfordians reply that act 1 of *The Tempest* deals with a shipwreck and has Ariel visit the "still-vexed Bermoothes." They argue that this is based on the widely reported wreck of the ship *Sea Venture* off Bermuda in 1609. This, of course, could make it impossible at least for Oxford to have been the *sole* author, since he died in 1604. But an earlier Bermuda shipwreck occurred in 1593, and Oxford was an investor in one of the wrecked ships. Besides, the Bermuda area had long been known as one in which fierce storms occurred and ships were often wrecked. Sir Walter Raleigh also had a ship wrecked in the area before Oxford's death.

Stratfordians argue that details in *The Tempest* are specific allusions to the particular 1609 shipwreck. For example, Caliban says that when Prospero first came to the Island he "strok'd me, and mads't much of me; and woulds't give me water with berries in't." The shipwrecked sailors of 1609, having landed on an island with no fresh water, made a drink of crushed cedar berries.

Was Caliban's "water with berries in't" a reference to this? It could be so. But Caliban's island did have fresh water; and Caliban knew where it was and where the berries grew. Would he have found it remarkable that someone put berries in the water? Possibly, what Prospero offered Caliban was wine. Grapes were sometimes called "berries" in Shakespeare's England; and wine could have been included in the ample chest Gonzalo prepared for Prospero before he was put to sea.

On the other hand, later in the play, when Stephano gives Caliban wine, he is very taken with it and does not speak of it as something he has tasted before. But "woulds't give me water with berries in't" suggests that Prospero had merely offered the drink, not that Caliban actually drank it. If so, Caliban first tasted wine when he got it from Stephano.

In any event, even if such lines as the "still-vexed Bermoothes" and "water with berries" did refer to the 1609 shipwreck, the lines could have been added by someone else to give a current feel to a play written before 1604.

The Winter's Tale is generally dated as of 1610, since we have a recorded performance in 1611. But we cannot rule out the possibility that there were unrecorded performances before 1604. The play is listed in the Account of the Revels in 1611 as *The Winter's Night's Tale*. Could it have been the same play as that entered in the Stationers' Register in 1594 as *A Wynters Nightes Pastime*?

Henry VIII is another of the plays unprinted until 1623. The play is said to have been first mentioned in 1613, the year in which it is generally considered to have been written. But Edward Alleyn, Henslowe's son-in-law, made a list of costumes years earlier, including a "Harrie the VIII gown." Was it from Shakespeare's play? The *Henry VIII* performed in 1613 includes lavish praise for Elizabeth, but also for her successor, James I, which would suggest a creation date after 1603. But some scholars believe this part of the play was added by a separate hand, possibly by the young playwright John Fletcher.

One factor that makes it difficult to assign certain dates to the plays is that they were often revised. Shakespeare, more than any other playwright of the period, revised and reworked his plays. Indeed, some plays may contain writing from several different periods. *All's Well That Ends Well* and *Love's Labour's Lost* are examples of plays exhibiting diverse styles. Thus, a play that contains passages deemed mature and self-assured, or that refer to some event at a particular time, and, for either of these reasons, is assigned a composition date late in the time line, may indeed have been written, for the most part, at a much earlier date. It may have been subsequently revised—by Shakespeare or someone else—possibly adding some event after the initial version to give the play an up-to-date feeling.

Some plays, such as *Henry VIII* and *Pericles*, are often said to have had two different authors. Shakespeare may have written a substantial part of such plays before 1604 and one or more others may have finished or added to them thereafter. Other plays like *Macbeth* may have been partially written before 1604 but left incomplete. The same may be true of *Timon of Athens*.

Another factor often overlooked in seeking the composition dates of a play is the source material on which the play is based. If the basic storyline of a play comes from a source that was not written until after 1604, the play was not written by Oxford. Strikingly, *no confirmed source for any of Shakespeare's plays was written after 1603*. Before that, Shakespeare based his plays not only on ancient works, but also on sources that were comparatively recent at the time, such as Hollingshed's *Chronicles*, Harrington's *Ariosto*, and Harsnett's *Popish Imposters*. The last current sources used by

Shakespeare were Harsnett, probably used for *King Lear*, and Florio's translation of Montaigne's *Cannibals*, used for *The Tempest*. Both source works appeared in 1603. Why did the playwright not use sources created after 1603? Was he dead?

There are things besides plays that Shakespeare may have written after 1604. But the evidence is not persuasive. An example is a poem published by Thomas Thorpe in 1612 entitled *A Funeral Elegy in Memory of the Late Virtuous Master William Peter of Whipton near Excester*. The poem is signed "W. S.," and the claim was made that it was the work of Shakespeare. Since William Peter was murdered in 1612, if the funeral elegy poem is *really* about his death and was *really* written by the Bard, Oxford, who died in 1604, could be ruled out at least as having been the *sole* Shakespeare.

It certainly seems that, by using the initials "W. S.," Thorpe (who also published the sonnets) intended to convey the impression that the new poem was by Shakespeare. Joseph Sobran contends that the poem could not be about William Peter of Whipton, because Peter had been married only three years at the time of his death, while the poem refers to a man married nine years when killed. He points out that the poem refers to Peter *and the poet* being in their youth and that the Stratford man was forty-seven at the time. Sobran's view is that Oxford wrote the poem in his youth about someone other than Peter and that Thorpe had it for years and trotted it out when Peter was murdered in 1612.

Sobran may be in error in assuming the subject of the poem was married nine years. The poem refers to a woman's sharing Peter's bed for nine years, and to "conjugal love," which might support Sobran's analysis. But it is possible that Peter and his wife lived together for six years before they were married. It happened—even in Elizabethan times. Also, it is one thing to attach the initials "W. S." to a poem. It seems quite another to pretend that the poem is about the murder of William Peter and put that representation in the title, if the poem is really about someone else murdered years before.

It is likely, however, that the poem is not by Shakespeare at all but by a lesser poet, John Ford. The poem is not consistent with Shakespeare's work, and it is quite consistent with Ford's. Professor Donald Foster of Vassar, apparently the first to announce the view that Shakespeare wrote the *Elegy*, has since changed his opinion and had sufficient academic integrity to admit his error. Now, like most scholars who have examined the matter, Foster believes the poem is by Ford. Probably, Thomas Thorpe, having done well with the sonnets, simply tacked the initials "W. S." onto Ford's poem to enhance sales but lacked the courage to misappropriate the entire name "William Shakespeare."

What, then, can we conclude about the Shakespearean works that may have been written after 1604? Do they squarely eliminate the possibility that Oxford was the sole author of the Shakespeare canon? No. Do they decrease the likelihood that he was? Absolutely. The existence of a significant number of plays, the performance of which was not recorded or written about until years after Oxford's death, certainly tends to support the inference that at least some of those plays were written or at least rewritten by someone other than Oxford after his death, and that he was not the author, or at least not the sole author, of the Shakespeare canon.

Naturally, the First Folio also creates a serious problem for the Oxfordians, as it does for every candidate except the Stratford man. The prefatory material describing Shakespeare as a "friend and ffellow" of Heminge and Condell and as the "Sweet Swan of Avon" and referring to his Buskin treading a stage and his "Stratford Moniment," seems squarely intended to link the playwright with the Stratford man.

There is the possibility that Jonson, Digges, Heminge, and Condell all really believed that the Stratford man was the playwright and were unaware that he was merely the front for some nobleman, such as Oxford. This seems most unlikely. These men were close to the London theatre and literary scene. It is hard to believe that they would not have known the truth.

As we have discussed, the other possibility is that the prefatory statements are a deliberate hoax, designed to perpetuate the false attribution of Shakespeare's works to the Stratford man. Seeking to demonstrate this, Charles Ogburn presents an elaborate scenario. According to Ogburn, Southampton was the love child of Elizabeth and Oxford (remember those rumors?). Oxford, an accomplished poet, wrote the sonnets, intending the "fair youth" sonnets for his own natural son. He also wrote plays for the common theatre. Burghley, with the queen's assent, decreed that Oxford must write, if at all, under another name. Oxford complied, using "Shakespeare" as his pseudonym and ultimately paying an actor with a similar name to front for him. In this way, Oxford was able to communicate potentially "dangerous" ideas, like the deposition of Richard II, that would never have been allowed under his illustrious name and title.

Ogburn's thesis is that Oxford's family, anxious to protect the family name and fearing the displeasure of James I, sought to continue the deception, even after Oxford's death. They enlisted the aid of Ben Jonson in creating the hoax of the First Folio.

Parts of Ogburn's theory are unpersuasive. There is no real evidence that Oxford had an affair with the queen, much less that they had a secret love child and that he was Southampton. Moreover, even if we could accept that a father wrote sonnets expressing what seems to be romantic, if not sexual, love for his son and that the sonnets suggest that the "son" has betrayed the "father" with another man and another woman, no father writes to his son that the boy has been "pricked out" with something of no use to the father, as Shakespeare does in Sonnet 20. Common sense seems to dictate that, if Oxford wrote the sonnets, the fair youth was not his son. And if, by the early sonnets, Oxford was urging Southampton to marry Burghley's granddaughter, he would have been urging a marriage of his son to his own daughter, not a likely scenario.

Until the First Folio, there had been no direct and explicit linkage of the Stratford man with the poems and plays. In 1622, the year before the Folio's publication, Henry Peacham compiled a list of outstanding Elizabethan poets. Oxford was first on the list. Shakespeare, although well known by then, was not even listed. Possibly Peacham believed that Oxford had written the poems attributed to Shakespeare.

Did Oxford's family foster the Stratford man-as-author hoax after Oxford's death? Did they scheme to create the First Folio and the Stratford monument? Oxford's widow died in 1612. We cannot know what part, if any, was played by Oxford's son, the eighteenth earl. He died of a fever in 1625 after fighting valiantly in battle. He may or may not have participated in the publication of the First Folio in 1623.

But the Folio was dedicated to Oxford's son-in-law, the earl of Montgomery, and to Montgomery's brother, the earl of Pembroke. Both men, extremely powerful, probably spoke and acted for Oxford's family at the time, especially if Oxford's son was off pursuing a military career.

Pembroke was Lord Chamberlain. Between 1616 and 1621, he raised the annual stipend paid to Ben Jonson from 20 to 200 pounds, a striking increase and one that was granted when the First Folio may have been in the planning and preparation phase. Jonson, of course, played a key role in the Folio's preparation and publication. In addition to his own foreword (so overblown and at variance with his earlier statements about Shakespeare), he may also have written the material attributed to Heminge and Condell.

In fact, everyone who contributed to the prefatory material in the First Folio was associated with Jonson in one way or another. Was Jonson paid by the family to perpetuate a hoax on their behalf? This possibility does not depend on accepting that Oxford was Elizabeth's lover or that Southampton was their love child. There were other reasons why the family may have acted to perpetrate such a hoax.

Joseph Sobran presents another such scenario. According to Sobran, Oxford and Southampton were homosexual lovers, and Oxford wrote *Venus and Adonis* and the "fair youth" sonnets in praise of the young earl. Sobran's thesis is that the Stratford man worked for Oxford as an actor and "front" and that he went back to Stratford on Oxford's death in 1604. By 1623, Southampton had married and was a rich and honored nobleman. Both Oxford's family and Southampton sought to perpetuate the myth that Shakespeare was the Stratford man to avoid any attention being paid to the homosexual relationship between Oxford and Southampton. This is why, Sobran says, the First Folio makes no mention of *Venus and Adonis* or *The Rape of Lucrece* or, indeed, of Southampton, and why it affirmatively ties the name Shakespeare to the Stratford man.

Sobran's thesis is plausible. We have already discussed the possibility of a homosexual relationship between the two earls. It certainly *could* have existed. If so, Sonnet 20, about the youth being "pricked out" with something of no use to the poet, might have been included as a "blind" to throw any reader off the trail. The references to the danger of the relationship bringing shame to the youth tends to support this possibility. But it remains just that—a possibility.

Certainly, if there was a homosexual relationship, it would explain why the Oxford family, and Southampton as well, would want to direct attention away from it and why using Jonson and his associates to create the First Folio, tying the works of Shakespeare to the Stratford man, might have seemed a splendid idea (and one that succeeded). But, here again, "might" is the best we can do.

Since the sonneteer promised the fair youth mortality through his "gentle verse," it is likely that he expected at least some of the sonnets to be published. It is understandable, however, that his family, and the family of the fair youth, might want to disavow them.

Despite his erudition, his poetry, and his vital interest in literature, some aspects of Oxford's life may be difficult to square with the feelings and philosophy expressed by Shakespeare, just as the petty, litigious career of the Stratford man seems difficult to reconcile with the works of the great Bard. Oxford was a well-known dandy, fond of extreme Italian fashion. Shakespeare showed little respect for men who were unduly concerned with the latest fashions, as for example, Parolles in *All's Well That Ends Well*. Parolles, who has "a very good tailor," is called "a jack-an-apes with scarfs" and "a snipt taffeta fellow." According to the wise Lafeu, "There can be no kernel in this light nut; the soul of the man is his clothes."[4] Did the fashion-conscious Oxford write these lines? Perhaps, if he were an extraordinary man with a puckish ability to make fun of his own proclivities. But then, if Oxford wrote the Shakespeare canon, he certainly was an extraordinary man.

Oxford was also an uncontrollable and irresponsible spendthrift, creating financial problems that plagued him most of his life. More significantly, Oxford was widely known for his violent temper and arrogant, unpredictable behavior. As a youth, he had stabbed one of Burghley's servants in the leg, leading to the man's death. The servant had been quite drunk, so perhaps Oxford was not at fault. In Italy, he supposedly issued an open challenge to meet any man in single combat. He even declined Elizabeth's request that he exhibit his dancing skills (which reportedly were prodigious) for the French ambassador, responding that he would not entertain Frenchmen.

Oxford had heated arguments with Burghley, his guardian and father-in-law, and apparently swore to kill his sister's intended husband. He had a widely reported spat on a tennis court with the soldier-poet Sir Phillip Sydney. Oxford called Sydney a "puppy," leading Sydney to challenge him to a duel, which would have happened had it not been forbidden by the queen.

We have already discussed Oxford's treatment of his wife and his serious and bitter controversy with Lord Henry Howard, who accused him of buggery. When Oxford fathered a child by Anne Vavasor, one of the queen's ladies-in-waiting, Elizabeth was so incensed that she sent Oxford,

---

4. In *Cymbeline*, when the loutish fop Cloten announces that he is a "gentleman," the response is, "That's more than some, whose tailors are as dear as yours, can justly boast of."

Vavasor, and their child to the Tower, where they were imprisoned for a few weeks. When Oxford reconciled with his wife, he was attacked by a relative of Vavasor. Each was wounded. Then, Vavasor's brother challenged him to a duel, which, like the Sydney duel, never took place. And these are just examples.

Does this vain, quarrelsome man square with Shakespeare's lofty sensibilities and apparent disapproval of violence any better than with the Stratford actor/trader? Maybe so; but Oxford's character flaws are, nevertheless, factors to be considered.

Notwithstanding those flaws and the problems created by his death in 1604, Oxford must be considered a strong candidate as at least *one* of the authors of the Shakespeare canon. Of course, there is nothing we can consider "proof." Still, if we could put aside the statements in the First Folio, the Stratford monument, Sonnet III (the "dyer's hand"), and the number of plays unpublished and unmentioned at the time of his death, Oxford's life, education, knowledge, and accomplishments seem a far better fit with Shakespeare than do those of the Stratford man.

21.

CHRISTOPHER MARLOWE

Marlowe is the "stealth" candidate. His activities are mysterious, and his early murder is highly suspicious. He could possibly have been Shakespeare, but his candidacy runs into some serious problems.

Marlowe was born in 1564, the same year as the Stratford man. Extraordinarily bright, he was a student at Cambridge, as well as an accomplished classicist. He translated Ovid himself. Given his intelligence, education, and proficiency as a scholar, it is less difficult to believe that he could have read and absorbed the diverse subjects reflected in Shakespeare's works than that the Stratford man mastered that daunting task.

Marlowe knew the leading literary figures of the day, as well as political figures such as Raleigh, and the younger members of many distinguished families. He was openly homosexual, which fits with the "fair youth" sonnets, except possibly Sonnet 20—the "pricked thee out" one.

Similarly, the references to the poet's disgrace and his concern in Sonnet 71 that the youth's reputation could be tarnished by their association, appear to fit Marlowe even better than Oxford and certainly better than the Stratford man. But Marlowe has the same age gap problem as the Stratford man. He appears to have been much too young to have written about what seems a vast difference in age between the youth's tender years and the poet's "tanned antiquity."

Sonnet III ("the dyer's hand") fits Marlowe far more easily than Oxford. The son of a shoemaker, Marlowe could well have complained that "Fortune . . . did not better for my life provide"; and, like the Stratford man, he had certainly used "public means" of earning a living.

But what about the "dark lady" sonnets, such as Sonnet 151, explicitly referring to the poet's physical lust for his mistress? Can we square this with Marlowe's homosexuality? Could he have been bisexual? It seems unlikely; but we can't rule it out.

Could the "dark lady" sonnets have been written about a man? It seems impossible. Shakespeare repeatedly uses terms like *her*, *she*, *my mistress*, and a *goddess*. True, such terms are jokingly used today by some gay men in describing their male lovers, but there may not have been any such satirical usage in the sixteenth century, and, in any event, the tone of at least most of these sonnets is hardly jocular.

Marlowe was an accomplished playwright and poet. While still in his twenties, he wrote *Tamburlaine the Great: Doctor Faustus*; *The Jew of Malta*; *Edward II*; *Dido, Queen of Carthage*; and other plays, as well as excellent and quite striking poetry. According to Edmund Malone, "Christopher Marlowe was the most popular and admired dramatic poet of that age previous to the appearance of Shakespeare."

Some of the subjects Marlowe chose were similar to those chosen by Shakespeare. For example, *The Jew of Malta*, like *The Merchant of Venice*, is about a dysphoric Jew living among hostile Christians in a European city.

But it goes beyond the similar subject matter. There is a strange and unexplained fact concerning the works of the two men. In many instances, Shakespeare's actual expression is so similar to Marlowe's that it is difficult not to conclude either that the lines were plagiarized, that the two worked together, or that they were the same person.

For example, in *The Passionate Shepherd to His Love*, Marlowe gives us these lines:

> *By shallow rivers, to whose falls*
> *Melodious birds sing madrigals.*
> *And I will make thee beds of roses,*
> *And a thousand fragrant posies.*

Compare Shakespeare's *Merry Wives of Windsor*:

> *To shallow rivers to whose falls*
> *melodious birds sing madrigals;*
> *There we make our beds of roses*
> *and a thousand fragrant posies.*

This cannot be coincidence. Yet there seems no common source for the lines. Marlowe's *The Passionate Shepherd to His Love* was written before 1593, while *The Merry Wives of Windsor* is commonly dated to around 1600. Did Shakespeare steal the lines from Marlowe? Or was he, in fact, Marlowe simply reusing lines from his own earlier work?

Other lines, while not identical, are strikingly similar. For example, in *The Jew of Malta*, Barabas's thoughts are torn between his money and his daughter. He says:

> *O, my girl, my fortune, my felicity;*
> *O girl, O gold, O beauty, O my bliss.*

In *The Merchant of Venice*, Shylock has the same quickly shifting concerns. When his daughter Jessica runs off with her Christian lover, stealing Shylock's savings, he cries out:

> *My daughter! O my ducats!*
> *O my daughter!*

In *The Jew of Malta*, Marlowe writes "I . . . hold there is no sin but ignorance."

In *Twelfth Night*, Shakespeare writes, "I say there is no darkness, but ignorance."

And, again, in *The Jew of Malta*, Marlowe writes, "These arms of mine shall be a sepulchre."

In *Henry VI*, Part 3, Shakespeare says:

> *These arms of mine shall be thy winding sheet;*
> *My heart, sweet boy, shall be thy sepulchre.*

There are many more such similarities. For example:

> "Was this the face that launched a thousand ships . . . ?"
> Marlowe, *Doctor Faustus*

"... She is a pearl, whose price hath launch'd above a thousand ships." Shakespeare, *Troilus and Cressida*

"Nature doth strive with Fortune ... to make him famous." Marlowe, *Tamburlaine the Great*
"Nature and Fortune joined to make thee great." Shakespeare, *King John*

"The sun, unable to sustain the sight shall hide his head." Marlowe, *Tamburlaine the Great*
"The sun for sorrow will not show his head." Shakespeare, *Romeo and Juliet*

"... Whiskt his sword about, and with the wind thereof the King fell downe." Marlowe, *Dido, Queen of Carthage*
"... with the whiff and wind of his fell sword, the unerved father falls." Shakespeare, *Hamlet*

Some of Shakespeare's strikingly similar lines may be deliberate allusions to Marlowe or parodies of Marlowe's famous scenes, rather than simple plagiarism. For example, in a scene from *Tamburlaine the Great*, first performed in 1587, Marlowe has the great conqueror enter in a chariot drawn by two captive kings in harness with the bits in their mouths. Tamburlaine berates them, "Holla, ye pampered jades of Asia. What, can ye draw but twenty miles a day?" On stage, the scene must have created a sensation.

In *Henry IV*, Part 2, which was probably written ten years later, Shakespeare has Pistol bellow, in a speech of scrambled nonsense, "... and hollow pampered jades of Asia which cannot go but thirty miles a day." Given that the speech is by the ignorant Pistol, rather than a heroic character, and given that it makes no sense in its context, Shakespeare's line is almost surely intended as a parody of Marlowe's spectacular scene, not a theft of it. Does this prove that they were different men? No. A writer could parody his own earlier lines, just as well as those of a rival.

Scholars disagree on the extent to which Marlowe's style differs from Shakespeare's, particularly with respect to the Bard's later plays. Of course, one would not expect an author's work to remain the same as he gained experience and maturity.

Marlowe created high drama, in which conquering heroes are brought low and murderous villains their comeuppance. He also wrote some extraordinary lines, sometimes more characteristic of modern poetry than that of the sixteenth century. An example is Dr. Faustus on the impact of Helen's kiss. "Her lips suck forth my soul, see where it flies." The line could have been written by T. S. Eliot or e. e cummings.

Marlowe and Shakespeare, born in the same year, were rival playwrights and continued so even after Marlowe's death. Marlowe was the more successful during his lifetime, and his plays continued to draw enthusiastic crowds at Henslowe's Rose even after he died.

Gradually, however, Shakespeare surpassed Marlowe in public acceptance. With the occasional exception of *Doctor Faustus*, Marlowe's plays are very rarely performed today. Eventually, Shakespeare gained recognition as the better playwright. He did so not by originality of plot (almost all of his plays were based on earlier works by others), but by the skill with which he expressed those general story ideas and perhaps, most importantly, by his intensely human, multifaceted characters. He generally gave us heroes and kings flawed by weakness, indecision, vanity, or greed, and great textured villains, whose misdeeds could be related to psychological, physical, or sociological infirmity and who could evoke understanding and fascination in the audience.

As the court of his brother Edward IV rejoices over the defeat of the Lancastrians, Richard III hobbles about the stage on misshapen limbs and bends under the weight of his hunched back. In a great soliloquy, he tells us:

> But I,—that am not shaped for sportive tricks,
> Nor made to court an amorous looking glass;
> I, that am rudely stamp'd and want love's majesty
> To strut before a wanton ambling nymph;
> I that am curtail'd of this fair proportion,
> Cheated of feature by dissembling nature,
> Deform'd, unfinish'd, sent before my time
> Into this breathing world scarce half made up,
> And so lamely and unfashionable
> That dogs bark at me as I halt by them;—
> Why I, in this weak piping time of peace,
> Have no delight to pass away the time,
> Unless to spy my shadow in the sun,

And descant on mine own deformity:
And therefore,—since I cannot prove a lover,
To entertain these fair, well spoken days—
I am determined to play a villain,
And hate the idle pleasures of these days. . . .

By contrast, Marlowe gave us essentially one-dimensional characters. Dramatic, yes; but without the complexity, depth, or humanity of the great Shakespearean figures.

Perhaps we can best compare the two playwrights by comparing Shakespeare's *The Merchant of Venice* with Marlowe's *The Jew of Malta*. In *The Merchant of Venice*, Shylock is torn between competing emotional forces; while the character was certainly not meant to be heroic, Shakespeare shows us that his stubborn vindictiveness is relatable to the plight of the dysphoric Jew, a perpetual outsider in a land of hostile, mocking Christians.

Unlike Shylock, Barabas evokes no sympathy. He is a complete and remorseless villain, a ruthless murderer who kills his own daughter and slaughters an abbey full of nuns and countless others. He is a scheming traitor who betrays Malta to the Turks and then betrays the Turks to the Maltese. As Barabas tells the audience: "As for myself, I walk abroad nights, and kill sick people groaning under walls; sometimes I go about and poison wells."

Perhaps we can enjoy Barabas's boldness and ingenuity, but we never feel for him or really even understand him. Shylock is a person, with understandable feelings and emotions. Barabas is a caricature.

Also, Shylock is a deeply religious man. Barabas, perhaps reflecting Marlowe's own attitude toward religion, is a cynic and skeptic to the extent we have any clue at all as to his views. Some argue that Marlowe intended the real villain of his play to be the sanctimonious, hypocritical Christians, rather than Barabas. This seems wishful thinking. The reasoning would be more applicable to *The Merchant of Venice* and to the thesis that Shakespeare meant us to see the utter hypocrisy of characters like Bassanio, Jessica, and Lorenzo, and perhaps even Portia herself.

It is often said that *The Merchant of Venice* and *The Jew of Malta* not only deal with a similar subject, but are very much alike. There are similarities, of course; but there are enormous differences. Even aside from Shylock's being very different from Barabas, the plots are quite different. *The Jew of*

Malta has no Portia and no Antonio, and lacks most of Shakespeare's characters. Marlowe's characters, beyond Barabas, are not developed at all. And even Barabas's motivation, other than greed and viciousness, is difficult to fathom.

The pound of flesh, the court scene, the casket scenes, the ring device—all are missing from *The Jew of Malta*. Instead, we have military and political intrigue involving Turks, Spanish, and Maltese, plus multiple, and sometimes senseless, murders by the protagonist.

Perhaps most significantly, Marlowe's "mighty line," as employed in *The Jew of Malta*, simply cannot be compared to the soaring beauty of Shakespeare's lines in *The Merchant of Venice*.

And these are only a few examples. There are many more. Not only does Shylock go far beyond Barabas, Antony in *Julius Caesar* certainly exceeds Tamburlaine, and Prospero in *The Tempest* is a far more complex and intriguing character than Dr. Faustus. Marlowe has no answer for Falstaff or Iago or Lear and certainly none for Cleopatra, Rosalind, Queen Margaret, or Lady Macbeth. Indeed, Marlowe's female characters tend to be relatively inactive and vaguely drawn.

Even so, we cannot rule out the possibility that Shakespeare's work exceeds Marlowe's because it is the work of a single artist maturing and growing in both skill and perception as he replows old ground and brings his manifest intelligence to bear on areas yet unexplored. It may not be likely, but it is by no means impossible.

At least one statistical test supports that view. Dr. Thomas Mendenhall, a distinguished physicist, created a method of identifying the author of unknown works by comparing the frequency of words of particular lengths in the anonymous work with the frequency in the works of a known writer. Mendenhall claimed that his computation was like a fingerprint in that, at least as a matter of probability, the works of no two authors would show the same frequency pattern.

Mendenhall was retained by a staunch Baconian to compare the word-length frequencies of Shakespeare and Bacon. Unfortunately for the man who commissioned the test, the word-length frequencies in Bacon were far different from those in Shakespeare. Perhaps on a lark, Mendenhall tried a similar comparison of the frequencies in Marlowe and Shakespeare. Mendenhall was amazed. They were virtually identical. Certainly, if Mendenhall's test had scientific validity and was properly administered, this would be significant evidence that Marlowe wrote what has been attributed to Shakespeare.

And, having died in 1593, Marlowe qualifies as the "ever-living poet" in the 1609 dedication of the sonnets.

But the Marlovians face a severe obstacle. How could Marlowe be Shakespeare when most of Shakespeare's works were written after 1593, when Marlowe *died*. Or did he? Therein lies the mystery discussed in Calvin Hoffman's fascinating book *The Murder of the Man Who Was "Shakespeare"* and in Anthony Burgess's engaging *A Dead Man in Deptford*.

From the time he was at Cambridge, Marlowe was a government spy, operating both in England and abroad under the ultimate direction of Sir Francis Walsingham, Queen Elizabeth's chief of security. Among his other acts of espionage, Marlowe left Cambridge to attend a Jesuit seminary at Reims in order to report back on English Catholics who were involved there in plotting against the queen. When Cambridge tried to withhold his degree on the ground that he had abandoned his studies, the Privy Council itself intervened, stressing that his absence had been to render "good service" to "her Majesty." This got Marlowe his degree despite his extended absence.

Aside from being a spy, Marlowe belonged to Sir Walter Raleigh's "School of Night," a group of intellectuals who met and freely—and perhaps carelessly—discussed philosophical and religious subjects, such as the existence of God and the divinity of Christ. Raleigh's group included other men of high position, influence and, sometimes, genius, such as the young earl of Northumberland, called the "wizard earl," the poet George Chapman, and the brilliant polymath Thomas Hariot.

Being a spy, a homosexual, and a member of Raleigh's freethinking group earned Marlowe some dedicated enemies. In 1593, he was living at the estate of Sir Thomas Walsingham, his wealthy patron and a cousin of the spymaster Sir Francis Walsingham, who was now deceased. Evidently, Marlowe had been involved in a long homosexual relationship with Sir Thomas. Perhaps the Walsingham connection or his prior service as a spy gave Marlowe some measure of protection. Perhaps his enemies would at least need some "evidence" if they sought to destroy him.

But that "evidence" became available. The government arrested Marlowe's friend, Thomas Kyd, who had in his possession certain papers containing utterances considered blasphemous and atheistic. Under torture,

Kyd said the potentially fatal papers belonged to Marlowe. This was probably true.

On May 20, 1593, Marlowe was ordered to appear before the Privy Council. This was a frightening prospect, which could ultimately mean torture and even burning at the stake. Marlowe's friend Francis Kett had suffered death by burning for charges no more serious than those now made against Marlowe. With the evidence the authorities now had against Marlowe, there was little his wealthy patron could do to stop the proceedings.

Marlowe appeared before the council as ordered. Perhaps because of Walsingham's influence, he was temporarily and conditionally freed, but he was ordered to reappear before the council every single day, presumably because other evidence was being gathered against him. This put Marlowe in severe peril, as he and Walsingham certainly realized.

On May 30, 1593, Marlowe and three men spent the afternoon and evening at the home of a Mrs. Bull (possibly a brothel) in Deptford. One of the men was Ingraham Frizer, Walsingham's overseer and apparently a friend of Marlowe's. The other two, Robert Poley and Thomas Skeres, had evidently served as spies under Sir Francis Walsingham and were well acquainted with Marlowe. According to the story told by these three, they were sitting alone in a small room after supper, when Marlowe unexpectedly picked up a knife and launched an unprovoked attack on Friger, presumably over the suggestion that Marlowe should pay the check. According to their story, Frizer was able to wrest the weapon from Marlowe's grasp; and, as the fight continued, he stabbed Marlowe in the right eye, killing him.

Within thirty-six hours, an inquest was held before local jurors. The only witnesses were Frizer, Poley, and Skeres. The jury readily accepted their uncontradicted testimony. Marlowe's death was quickly recorded as self-defense on the part of Frizer. So Marlowe was dead and buried. Or was he?

Marlovians are correct in finding this story suspicious. Marlowe, in grave and imminent danger from the Star Chamber, is conveniently killed by a friend, who works for Marlowe's patron? Unconvincing.

Perhaps Walsingham was also involved in the expression of heretical or blasphemous views. Perhaps he feared that, under torture, Marlowe would implicate him or reveal their homosexual relationship. Perhaps he had Marlowe killed to prevent that. Or possibly Raleigh or some other powerful member of the "School of Night" arranged for Marlowe's murder to avoid what the playwright might reveal under torture. There is no evidence to support these alternative explanations. But they could be the case. Or Marlowe's "death" may have been staged to avoid a real and painful death and to permit him to live comfortably in some other land. But that doesn't mean he necessarily became Shakespeare.

Perhaps, however, he did. Perhaps, after his supposed "death," he was spirited off to Italy, where he spent the rest of his days writing poems and plays and sending them back to be palmed off as the work of a notoriously venal London actor who was paid handsomely for his cooperation and silence. Perhaps the manuscripts in Marlowe's hand were rewritten by a scrivener to avoid recognition. We know that, rather oddly, Walsingham left a bequest to a scrivener. Is that why "Shakespeare's" manuscripts never contained a "blotted line"? Is that why so many of Shakespeare's plays have lines so similar to Marlowe's?

If Marlowe was Shakespeare and was hiding out in Italy or some other distant place, he had ample reason not to speak out on the death of Queen Elizabeth or King James's son. Aside from the continuing need for secrecy, by the time word of these deaths reached him by sailing ship and he wrote an appropriate sentiment and sent his words on the long journey back to London, it would be far too late.

Some scholars have opined that early plays normally attributed to Shakespeare were, in fact, written at least partly by Marlowe. Prime examples are the three parts of *Henry VI*. But some have included *Richard II*, *Richard III*, and *Titus Andronicus* as well. If so, did Marlowe simply continue writing the works now attributed to Shakespeare after Marlowe's "death" in 1593?

In 1594, the year after Marlowe's "death," the Stratford man became a sharer in the Lord Chamberlain's Men, evidently the first time he had attained that status. Was that because he was now to be the recipient of all subsequent plays by the highly successful Marlowe?

While the evidence that Marlowe wrote the Shakespeare canon is hardly conclusive, it does exist. We have the use of the strikingly similar lines, and we know that nothing written by Shakespeare appeared in print until 1593, the year of Marlowe's "death." Over the next thirty years, two long poems, 154 sonnets, and thirty-six plays appeared under the name "Shakespeare."

Shakespeare's works contain what could be specific references to Marlowe's death. In *As You Like It*, probably written six years after Marlowe's "death," Touchstone muses that, when a poet's verses are not understood, "it strikes a man more dead than a great reckoning in a little room." Is this great reckoning the one that occurred in the little room in Deptford, where Marlowe was supposedly slain?

In the same play, Phoebe, a shepherdess says:

> *Dead shepherd! Now I find thy saw of might;*
> *'Whoever lov'd that lov'd not at first sight'*

The lines are identical to those of Marlowe in *Hero and Leander*. Shakespeare seems to be making an open and intentional reference to the "dead" poet.

There are lines in the sonnets that could also be construed as references to Marlowe's death. For example, in Sonnet 74, Shakespeare speaks of his own death as taking only his body, his least important aspect. He writes:

> *My spirit is thine, the better part of me:*
> *So, then, thou hast but lost the dregs of life,*
> *The prey of worms, my body being dead;*
> *The coward conquest of a wretch's knife,*

"The coward conquest of a wretch's knife"? Is that a description of Marlowe's "death"? If not, it is a very odd coincidence. Shakespeare's reference is to his own body being dead as a result of being stabbed by a knife. Why would the Stratford man, or even Oxford, suppose that he would be killed by "a wretch's knife?" In Oxford's case, perhaps "a rival's sword" or "the headsman's axe," but not "a wretch's knife." And, why would the Stratford real estate dealer envision any such violent death for himself? Was it Marlowe writing as "Shakespeare" and referring to his own faked death?

The first recorded reference to the sonnets was by Francis Meres in 1598. If Marlowe wrote them, was he having a love affair with Southampton, or whoever was the "lovely youth," after his supposed death? The sonnets seem to be written as the affair is taking place—not years later. Did the youth visit Marlowe in Italy?

Or was Marlowe hiding out on Walsingham's estate? That would seem far too risky. If Marlowe was the poet, it seems more likely that he wrote the sonnets before his "death" and in the course of the relationships they describe. But, if so, how would he know that his death would be by a "wretch's knife"? Perhaps Sonnet 74 and others were written after the murder plot was hatched or even after it was carried out, even though most of the sonnets had been written before.

The scenario would have to be something like this. In 1591 and 1592 Marlowe has a romantic, perhaps physical relationship with a younger man—possibly Southampton. He begins to write sonnets about his feelings. At the same time, he continues residing with his longtime friend Sir Thomas Walsingham. Perhaps, like many stylish Englishmen, he even has a "mistress" with whom he has a vague sexual relationship or at least fantasizes one. In May 1593, Marlowe faces possible torture and burning at the stake. The plot to stage his death is formed, and he writes Sonnet 74, telling the youth "never mind that my body will be the prey of worms and the victim of a 'wretch's knife,' you will always have my spirit." In ensuing years, the poems are privately read and attributed to "Shake-speare." Meres hears about them and, finally, in 1609, Thorpe publishes them. Meanwhile, Marlowe, hidden away in the hills of Tuscany or in a Venetian palazzo, is writing the plays and continues doing so until his actual death.

But what about the First Folio? What about the prefatory statements of Jonson, Digges, Heminge, and Condell linking the author of the plays to the Stratford man? Could they have really *believed* the Stratford man wrote the plays if Marlowe was the true author? Or were they continuing a hoax at the behest of the families of Southampton and Walsingham, to deflect rumors of homosexual relationships with Marlowe and to cover up Walsingham's participation in Marlowe's staged "death"?

There is a potential problem with the Marlovian faked death theory. Why would Marlowe have written under the name Shakespeare *before* he got into trouble with the Star Chamber in May 1593? He was not a nobleman and would have had no problem writing plays for the public theatre. He had done so quite successfully under his own name. After May 1593, he had a reason for pretending that William Shakespeare was the author of whatever he wrote. Before May 1593, he had no such reason.

Yet, some works may have been attributed to Shakespeare before 1593. If Marlowe wrote them, why were they not presented under his own name, rather than Shakespeare's?

Shakespearean scholars tend to date the creation of six to nine plays by the Bard in or before 1593. These include the three parts of *Henry VI, Titus*

Andronicus, and *Richard III*, plays sometimes attributed at least in part to Marlowe. Most of the plays written before Marlowe's "death" in May 1593, would not have been performed until after that event, when it might have made sense to announce the plays as being by William Shakespeare, rather than by Marlowe. But what about plays performed before May 1593? If Marlowe wrote them, there would have been no reason to present them under any name but his own.

Do we *know* that Shakespeare was credited as the author of any plays performed before May 1593? It seems likely; but it may not be the case.

We have seen that, in *The Teares of the Muses*, Edmund Spenser praised an author named "Willy" and expressed regret for the cessation of his playwriting. Spenser probably wrote this in 1590. It sounds as if "Willy's" plays had been performed before then. If "Willy" were Shakespeare (which is doubtful), and Marlowe were the true author, why would he write under Shakespeare's name? He wasn't yet in trouble with the Star Chamber. Of course, Willy was probably someone else entirely.

Henslowe's diary shows that Marlowe's plays were performed in 1592, including *The Jew of Malta* and *Tambercame* (*Tamburlaine*). But he doesn't record the name of the playwright.

All three parts of *Henry VI* were probably written in or before 1591. It would be reasonable to expect that they would have been performed by 1593. Henslowe's records show several performances of *Harey the vi*, a new play, in 1592; but there is no written record that the play was attributed to Shakespeare.

We know from Robert Greene that *Henry VI*, Part 3 had been performed by 1592. Greene's letter warns against "Shake-scene," who may have been the playwright, as well as an actor. If that were a reference to Shakespeare, why would Marlowe have used that name before he had a reason to disappear in May 1593? In 1592, Marlowe was a noted and successful playwright. If Marlowe wrote *Henry VI*, Part 3, there was no reason at that time to attribute its authorship to Shakespeare.

Perhaps it wasn't attributed to Shakespeare. Possibly, by "Shake-scene" Greene was not referring to Shakespeare, but to the actor Edward Alleyn, intending to make no mention of the play's author. Aside from the possibility that Greene may have attributed the play to Shakespeare in the 1592 letter, no one else did until 1619, when he was listed as the author of the play on the cover page of a quarto edition of what seems all three parts of *Henry VI*. Previous quartos had not identified the playwright.

Francis Meres's 1598 list of plays by Shakespeare does not include any of the parts of that play. This is not conclusive, but it must be taken as some evidence that it was not considered a Shakespearean play. By 1619, things were different. There was a strong commercial motive to ascribe a published play to Shakespeare, regardless of who wrote it. We simply do not know for sure who was identified as the author of the *Henry VI* plays prior to 1619.

But what about *Venus and Adonis*? Richard Field registered the poem with the Stationers' Company on April 28, 1593, without listing the author's name. Marlowe was called before the court of Privy Council on May 20, 1593. He was "killed" on May 30, 1593. Just eleven days later, in London, Richard Stonely bought a copy of *Venus and Adonis* by "Shakespeare."

Did Field rush to change the name of the author from "Marlowe" to "Shakespeare" in that brief time? Assuming that the poem was not published until shortly before Stonely bought it, there was plenty of time after Marlowe's "death" on May 30 for a quick change of the cover page. But why would Field make that change? The poem could still have been published "posthumously" under Marlowe's name. Possibly Field believed that the accusation of heresy and blasphemy and the tale of Marlowe's scandalous death would hurt sales and so used the pseudonym *Shakespeare*. But why *that* name, at that time? In the brief period between May 20 and June 10, 1593, had Marlowe or his patron already made a deal for the Stratford man to act as a front for Marlowe's future works? It seems a stretch, but it is not impossible. Marlowe probably knew the Stratford man from the theatre; and, if he didn't, Field knew them both and could have brought them together.

In 1598, Marlowe's unfinished *Hero and Leander* was published under his own name. Supposedly, this was the poem he was working on when he was killed. Why could *Hero and Leander* be published posthumously in 1598, under the name Marlowe, while, in 1593, *Venus and Adonis* had to be brought out as Shakespeare's? Possibly by 1598, the element of scandal had dissipated and there was no need to conceal the true author.

Marlowe's death is certainly suspicious, and he certainly can be considered a viable candidate. Greene's 1592 letter and the purchase of *Venus and*

Adonis in June 1593 could be taken as evidence against the Marlovian case, although hardly conclusive. But, of course, Marlowe has the same problems as Oxford and every other candidate but the Stratford man. His proponents must explain the First Folio and the Stratford monument, which seem plainly to connect Shakespeare to the actor and Stratford resident. Still, all things considered, Marlowe can't be ruled out.

22.

FRANCIS BACON

*F*or centuries, Bacon was considered the prime candidate to be the real "Shakespeare." Later, other candidates became more fashionable. But Bacon had many of the qualities that match what we can see in Shakespeare.

Born in 1561, the son of Sir Nicholas Bacon, he was classically educated and extremely intelligent, entering Cambridge University at twelve. Bacon was fluent in Greek, Latin, and European languages and was well versed in history, philosophy, religion, classical and European literature, and most other subjects referred to in the Shakespeare canon. He wrote widely and brilliantly on many subjects. His expressed views and feelings were quite similar to those of Shakespeare. In his own writings, he often quoted from the same sources as Shakespeare.

Bacon not only studied law at Gray's Inn, he became solicitor general, attorney general, and lord chancellor. Obviously, he was completely familiar with legal matters and legal terms. He seems to have had little or no experience with military campaigns or country sports, such as falconry. But, to the extent the plays deal with military matters, Bacon, a proficient scholar, could have read about them, or he could have discussed them with numerous friends who had such knowledge. The same is true of country sports. Still, the natural and metaphoric way Shakespeare used terminology from these various fields seems inconsistent with his usage having flowed from research or questioning others.

Bacon was fond of drama. As a law student at Gray's Inn, he put on sketches for his fellow students, lawyers, and aristocratic private audiences.

Shakespeare's works refer to Bacon's residence, St. Albans, many times. As we have seen, they never mention Stratford.

Bacon seems to have had a relationship with most of the major candidates for authorship of the Shakespeare canon. Burghley, who was Oxford's father-in-law, married Bacon's aunt. Bacon acted as the lawyer for Lord Stanley, another candidate, whose wife was Oxford's daughter and Burghley's granddaughter. We know of Bacon's relationship with the queen, and it is a reasonable bet that he knew Marlowe and the earl of Rutland as well.

Some contend that both Bacon and Essex were the sons of Queen Elizabeth and Leicester, who, the argument goes, were secretly married. There is little or no evidence supporting that contention. Besides, Bacon had a well-known father and mother. The primary "evidence" is that Elizabeth stayed from time to time at Canonbury Tower, an ancient structure owned by Leicester's father. A list of the Latin names of English monarchs was found inscribed on the wall of an upper room. After "Elizabeth," and before "Jacobus" (Latin for James), was a name that had been obliterated except for the first two letters: "Fr."

Was "Fr" Francis Bacon? Does this prove that Bacon was next in line to the throne or that he was Elizabeth's son? Hardly. If the claim were true, it might explain the queen's fondness for Essex and her repeated willingness to forgive him. But it would also mean that the queen assigned Bacon to manage the prosecution that led to beheading her own son and Bacon's own brother. It seems most unlikely.

Apparently, Bacon was homosexual. At least his mother thought so. She wrote letters to Bacon's brother, Anthony, objecting to Francis's male bed companions, who, she felt, were creating a serious risk of scandal. One of those bedmates was Antonio Perez, the Spaniard probably depicted as Don Armado in *Love's Labour's Lost*.

Bacon's homosexuality might seem consistent with the sonnets to the "fair youth," except for Sonnets 20 and 151 which suggest that the poet was heterosexual. *Venus and Adonis* and *The Rape of Lucrece* are dedicated to the earl of Southampton. The earl had no known relationship with the actor from Stratford, and such a relationship, while not impossible, would seem unlikely. A relationship with Francis Bacon would have been far more probable. Both men were associates of Essex; and they undoubtedly knew each other.

As in the case of Marlowe, Sonnet III (the "dyer's hand") can be more easily squared with Bacon than with Oxford. Bacon may have railed at fate for not providing him with vast wealth or an earldom. He did have a very "public" career as a lawyer and politician; and he may have felt that, in these pursuits, he had "almost" developed "public manners."

There are events in Bacon's life that can be related to things in Shakespeare's plays. But the relationship is not a particularly strong one. Bacon spent three years in Poitiers, traveling to other French places, such as Orleans, Maine, and Anjou. *Henry VI, Part 1*, is set in this area. Always plagued by financial problems, Bacon was evidently sentenced to a workhouse when he appeared unable to meet payments coming due on his bond. He was rescued by his brother Anthony. Was this the genesis of *The Merchant of Venice*?

There are things in the plays that militate against Bacon's authorship. If the character Polonius in *Hamlet* was meant to be Lord Burghley, it is unlikely that Bacon, a consummate politician, would have lampooned him, as Shakespeare did, particularly since Burghley's son, Robert Cecil, was a powerful man himself and no friend of Bacon. A great peer like Oxford might have gotten away with mocking Burghley. It is not something that the careful, ambitious Bacon was likely to try, even though Burghley was married to his aunt. Similarly, it seems most unlikely that Bacon would have written the deposition scene in *Richard II* that so enraged the queen.

Some contemporaries evidently believed that Bacon wrote *Venus and Adonis* and *The Rape of Lucrece*. Joseph Hall criticized the author of these poems. John Marsden replied, indicating, by the use of Bacon's motto in a cryptic line, that he understood Hall's criticism to be an attack on Bacon. Curiously, what both Hall and Marsden wrote was suppressed and burned by order of the archbishop of Canterbury, which suggests that someone quite powerful was annoyed.

The somewhat self-effacing tone of the dedications to Southampton seem to fit Bacon's status and position better than that of Southampton's fellow earls Oxford, Stanley, or Rutland.

A huge mural depicting the last scene of *Venus and Adonis* was uncovered on the walls of an inn near Bacon's home. Some Baconians make much of this, and claim that the room was the meeting place for a secret society—probably Rosicrucian—of which Bacon was the leader. This is not impossible; but the claim goes far beyond what is warranted by the evidence. *Venus and Adonis* was a highly popular work. The fact that it was the subject of a painting on a wall near Bacon's home is not significant evidence that Bacon wrote the poem.

A curious document was discovered in 1867 in the London residence of the duke of Northumberland. On the torn and faded cover sheet of some old manuscript pages were scribblings in at least two hands. Some of the writing was upside down in relation to the rest, and much of it was jumbled, incomplete, and, to some extent, indecipherable. Bacon's name is at the top right-hand side of the cover sheet, followed by what appears to be a list of the items that were once attached to the cover sheet. Some of these items were no longer there when the document was found.

The words *By Mr. ffrancis* and *By Mr. ffrancis Bacon* and *Bacon* are repeated over and over again at random places on the cover page interspersed at random with other words and names, such as *Thomas*, which is repeated four times, along with *Thom Thom* and *Thomas Nashe*.

After one of the scribblings of *By Mr. ffrancis Bacon* is a repetition of the word *Bacon*, below which is scrawled what appears to be *Each of it By Mr.* and *mmmf By Mr.*

This strange jumble of words is followed by the words *Essaies by tje sa,e aitjpr* after which is a word that appears to be *printed.* Below this is a space followed by the words *William Shakespeare* and *Shakespeare,* under which is the following list:

> Rychard the second
> ffrauncis
> Rychard the third
> Asmund and Cornelia
> Ille of dogs frmnt

Just to the left of this is another *By Mr. ffrauncis Bacon,* followed by two more repetitions of *Bacon,* some indecipherable words, and a repetition of *Asmund and Cornelia.*

To the right of the list is the word *Thomas,* repeated twice, as well as *Thom Thom.*

Below the list is *By Thomas Nashe,* followed by *William Shakespeare* repeated four times, *Shakspeare* repeated three times, *Shak* three times, *Sh* four times, *Wm* twice, and *Will* once. All of these are scattered and scrawled at random near the bottom of the page.

The cover sheet also contains an inaccurate repetition of a line from *The Rape of Lucrece,* plus an erroneous version of Shakespeare's famous long word, rendered here as *Honorificabilertudine.* The actual word, uttered by Costard in act 5, scene 1 of *Love's Labour's Lost,* is *honorificabilitudinitatibus.*

Baconians conclude from this jumble of scrawled words that the writer was revealing Shakespeare's true identity as "ffrauncis Bacon." They are reading far too much into the hopelessly ambiguous scribbling. It is more likely just the random doodling of someone thinking at the time of Bacon, Shakespeare, and Nashe.

Bacon loved cryptology, invented a sophisticated code, and wrote a book on the subject. It would be reasonable to believe that, if Bacon wrote the poems and plays under Shakespeare's name, he might have left a coded clue to his own authorship. For decades, amateur and professional cryptologists have attempted to find anagrams or cryptograms in Shakespeare that amount to such a clue. Some, aided by a great deal of wishful thinking, have claimed success. But they find their clue only by leaving out letters or words or they come up with highly ambiguous messages that might have nothing to do with Bacon. So far, none of the Baconian cryptological proof is compelling. By employing the same subjective methodology to the vast Shakespeare canon, one could find "clues" suggesting that the author was virtually anyone from Babe Ruth to Mao Tse Tung.

Baconians also claim that the Droeshout engraving of Shakespeare spells out the initials of Francis Bacon. Just as I am unable to see a mask in this portrait, I cannot discern Bacon's initials. These are the kinds of assertions that tend to discredit the Baconian position. But there are legitimate arguments for Bacon's authorship and, while his candidacy has fewer proponents today than in the past, it can, by no means, be disregarded.

Neither Bacon nor Oxford ever mentioned William Shakespeare despite his renown as a playwright. This is particularly odd in the case of Bacon, who wrote volumes of nonfiction, was quite interested in drama and theatrical works, and lived for years after Oxford's death, giving him far greater opportunity to become familiar with Shakespeare's works.

We have seen that Ben Jonson had some unkind things to say about Shakespeare until around 1620. It was around that time that Jonson became a close associate of Bacon. In 1620, Jonson was living with Bacon at Gorhamsbury and became his literary assistant. From about that point on, we find no further slurs from Jonson about Shakespeare. We do find in Jonson extraordinary praise of Bacon, such as: "He who hath filled up all numbers, and performed that in our tongue which may be compared or preferred either to *insolent Greece or haughty Rome* . . . so that he may be named and stand as the mark and acme of our language."

Now compare what Jonson said about Shakespeare in heaping lavish praise on the Bard in the introduction to the First Folio. After referring to Shakespeare as "Soul of the age; the greatest writer of ancient or modern time," Jonson says, "Leave thee alone for the comparison of all that *insolent Greece or haughty Rome* sent forth. . . ."

Here again, having used the comparison to "insolent Greece or haughty Rome" in praising Bacon, Jonson uses the very same words in praising Shakespeare. Either Jonson—an extraordinarily articulate writer with a large vocabulary—found himself unable to come up with words to praise Shakespeare different from those he had already used to praise Bacon, or he had forgotten using those words before, or—dare we say it?—he considered them the same man. The last may be possible, but it seems the least likely explanation.

In 1637, Jonson went on to say about Shakespeare: "I loved him this side of idolatry as much as any." This about the man he had treated so disparagingly in so many of his earlier writings.

What happened in or around 1620 to change the earlier insults into the overblown praise of the later years? Did Jonson change his mind about Shakespeare? Was he paid to change his mind? Whichever is the case, why did it happen? If he changed his mind, was it because he came to know and respect Bacon and learned that Bacon *was* Shakespeare?

There are certainly similarities of philosophy and even schematic thought between Bacon and Shakespeare. In fact, there are points on which Shakespeare changed his thinking, as and when Bacon did. For example, in *Hamlet*, probably written in the very early 1600s, the playwright indicates a belief in the moon's controlling the tides. All the quarto editions of *Hamlet* make the same point. This was also Bacon's view, as set out in his early writings. In 1616, however, Bacon changed that view. In *De Fluxo et Refluxo Maris*, he reversed his thinking on the point.

In 1623, in the First Folio version of *Hamlet*, Shakespeare's earlier view of the relationship between the tides and the moon is abandoned, just as Bacon abandoned the same theory.

Does this prove that Shakespeare *was* Bacon? By no means. It does, however, appear to prove *some* things. Seemingly, Oxford couldn't have made the change in *Hamlet* to reflect Bacon's revised view published in 1616. Oxford died in 1604. If he wrote *Hamlet* before his death, someone apparently revised it later, after seeing Bacon's changed version. The Stratford man died in 1616, but earlier in the year than Bacon's revised *De Fluxo* was published. Although he might have seen a prepublication copy out in Stratford, it seems unlikely. The 1623 revision in the play as it appeared in the First Folio may have been to conform to Bacon's thinking. But this doesn't mean the reviser *was* Bacon. It could have been Jonson. He was heavily involved with creation of the First Folio and he was certainly an admirer of Bacon.

There are lines of Shakespeare that are strikingly similar to lines written by Bacon. We have already talked about the reference in Sonnet 76 to keeping "invention in a noted weed," meaning garment. And we have Bacon writing, "I have in a despised weed, procured the good of all men." Since *weed* was a word that, if not commonly used, was at least known in Elizabethan times, its use by two different writers would not be extraordinary.

But Bacon made a series of entries in a work called *The Promus of Formularies and Elegancies*, a work now in the British Museum. This was a collection of phrases and humorous lines that evidently appealed to him. Over and over again, the same or very similar lines appear in Shakespeare. Thus, for example:

A fool's bolt is soon shot. (Bacon, *Promus*)
A fool's bolt is soon shot. (Shakespeare, *Henry V*)

Seldom cometh the better. (Bacon, *Promus*)
Seldom cometh the better. (Shakespeare, *Richard III*)

All is not gold that glisters. (Bacon, *Promus*)
All that glisters is not gold. (Shakespeare, *The Merchant of Venice*)

Make use of thy salt hours (Bacon, *Promus*)
Make use of thy salt hours (Shakespeare, *Timon of Athens*)

Who dissembles is not free. (Bacon, *Promus*)
The dissembler is a slave. (Shakespeare, *Pericles*)

Good wine needs no bush (Bacon, *Promus*)
Good wine needs no bush (Shakespeare, *As You Like It*)

Thought is free. (Bacon, *Promus*)
Thought is free. (Shakespeare, *The Tempest*)

Is this coincidence? Did Shakespeare steal from Bacon's notebook? Did Bacon note phrases in Shakespeare that caught his fancy?

None of these explanations is totally satisfying. The last seems unlikely, since dates on Bacon's *Promus* indicate that it was written between early December 1594 and the end of January 1595, before publication or recorded performance of the Shakespearean works that used the same or similar phrases. Of course, as we have said, those plays could have been written at an earlier time and not published or even performed without the performance's being noted.

What is also possible is that Bacon and Shakespeare took the same phrases from the same sources. Frequently, two or even more writers in this period used the same phrase, and a common source was often the most likely explanation.

Did Bacon have the motivation to pretend that someone else wrote the Shakespeare canon if he was the true author? Yes; as an ambitious lawyer and politician, he would not have wanted the queen (or, later, King James) to see him at least publicly known as the author of plays for the common theatre.

But what of the First Folio? If Bacon wrote the Shakespeare canon, Ben Jonson must have known it. Would Bacon have participated in a ruse to perpetuate the notion that Shakespeare was the Stratford man? Certainly, if it served his interests. Would Bacon have had the wealth and influence to carry out a hoax on that scale? Possibly, if he had the cooperation of Southampton's family, seeking to fend off any inference of a homosexual relationship between Bacon and the young earl that might be drawn from the sonnets.

Of all the candidates, Bacon has been considered the most celebrated thinker and philosopher, one who best fits the thoughts expressed in the Shakespeare canon and the sublime manner in which "Shakespeare" expressed them.

Listen, for example, to what Emerson said of Bacon:

Let Bacon speak and wise men would rather listen though
the revolution of the Kingdoms was on foot. . . .

FRANCIS BACON ✠ 259

> The book of Lord Bacon that gets out of libraries . . . is
> his Essays. Few books ever written contain so much wis-
> dom and will bear to be read so many times. . . . They are
> clothed in a style of such splendor that imaginative per-
> sons find sufficient delight in the beauty of expression. . . .
> . . . It is the survey of a superior being, so commanding, so
> prescient as if the great chart of the intellectual world lay
> open before him.

No one ever said such things about Oxford, Marlowe, Stanley, Rutland,
or any other candidate for the Shakespeare authorship. Certainly, no one
said anything comparable about the Stratford man—unless one can consider Jonson's praise in the First Folio to be a comparable paean.

And listen to Shelly:

> Lord Bacon was a poet. His language has a sweet and ma-
> jestical rhythm which satisfies the sense no less than the
> almost super-human wisdom of his philosophy satisfies
> the intellect.

Yet James Spedding, the nineteenth-century authority on Bacon, who
wrote fourteen volumes on Bacon's life and works, was positive that his
writing style was so markedly different from Shakespeare's that it was impossible for Bacon to have been the Bard. Of course, despite his many years
of Bacon scholarship, Spedding may not have been an expert on writing
styles. And most of Bacon's writings were nonfiction and prose, while
Shakespeare wrote fiction and poetry. Naturally, this makes their styles
somewhat difficult to compare.

There are some striking aspects of Shakespeare's works that distinguish
him from other writers of the time. As we have said, Shakespeare's characters, unlike those of earlier dramatists, are not black or white, not all good
or all bad. His heroes are usually flawed, like Hamlet. His villains, while
committing dark deeds, have an understandable side—like Shylock. We
comprehend the reason for their wrongdoing, even in such archvillains as
Richard III.

Moreover, good and bad things happen, not because of the gods or bad
fortune, but because of the actions of the characters themselves. They bear
the responsibility for their own acts and suffer their consequences.

These are modern concepts, extremely advanced for a sixteenth-century writer. Which of the candidates reflects this kind of thinking? Probably Bacon more than any of the rest. And, unlike Oxford and Marlowe, Bacon has no problem with the dating of the plays. He lived long enough to have written everything in the First Folio.

Could Bacon have written all or a substantial part of "Shakespeare's" work? Certainly. Do we have anything that approaches proof of this? Certainly not. Can we rule him out? By no means.

23.

WILLIAM STANLEY, EARL OF DERBY

Stanley has enjoyed considerable support as the true Bard, particularly among the French. He was born in 1561, descended from a distinguished family famous for switching from side to side in the Wars of the Roses and for considering family advancement above all else. His great-great-great-grandfather was the Stanley who betrayed Richard III at the Battle of Bosworth Field and crowned Henry Tudor Henry VII after the battle. Stanley was also a great-great-great-grandson of Henry VII himself, his mother having been a direct descendant of that first Tudor king.

Stanley was educated at Oxford and studied law at Lincoln's Inn. He was widely traveled, visiting at least France, Italy, and Spain. He married Oxford's daughter (the one rejected by Southampton).

Acting companies regularly performed at the Stanley family home; and Stanley appeared in private performances as an amateur actor. There is evidence that he even wrote plays for the public theatre but concealed his authorship. In June 1595, a Jesuit spy reported to his superiors that Stanley was busy writing comedies for common players. No such works ever appeared under his own name.

In 1594, Edmund Spenser wrote a poem celebrating various writers, mostly with disguised names. Two of those mentioned were Stanley's just deceased brother Ferdinando and his widow. Just after those two, Spenser mentioned another writer called "Aetion," whom he described as "last" but "not least," and as a "gentle shepherd." This may (or may not) have been a reference to the author of the Shakespeare canon. At the time, "gentle" often meant "of noble birth," and that was certainly not true of the Stratford man. Here, once again, we come to family crests. *Aetion* is Greek for "man of the eagle," and the Stanley crest featured an eagle holding a child. It was a family legend that the Stanleys were descended from a child that had been abducted by an eagle. The Eagle Tower was a part of the Stanley family home, which was sometimes called the "Eagle's Nest."

It is quite probable that, by "Aetion," Spenser meant Stanley. But it does not follow that he was saying that Stanley was Shakespeare. Writing in 1594, a fairly early date in terms of Shakespeare's career, Spenser may have considered Stanley an author deserving of mention, while overlooking or deliberately omitting the Bard. "Aetion" may well have been Stanley, but Stanley may still not have been Shakespeare.

There is, however, other evidence supporting Stanley's candidacy. In 1610, John Davies, a close friend of Stanley, wrote his poem dedicated to "our English Terence, Mr. Will Shake-speare." We have already discussed the claim that "Terence" allowed other writers to use his name on works they did not wish to acknowledge publicly. If that claim is true, the reference to "our English Terence" could describe someone who "fronted" for Stanley, since he apparently wrote poems or plays that were never published under his own name. But the same could be said about Oxford, Bacon, and other candidates.

Davies's poem seems to refer to "Shake-speare" in the present tense, indicating that he was still alive. Stanley was (he died in 1642). Oxford was dead. So was Queen Elizabeth and (maybe) Marlowe. But Stanley, Bacon, and the Stratford man were still alive. Stanley's name, of course, fits the "Will" sonnets, and his initials were "W. S.," like those of the "old player" from *Willowbie His Avisa.* We do not know how the "fair youth" or the "dark lady" sonnets square with his life.

Many scenes in Shakespeare's plays are set in the area in which Stanley was raised, and the household books of Stanley's family show the retention of a "falconer" on the permanent household staff and record the enthusiasm of Stanley and his brother Ferdinando for hunting and hawking.

The French Stanleyites point out that *Love's Labour's Lost* is a perfect embodiment of French aristocratic conversation of that age; and, as we have said, the play follows events that had occurred in the court of Navarre during the reign of Henri of Navarre, who later became Henri IV of France. The characters are similar to actual characters at that court at that time. The play is thought to have been written in 1591. The Stratford man was only twenty-seven. It is probable that he had been in London only a few years. It is most unlikely that he could have acquired the knowledge of the language, manners, characters, and events necessary to write the play.

Stanley, however, was in Europe at about the right time. The French Stanleyites assert that Stanley was actually in Navarre in that period and that he wrote the play based on what he actually heard and saw there.

There is another element in the play that may support Stanley's candidacy. Holofernes, the pedantic schoolmaster in *Love's Labour's Lost*, seems to have been based on Stanley's stiff and unwelcome traveling companion, Richard Lloyd. In the play, Holofernes writes, in all seriousness, a silly, stilted masque called "The Nine Worthies." This is performed for the other characters, who laughingly deride it. The real Lloyd had actually written a boring, pedantic work by that very title. It seems fairly clear that Shakespeare was satirizing Lloyd and his masque in *Love's Labour's Lost*.

This, of course, does not prove that Stanley wrote the play. He may have jokingly described Lloyd and "The Nine Worthies" to the true author. If so, the author was probably someone of Stanley's own class—someone, for example, like Stanley's father-in-law Oxford or his family lawyer Bacon. It is difficult to imagine Lord Stanley making fun of his traveling companion to a common actor from Stratford.

According to the Stanleyites, *Hamlet* also owes a debt to the court of Navarre (and Stanley's assumed visit there). Helene, a young girl at the court, had a tragic love story quite similar to that of Ophelia. Stanley could have heard the story. So, of course, could Bacon or Oxford or maybe even the Stratford man.

The Tempest is urged as another tie to Stanley. "Ferdinand," son of the king of Naples, is supposedly, in one place, actually written as "Ferdinando," the name of Stanley's brother, who was the hereditary ruler of the Isle of Man. Some believe that a small island nearby was the setting for the play. *The Tempest* treats mysticism and the occult in a generally favorable way; and these were matters that intrigued Stanley.

Stanley's older brother Ferdinando was a Catholic sympathizer. As a direct descendant of Henry VII, he was also a prime candidate to succeed to the throne on Elizabeth's death. He was, accordingly, regarded with great mistrust by Burghley, a staunch Protestant, and by others of like mind surrounding the queen. Ferdinando died at 35, apparently the victim of arsenic poisoning. There is considerable dispute as to whether he was killed by the Catholics for having betrayed a Catholic agent to clear himself of suspicion, or was killed by agents of Burghley, so that Stanley could inherit Ferdinando's title and estates and then marry Burghley's granddaughter.

It has been reported that Ferdinando attempted unsuccessfully to disinherit Stanley, possibly because he was less sympathetic to Catholics, or possibly because, as George Carey rather nastily put it, in a letter to his wife, Stanley was a "nidicock" (i.e., a fool).

Carey was not without bias in the matter, however. His wife's sister, Ferdinando's widow, would have received a vast inheritance if Ferdinando had succeeded in disinheriting his brother. Besides, Carey suffered from syphilis, and may have had his own problems with mental acuity. A contemporary rhyme about him contains the lines:

> Quicksilver is in his head,
> But his wit's dull as lead.

Supporting this view is the fact that, in the same letter to his wife, Carey tells her that Ferdinando died not only of poisoning, but also of "witchcraft and enchantment." He adds the probably false and certainly malicious gossip that Southampton's mother was about to marry the vice chamberlain and that both had "the pox" (gonorrhea).

Obviously, the works of Shakespeare were not written by a "nidicock." But then we cannot assume that Stanley was one just because Carey said so.

Certainly, there is cogent evidence supporting Stanley's candidacy. As in the other cases, however, it is far from conclusive.

24.

ROGER MANNERS, EARL OF RUTLAND

Rutland is an intriguing but less popular candidate. He may have played some part in creating the characters and events in *Hamlet*. Other, more debatable factors can also be construed as supporting his candidacy.

Rutland was born at Belvoir, the Manners family estate, on October 6, 1576. He was well educated, spending seven years at Cambridge starting in 1587. He certainly had the opportunity to learn the "inside" Cambridge terms that appear in Shakespeare. Rutland's father died in February 1588, when Rutland was still only eleven. The young man became a royal ward, and, as in the case of Southampton, Burghley was appointed his guardian. Most of the guardianship duties, however, were carried out by Burghley's nephew, Francis Bacon.

Rutland traveled widely in Europe for five years, including many parts of Italy. His knowledge of things Italian was enhanced by attending the University of Padua, where he enrolled in 1596. His family's library at Belvoir contained a vast collection of books, including many rare volumes used in Shakespeare's works. Rutland studied at the Inns of Court and would have acquired sufficient knowledge of the law and legal terminology to have written the Shakespearean plays. He also played tennis and so knew the tennis terms used in *Henry V*, act 1, scene 1. He frequently engaged in hunting and falconry and so met that requirement as well.

Rutland saw active military service, primarily in Essex's Irish campaign. He participated in the attack on Cohir Castle, which resembled the siege of Honfleur as portrayed by Shakespeare in *Henry V*, apparently written in the same year as the Cohir attack, 1599.

Rutland was associated with Essex at the time of his rebellion. He confessed, implicating Essex and others. His own role was fairly slight. He was not one of the conspirators and had no advance knowledge of the rebellion. Evidently, he believed that Essex was in danger of being assassinated by his rivals and intended not only to help defend him, but to implore the queen to intercede on his behalf. Although freed from the Tower, he was fined £30,000 by Elizabeth—a huge sum.

Given Elizabeth's efficient security service, it is most unlikely that she was ignorant of Shakespeare's true identity. One explanation for why the author of *Richard II* was not singled out for punishment, like the authors of other "dangerous" writings, is that he had already been punished under a different name. Did the £30,000 fine imposed on Rutland include punishment for writing the royally unacceptable play?

Rutland was friendly with the earls of Southampton (Henry Wriothesley) and Pembroke (William Herbert). If he was Shakespeare, this might explain the dedications in *Venus and Adonis* and *The Rape of Lucrece*, as well as "Mr. W. H." of the sonnets.

If Rutland authored *Venus and Adonis*, he was only sixteen when it was published, and younger still when it was written. Indeed, at least fourteen of Shakespeare's plays were written before Rutland was twenty. This may seem unlikely, but it's certainly not impossible. Mozart, Byron, Raphael, and other prodigies have accomplished similar and perhaps even greater feats at very early ages.

The sonnets are more difficult. They were written when Rutland would have been twenty-two, maybe even earlier. Yet, as we have seen, they appear to be the musings of a much older, mature man, directed to a much younger man. Rutland would seem far too young; and, if Southampton was the "lovely youth," he was older, not younger, than Rutland. Rutland would seem possible as the poet only if the sonnets were fiction or merely poetic exercises unrelated to actual people and events.

Rutland's family home contained a fresco copy of Correggio's *Io and Jupiter*. The original painting was in Milan. Shakespeare refers to this painting in *The Taming of the Shrew*. This does not tell us that Rutland was

Shakespeare. Possibly, the author saw the painting in Milan or at Rutland's home, or he may simply have heard it described.

There is, however, a connection with *Hamlet* that might give us pause. In the reign of James I, Rutland was appointed a special ambassador to Denmark, where he visited the castle at Helsingör (Elsinore). Between the original and the final version of *Hamlet*, alterations were made to the text to make the names of characters fit actual Danish names and to make the references to Danish places and scenes more accurate. Assuming that Rutland was the source of this information, however, it does not follow that he wrote *Hamlet*. Someone else with less knowledge of Denmark may have originally written the play and then received help from Rutland in revising and correcting it.

John Michell, who has written a generally excellent book on the Shakespeare authorship question, discusses the studies made by "the most learned of the Rutlanders, Célestin Demblon." Michell tells us of Demblon's unique findings:

> At Padua University Demblon made a striking discovery. Rutland studied there during his Italian tour, and in the same register that records his entry on 28 March 1596 are the names of his two Danish fellow-students, Rosencrantz and Guildenstern.

Striking indeed! But incorrect. The university records are still there in Padua. Rutland is in the register for March 28, 1596, just as Michell and Demblon report. But there is no sign of Rosencrantz or Guildenstern—not then, or at any time ten years before or after Rutland. There were Rosencrantzes and Gyldenstjernes among the sixteenth-century students at the University of Wittenberg, where Shakespeare tells us Hamlet studied. But they are not in the records at Padua. And there is no record of Rutland's having studied at Wittenberg.

Other facets of Rutland's life fit the pattern of Shakespeare's plays. Despite his release from the Tower, Rutland continued in disfavor with Elizabeth after Essex's rebellion. He would never regain his status at court until the queen's death in 1603, which might explain Shakespeare's silence on that momentous event—if Stanley was Shakespeare. James I, who sometimes regarded those disfavored by Elizabeth as potential supporters, forgave Rutland and treated him honorably.

Nevertheless, Rutland went through a period of worry and melancholy.

Like Timon of Athens, his financial condition had become precarious. His marriage had become something of a sham (possibly, he was impotent). Like Othello, he may have been filled with jealousy. According to Jonson, a handsome courtier, Sir Thomas Overbry was in love with Lady Rutland. Rutland's health had never been good since he suffered a severe illness (probably malaria) in Italy. Now, it worsened.

In this period, Shakespeare seemed to move away from fairly light-hearted crowd-pleasing comedies toward tragedies steeped in melancholy, treachery, and violence. If traditional dating is accepted, he turned to plays like *Othello*, *Macbeth*, and *King Lear*. Yet, nothing in the life of the Stratford man suggested such a change in his outlook at that point in time, unless it was his fortieth birthday. But there seems no evidence that merely turning forty wrought any such dramatic change.

When Shakespeare wrote *The Tempest*, there were indications that he was tired and ill and that he anticipated—possibly even embraced—death. E.K. Chambers points out that, toward the end of the play, "the weary magician drowns his book and buries his staff certain fathoms deep in the earth." At the end, Prospero tells us "Every third thought shall be my grave."

Rutland died on June 26, 1612, after a long illness. Most scholars believe that none of Shakespeare's plays were written after this, although work may have been done by others on *Henry VIII*, a play which Shakespeare may have started before that.

The Stratford man basically retired to Stratford around 1612. Was that because, with the death of Rutland, his fronting arrangement was over? He lived on until 1616. Were no plays written after 1612 because the real Shakespeare was dead? Possibly, but it is equally arguable that, in 1612, the aging Stratford man simply decided to retire and stop writing plays.

On Rutland's death, his brother Francis Manners succeeded to the title. He was the earl of Rutland whose records showed a 1613 payment to "William Shakespeare" and "Richard Burbage" with respect to the new earl's impresa. It is not inconceivable that Francis, knowing of a long relationship between his deceased brother and the Stratford man, called upon the actor to bring his knowledge of scenery and set decoration to bear upon the creation of the impresa. While there is evidence supporting Rutland's candidacy, the evidence seems considerably less compelling than that supporting the candidacy of his rivals.

25.

QUEEN ELIZABETH

*T*he queen is not a very likely candidate, but her candidacy is great fun. She certainly had the education and background to have been the author, although we might quibble about the use of Cantabrigian terms. She was totally familiar with the classics and was fluent in Greek, Latin, and a number of European languages.

She wrote poetry that was quite good and loved plays. She had a strong motive to keep her authorship concealed. Most of her subjects would have considered it quite unseemly for the queen to write plays for the public theatre.

Dr. Lillian Schwartz, an expert in computer matching of faces, had worked on the similarities between the Droeshout etching of Shakespeare in the First Folio and portraits of others. Running the image of Elizabeth and Droeshout's Shakespeare through her computer they came out the same, feature for feature, except for the beard. Shakespeare's face, Dr. Schwartz said, was that of the queen.

George Elliot Sweet has written an entire book devoted to the theory that Elizabeth was the great Bard. It has been argued that the queen wrote the "fair youth" sonnets about Essex, with whom she appears to have been in love (or at least infatuated). She was much older than he, and that fits. The sonnets refer to the author's lameness, which could mean Elizabeth's rumored sexual infirmity or, given her age, some other debilitating condition. Sonnet 20, which punningly refers to God's having "pricked thee out" with something that is of no use to the author, suggests a male author and a nonsexual relationship. But, here again, it could refer to the queen's sexual dysfunction—if she had such a condition.

Sonnet 76 includes the line "Why write I all still one, ever the same." This is one of the lines cited by the Oxfordians in support of their case. But, in Latin, "ever the same" is *semper eadem*, which was Elizabeth's motto.

It has been suggested that the "dark lady" sonnets, describing a devious but compelling woman, refer to Lettice Knollys, the queen's cousin. Elizabeth despised Lettice for secretly marrying Leicester—the queen's dear "Robin"—and then being unfaithful to him. But that would eliminate Essex as the fair youth, since the young man of the sonnets has an affair with the dark lady and Essex was Lettice's son. Sonnet 151 expresses the poet's physical lust for the dark lady in obviously masculine terms, which do not fit Elizabeth at all.

If Essex was the fair youth of the sonnets, Lettice would, instead of the dark lady, be the "mother" referred to when the poet says the youth's face recalls "the lovely April of [his] mother's prime." But writing that would also seem inconsistent with Elizabeth's feelings of resentment toward Lettice.

The "Will" sonnets also pose a problem for those who argue the queen's authorship. Oxford, although a non-William, at least had "Willy" as a nickname. Elizabeth did not. No one appears to have called the great queen "Willie" or "Will" or anything similar.

Another impediment to the queen's authorship is the fact that a number of the plays became known only after Elizabeth's death in 1603. Of course, as in the case of Oxford, they could have been written earlier or could have been unfinished at her death but completed later by others.

More telling, however, is the scene in Richard II that portrayed the deposition of a reigning monarch. Elizabeth deplored and suppressed that scene. It seems inconceivable that she would have written it. And Shakespeare makes some unkind comments about virginity in *All's Well That Ends Well* and again in *A Midsummer Night's Dream* that are most unlikely to have been written by the queen.

Of course, Shakespeare's strange silence on the queen's death could be taken to support Elizabeth's cause. Had the Bard died with the queen?

Was it the queen who resented Greene's vitriolic attack on "Shake-scene," this "upstart crow"? Was it she who forced Henrye Chettle, the printer, to issue an abject apology? If so, why? Was she "Shakespeare"?

When Christopher Marlowe was about to be denied his degree from Cambridge on the ground that he had been absent too long from his studies, someone very important interceded with the university and got Marlowe his degree. Was that important person Elizabeth? Had Marlowe's demonstrable absences been the result of his working with the queen on early plays? More likely, the government interceded because Marlowe had been working abroad as an effective English spy.

Notwithstanding the asserted similarity of her face to that of an un-bearded Bard, if we limit ourselves to the facts we actually know, the case for the great queen's being the sole or even the primary author of the Shakespeare canon is not a strong one. Still, it has been seriously contended that she was. As Hemingway put it in the final lines of *The Sun Also Rises*, "Isn't it pretty to think so?"

26.

GROUP AND COLLABORATION THEORIES

The concept of a group of co-authors creating the Shakespeare canon is flexible enough to fit the known facts and is emotionally satisfying. The motivation is there—writing plays would likely have been seen by the public as unseemly for such distinguished people, and having a conspiracy to keep a relatively harmless secret might have been seen as fun.

The stupendous vocabulary, many times that of highly educated men of the times, argues for more than one person as the author.

There are strong indications, set out in Brian Vickers's well-reasoned book, that some plays, such as *Titus Andronicus*, *Timon of Athens*, *Henry VIII*, and *Pericles*, contain significant contributions by more than one playwright. As we have seen, other plays seem to involve more than one creator not so much because of the writing style, but seemingly from the author's philosophy—his point of view.

And there is the sometimes uneven quality and mood of the sonnets. Some are seemingly written for momentary amusement, filled with puns and puckishness. Others seem to bare the poet's soul. Others are bawdy in tone. Are they the work of one person of changing moods, or the product of a group, a collaboration, with each collaborator in turn providing a sonnet for the other's enjoyment or even for the others to read and revise?

The idea of a group of highborn friends gathering to write the works of

Shakespeare is an appealing one. We can imagine Bacon, Oxford, Stanley, and Rutland—even Marlowe—gathering in secret with the queen, assigning tasks between them, exchanging drafts and enjoying themselves immensely, while fooling the public by feeding their combined work to the actor from Stratford, quite ready to take payment for posing as the poet and playwright.

The group concept would explain why there seem to be things in and about Shakespeare that, at least arguably, relate to each of these people.

The problem is that, with so many participants, it would seem virtually impossible to have kept the secret. And there is not a shred of evidence—not a hint anywhere—that such a group ever met and wrote anything.

On the other hand, two such authors sharing the secret and joining in creation of the Shakespeare canon is easier to accept. One plausible combination is Oxford and Stanley, using the Stratford man as a front to market their product. We know that Stanley married Oxford's daughter, and the two noblemen-writers became not only family but friends. Did they work together on the plays, with Stanley going on after Oxford's death in 1604 to finish the plays they had started together and perhaps to start new ones on his own? Stanley had plenty of time to do that. He lived until 1642.

But if Stanley was writing new plays after 1604, why did he stop in 1623 with the publication of the First Folio? If the Oxford family was in favor of perpetuating the idea that the Stratford man was the sole author of the plays, it seems likely that Stanley would have joined with Oxford's other son-in-law Montgomery and Montgomery's brother Pembroke in fostering that myth. If so, Stanley probably would have ceased writing *more* plays after the First Folio to avoid exposing the scheme.

Oxford and Stanley had another thing in common, besides nobility, wealth, education, travel, talent, and a relationship through marriage. Their families had combined to provide Elizabeth's grandfather Henry Tudor with an upset victory in 1485 at Bosworth Field. That triumph over Richard III put Henry on the throne and created the Tudor dynasty. It was an earl of Oxford that led the Tudor forces (mostly French, Scots, and Welshmen) who fought their way up Ambion Hill, pushing Richard's loyal men back and forcing Richard to take a desperate gamble.

Riding headlong across the field toward Henry Tudor, Richard intended to engage Henry in individual combat, and to kill him, ending the battle with a single stroke. Richard was a noted warrior, Henry was not.

Unfortunately for Richard, just before he reached Henry, the numerous red-jacketed troops of Sir William Stanley crashed on Richard's right flank, overwhelming and killing him.

Sir William and his brother, following Stanley family tradition, had promised both Richard and Henry Tudor their support and had stood aside while the fighting progressed, waiting to see how the battle went before taking a side. When it was over, it was Lord Stanley who placed the crown on Henry's head, making him Henry VII.

This may seem like ancient history, but it was not so remote to Queen Elizabeth. Her grandfather's claim to the throne had been an extremely weak one, and Richard III had assembled a larger force than Henry's. He was a skilled military leader, and he occupied the high ground on Ambion Hill when the battle started. Elizabeth was well aware that she owed her crown, and indeed her life, to the forebearers of Oxford and Stanley and what they did on that fateful summer day in 1485. This may have played a part in her overlooking Oxford's "mistakes," her generosity to him, and her willingness to forgive even the writing of *Richard II*.

A collaboration between Oxford and Stanley could make sense. But, the combination could have been Oxford and Bacon or Bacon and Stanley, or there may have been no such collaboration at all.

Part IV

SUMMING UP

✠

27.

SUMMING UP

*H*aving considered the evidence for and against the Stratford man and each of the major alternative candidates, what can we conclude?

First, we must acknowledge that there is no quick, easy, and certain answer. Our conclusion will depend on the interpretation and weight given to the evidence for one side or the other. Like the members of a jury, we must apply our own instincts and judgment to that evidence in deciding which version (actually, which of several versions) is the truth. Like the members of a jury, our conclusions may differ. Notwithstanding the dogmatic assertions of some Stratfordians, these are serious issues.

Second, the Shakespeare canon is, in general, far more consistent with the background, education, experience, and outlook of Oxford, Marlowe, Bacon, and Stanley than with what we know of the Stratford man. If we could but ignore such evidence as Sonnet III, the First Folio, and the Stratford monument, we could feel comfortable in concluding that the great Bard was probably one of those exceptional men.

But, of course, we cannot ignore that evidence. In Sonnet III, Shakespeare complains that, because he was not better provided for by fortune, he has turned to "public means," which lead to "public manners"; this certainly fits with the Stratford man's earning his living in the public theatre.

It could also fit Marlowe or Bacon. Conceivably, even Oxford could have used these self-deprecatory lines as a sort of poetic conceit.

Or, since some of the sonnets were likely intended for publication (otherwise, how would they give the lovely youth "immortality"?), Sonnet 111 could have been a ruse to throw the public off the track and to further the belief that Shakespeare was the actor from Stratford.

Finally, the Stratfordians could be correct that the sonnets are fiction or mere poetic exercises without autobiographical content.

Unquestionably, however, Sonnet 111 must be considered significant evidence for the Stratfordian case.

The First Folio is, of course, even more powerful support for the conclusion that Shakespeare was the Stratford man. Trying to avoid that conclusion by reaching for a strained construction of the language or conjuring up alternative meanings for such phrases as "Sweet Swan of Avon," "Small Latin and less Greek," thy "Buskin" trod "a stage" and "thy Stratford moniment" seems hopelessly unavailing.

Construed as it was almost certainly intended, the First Folio seems plainly to say that Shakespeare, the playwright, was Shakspere, the actor from Stratford-upon-Avon.

That, of course, does not end the matter. Anti-Strats may argue that Jonson, Heminge, and Condell did not know the true identity of the poet and playwright. But this seems virtually impossible.

If there is any answer to the First Folio, it more likely lies in the possibility that the project was a deliberate hoax, designed to confirm and establish forever the false impression that Shakespeare was the Stratford man. There were people with solid motives for perpetrating such a hoax, and they had the influence and the means to bring it off.

If this were a court of law, one could properly argue that a heavy burden must be placed on the anti-Strats to prove that the written statements of otherwise reputable men, accepted for centuries as the truth, were, in fact, a tissue of lies. There is, in law, a presumption against fraud. In many jurisdictions, that presumption can be rebutted only by "clear and convincing evidence."

There is evidence supporting the existence of such a hoax. We have Ben Jonson's prior inconsistent comments on Shakespeare, the large fee he received from an Oxford relative, the powerful motive on the part of the Oxford and Southampton families to create and cement the false impression that Shakespeare was the Stratford man and, of course, all of the other evidence we have examined suggesting that the Stratford man was *not* the great Bard and that one of the other candidates was.

Obviously, if we are convinced by all that other evidence that the Stratford man was definitely *not* Shakespeare, we would necessarily reject the First Folio as a fraud or mistake. But can we say that? It seems the *most* one could reasonably conclude is that, based on all the evidence, he was *probably* not the Bard and that there is *some* evidence consistent with the First Folio's having been concocted to create a false impression. Is that enough? If a jury found that such a hoax was perpetrated, would an appellate court hold the evidence sufficient to affirm their verdict? Probably. But the question is a close one.

Of course, we are not in a court of law. We have far greater latitude to apply our own judgment and human experience to the evidence and to reach our own conclusion—one no appellate court can overturn.

The Stratford monument is another serious obstacle in the path of the anti-Strats. It seems squarely to tie the Bard to the Stratford man. However, the work of Dugdale, Rowe, and Thomas is evidence that the figure originally had no quill and was clutching what looks like a grain bag and that it was subsequently altered—perhaps when "repaired" in 1748—to fit the desire of the city fathers for a more distinguished bust of the great Bard.

Yet we have Vertue's eighteenth-century sketch showing the quill and (strangely) writing on a pillow. Was the alteration made between 1730, when Thomas checked on Dugdale's earlier portrayal, and 1737, when Vertue made his sketch? Or was the quill added from Vertue's imagination and then embodied in the revised monument in 1748?

Of course, even if the figure did have a pen and was writing on a pillow from the beginning, the monument could have been a part of the same hoax as the First Folio.

Here again, a court of law would likely place a strong burden of proof on the anti-Strats to show that the monument was a fraud from its inception. The evidence would essentially be the same as that used to show that the First Folio was bogus, including all the evidence supporting the inference that the Stratford man was not, in fact, Shakespeare.

And what is that evidence? In summarizing it, we might begin with the seemingly vast gap between what we know of the Stratford man and the overwhelming body of varied information and learning, the facility in ancient and modern languages, and the superhuman vocabulary present in the Shakespeare canon.

Yes, some of the anti-Strats' examples are overstated, an unfortunate characteristic of advocacy—even sincere advocacy. But there is still too much in that supreme body of work for one to readily accept that it was the creation of a man who appears to have been a small-minded actor and trader of limited education and experience. The cry of "genius" seems an unpersuasive response, as does the claim that all of this is the product of a fine grammar school education, plus diligent research.

Despite the struggle of the Stratfordians to glorify the learning in the Stratford grammar school in the 1570s (assuming that the Stratford man ever attended the school and that he completed its curriculum), that limited education and what we know about the Stratford man's experience cannot be squared with the gigantic vocabulary and immense body of diverse knowledge manifested in the Shakespeare canon.

There is also the question of outlook, of Shakespeare's view of life and people. While Shakespeare might not be the first great artist whose actual life and attitudes were at variance with the expression of his art, it remains difficult to reconcile the litigious small-town land and grain speculator, striving to be deemed a "gentleman," with the soaring humanity, extraordinary sensitivity, and revulsion at hypocrisy and pretense found in Shakespeare's body of work.

More evidence lies in the matter of the Stratford man's writing—if, in fact, he could write more than his own name. Often, rural men in the sixteenth century learned to sign their names but nothing else. We have seen the six awkward, childish signatures of the Stratford man. We might have explained the three on his will as the result of the illness that led to his death. But his signature on his deposition in *Belott v. Mountjoy* was made in 1612, when he was apparently in good health. Yet it is even shakier and more uncertain than those on his will. The two signatures on the Blackfriars gatehouse documents are scarcely better than the one on the deposition.

We also have the comment of William Beestow, son of a fellow actor, that, "if invited to writ, he was in paine."

How do we reconcile this evidence with Shakespeare's having written by hand thirty-six plays, 154 sonnets, and two long narrative poems? The reconciliation becomes even more difficult when we consider Ben Jonson's comment that "players have often mentioned it as an honour to Shakespeare that in his writing (whatsoever he penned) he never blotted out a line."

And we have no report—none at all, even second- or thirdhand—of anyone who claims ever to have seen the Stratford man, in his entire lifetime, writing anything at all. How is that possible?

Nor do we have anything that we know is his writing. There may be explanations for the absence of all the manuscripts. But where are the letters we would expect of the amazingly articulate Shakespeare? If he was the Stratford man, where are the letters to his wife, his beloved daughter Susanna, his son-in-law John Hall, his friends and associates in Stratford, or his "ffellows" in London?

Every inch of Stratford and London has been scoured for centuries by scholars and researchers seeking any scrap of paper the man ever wrote. Evidently, not a scrap exists; and it would not be unreasonable to conclude that not a scrap ever existed, or that, if the Stratford man left writings of any kind, someone set out to eliminate them.

The will also creates problems for the Stratfordians. There are certain plausible explanations for why literary property or the interests in the two theatres might not be mentioned. But these are merely reasonable suppositions. Given the nature of the man and of the will, these omissions are, at the very least, suspicious.

And, if Shakespeare was the Stratford man, why do Henslowe's records fail to list any payment to him for his plays, at least some of which played at Henslowe's Rose?

And what of the childish doggerel on his tombstone? Perhaps it is worth considering again:

> Good frend for Jesus sake forbeare
> to digg the dust enclosed heare!
> Bleste be ye man yt spares thes stones,
> And curst be he yt moves my bones.

Is this the great Bard?

Nor have the Stratfordians dealt convincingly with the sonnets' dedication to "our ever-living poet"—manifestly a reference to someone already dead, but considered "immortal" because of his works. The Stratford man was very much alive at the time, while Oxford and Marlowe were dead (or, in Marlowe's case, perhaps pretending to be). That the poet was dead is also suggested by the fact that someone else wrote the dedication and that the publication was entitled *Shake-speare's Sonnets*, suggesting there would be no more.

Similarly, the failure of Shakespeare to speak out at the death of the queen in 1603 or that of the prince of Wales in 1612 might suggest that he was no longer alive or that, as an aristocrat, not publicly perceived as the famous poet and playwright, he felt free to express his feelings on these events privately, in his own name, or not to express them at all.

Even more telling is the fact that, despite the fame Shakespeare had achieved by 1616, no one spoke out on the death of the Stratford man that year. How is that possible, if the deceased was perceived by the literary world to be Shakespeare, the esteemed poet and playwright? Where was Ben Jonson then? Where were the soaring accolades that appeared seven years later in the First Folio? Where were the outpourings of grief that followed the deaths of even lesser-known writers? There were none, so far as we know.

And why did William Camden, who had written high praise for Shakespeare and his works, and who knew the Stratford man and approved the grant of his coat of arms in 1596, fail to include the Stratford man in his list of "Stratford Worthies" published in 1605? And how could Camden not list the death of the Stratford man in his "Annals" of that year, if he thought it was the great Bard who had died?

The sonnets themselves (with the exception of Sonnet 111) seem to fit Oxford far more than the Stratford man. With that one exception, nothing in them fits anything we know about the Stratford man.

Although many authors' works reflect elements of their real experience, little, if anything, of the Stratford man's life and residence seems reflected in the plays, save the possibility that he really was arrested for stealing deer (and so depicted Sir Thomas Lucy as Justice Shallow), and some brief references to calf slaughtering, sheep raising, chevarie, and the like. Where are the moving descriptions of rural life in Stratford, the trenchant portrayals of characters living there? Where do we find the theme of a young man trapped into marrying an older woman he has impregnated? What play gives us the emotions of a man impelled to abandon his wife and children? Where are the Dickensian adventures of a rustic young man newly come to make his living among the stews, thugs, and rascals of London?

None of these things seem present. Instead, we get plays about people and relationships that appear to have no bearing at all on what we know of the Stratford man's life—things that seem more akin to the lives and experiences of men like Oxford, Stanley, and Bacon. Notwithstanding Professor Greenblatt's thesis that the plays reflect the personal responses of the Stratford man to events he may have experienced, they do not appear to describe the kind of places and events that probably marked his existence.

Nor does it seem wholly credible that all of the plays were originally written as commercial pieces to be successfully performed in the public theatre. An example is *Hamlet*'s original four-hour running time. This probably exceeded the daylight hours essential to performance in an open-air theatre that started in the midafternoon, and it certainly exceeded the attention span of the groundlings, a problem made more critical by the absence of bathrooms. Would a stagewise actor and theatre owner have written a play that long? *Richard II* and *Troilus and Cressida* created similar problems.

A good case can be made for the proposition that Shakespeare was writing not just for a company of actors to stage a commercial "hit," but at least in part, to set down for posterity his ideas, feelings, and views on fundamental issues. We know from the sonnets that his eye was on literary immortality. In Sonnet 81, for example, he tells the fair youth that his "monument shall be my gentle verse which eyes not yet created shall o'er read," so that when all people alive "are dead; you still shall live—such virtue hath my pen."

The Stratfordians argue that, since the anti-Strats can't agree on who Shakespeare was, he must have been the Stratford man. That, of course, is a patent *non sequitur*. The same argument might be made on behalf of any of the other candidates. Baconians might argue, for example, that since the disputants can't agree on whether Shakespeare was Marlowe, Oxford, or the Stratford man, he must have been Bacon. There are sound and responsible Stratfordian arguments. This is not one of them.

What, then, is the correct conclusion? Who, finally, was Shakespeare? If we are to be honest and objective, we must conclude that, given the present state of the evidence, there is no "right" conclusion, that the identity of Shakespeare is a matter on which reasonable minds may differ—and may always differ.

My own opinion? I believe the Stratford man did play a significant part in the creation of the plays, but that someone else originally created them and wrote the poems as well. I believe that original author was brilliant, highly educated, and widely traveled—probably a nobleman. But there are aspects of the plays that suggest a contribution by someone with "street smarts" and a shrewd nose for what would play in the public theatre. Many of the plays contain earthy, bawdy humor, as well as overly broad and "lowlife" characters that seem clearly designed to please a common theatre audience. And there are those seemingly inconsistent attitudes—the gratuitous whiff of bigotry—so difficult to understand.

I think one man, aristocratic and highly educated, wrote the sonnets, but that, in creating the plays or revising them, he listened to another voice—that of someone with a crass but practiced commercial eye and a sound knowledge of the theatre—and that each brought to the table the things that he knew best.

The stage directions published as a part of the plays reflect that shrewd knowledge of the theatre and of effective dramatic presentation. They follow a general pattern that can be made to follow the life of the Stratford man—who, in my view, was part of the team responsible for making practical suggestions and transferring the manuscript successfully to the stage. In the early plays, before the Stratford man became a sharer in the Lord Chamberlain's Men, the directions are quite full, suggesting that he did not expect to be a significant participant in the preproduction process. Then, when he became a co-owner of the company, the directions are more sparse, as if he knew he would be intimately involved with preparing the actors and stage personnel for the play's performance. Finally, in the later plays, the directions become more extensive once again. Was this because he was now living primarily in Stratford and aware that he would have to rely on others to see that the plays were effectively presented?

Consider this scenario. The earl of Oxford writes poems and plays beginning as early as 1580, or even before that. Like many competent writers, he is critical of his own work—is something of a perfectionist. As time goes on, some of the plays are shown to others and are privately performed. Other plays are put aside, as many authors put aside material with which they are not satisfied.

Oxford yearns to try his hand at the public theatre. He feels he cannot. The queen would never permit it. Perhaps he even asks her or asks his father-in-law Burghley. The answer is a resounding "no," certainly not under his own name. Writing under a pseudonym is not specifically forbidden, but he knows it still creates a risk of displeasing the queen. He needs added cover. He realizes that there might be a similar problem with poems, especially if, like *Venus and Adonis* and *The Rape of Lucrece* (and like the sonnets he has already started writing), they are somewhat erotic in content.

Oxford hears of a hustling, provincial actor named Shaksper who is working in London. He is doubly intrigued, because the man's family name reminds him of the arms of his own subsidiary title, Viscount Bolbec—a rampant lion shaking a spear.

They make a deal. Oxford will write and supply plays—and perhaps poems as well. When the plays are ready, they will be performed and published under the actor's name—but not quite that name. Perhaps a more dramatic version, cryptically suggesting Oxford himself. Henceforth, the name will be *Shakespeare*. To the actor, it sounds quite splendid. He will, of course, be well paid for his assistance—and his silence.

Oxford has an incomplete play called *Titus Andronicus* that he thinks might work for the public theatre. Somewhat insecure about the techniques of writing for the groundlings, he is referred to George Peele, a "professional," who, for a price, will help complete the play. Oxford, of course, acts through an intermediary, and Peele is not told the identity of his collaborator. He will be paid for his assistance, but he will not be acknowledged as a co-author when the play is performed. But Oxford is displeased with Peele's work and, for the moment, puts *Titus* aside. Next time he seeks help with a play, he will aim higher.

In writing the three parts of *Henry VI*, he turns for advice and assistance to Christopher Marlowe, a highly successful playwright he has met through Walter Raleigh and whom he is confident will keep his secret. He likes Marlowe's ideas and uses them in the plays, which he delivers to the Stratford man. They are performed and attributed to Shakespeare in accordance with the arrangement. But the Stratford actor does more than he promised. He also makes stage-wise comments on the plays and adds knowing stage directions.

For example, Oxford depicts Joan of Arc as a dedicated and heroic peasant girl who firmly believes in her visions and God-given powers and is sincerely determined to avenge the humiliating setbacks suffered by her country. But the actor, by now a theatre-wise "pro," realizes that this sympathetic portrait of Joan has to change if the groundlings are to be pleased. He suggests exposing her ultimately as a charlatan, harlot, and witch.

He also suggests a surefire, crowd-pleasing line. When Joan finally convinces the duke of Burgundy to switch sides, deserting the English and joining the French, she tells him to his face that he's acting like a typical Frenchman, switching sides again and still again. Oxford sees the inconsistency in the portrayal of Joan and realizes that her anti-French insult to Burgundy makes no sense at all. But against his better judgment, he relents. The Stratford man proves correct. The audience loves the play and roars with approval at Joan's absurd insult to the French. The play is a financial success. The young actor is very pleased and perhaps a bit boastful.

Robert Greene, a university-educated playwright, has come upon hard times. Drink and disease have reduced him to a miserable and penurious state. Somehow he manages to see a performance of *Henry VI*, Part 3 at Henslowe's Rose. He has had a furious dispute with Edward Alleyn, the actor who plays Richard, duke of York. Alleyn is co-owner of the theatre company and considers himself a playwright as well.

While Greene lies drunk and near death in a shoemaker's flat, he writes an angry letter, meant to be a part of a work called "A Groatsworth of Wit." He warns those he considers his own group (i.e., university-educated playwrights), against Edward Alleyn, whom he accuses of being a "Shake-scene" and "an upstart crow beautified with our feathers," in other words, a ham actor who's using "our" material to get ahead. But the letter is ambiguous. Even though Greene doesn't mean it, or even think about it, the word *Shake-scene* is construed as a reference to the playwright, thought to be a young actor named Shakespeare.

Before publishing the letter, Greene dies. Printer Henrye Chettle manages to get hold of the letter and "A Groatsworth of Wit." Although he's not sure who or what Greene meant by his letter, he prints them together.

Then the sky falls in. Word comes down from persons of enormous status and power that Chettle has made a big mistake. Chettle doesn't know it, but Oxford is outraged. He has construed Greene's letter as an attack on the play and the playwright and even an implication of plagiarism.

But Chettle is no fool. He realizes that someone very powerful has a close connection to Shakespeare and to *Henry VI*, Part 3. Chettle publishes an abject, if somewhat confused, apology. He's had, he says, complaints about Greene's letter from two of the "play-makers" Greene was warning against "Shake-scene." One he doesn't care about (that's Marlowe). But the other is admired "by divers of worship," that is, persons of high station.

Chettle expresses regret that he did not take greater care to spare him. This makes it seem like the second "play-maker," the one Chettle didn't spare, is the person Greene was attacking as the "upstart crow." If so, Greene would have been warning that play-maker against himself. But, after all, Chettle is nervous and certainly not at his best.

Notwithstanding Greene's attack, each of the *Henry VI* plays succeed. Encouraged, Oxford supplies the actor with other plays. He includes *Titus Andronicus*, despite his doubts about Peele's work and even about his own. But *Titus* is a surprising success and is performed repeatedly. Meanwhile, Oxford gives the Stratford man *Venus and Adonis*. He has dedicated the long erotic poem to the earl of Southampton in language Oxford thinks a commoner might use in writing to the highborn earl. The Stratford man takes *Venus* to his fellow townsman Richard Field to be printed. It achieves very significant sales. Oxford delivers *The Rape of Lucrece*, another such poem. It too is successful. "Shakespeare" is becoming famous.

Now, more plays follow, one after another. At this point, Oxford no longer feels the need for outside help. The plays are performed, and some are published. The Stratford man makes more shrewd suggestions that help the plays achieve commercial success. Sometimes these are minor insertions like Marian Hacket, the fat alewife of Wincot, or the idea of satirizing the arms of Sir Thomas Lucy. Sometimes they are more substantial.

In writing *The Merchant of Venice*, Oxford wants Shylock to be very different from Marlowe's murderous Barabas in *The Jew of Malta*, and he wants no part of Marlowe's gruesome ending with Barabas boiled to death in a cauldron. Oxford has written a moving speech for Shylock that portrays with great sympathy the plight of the diasporic Jews Oxford has observed on his European travels. Near the end of the play, he has Portia save Antonio by outwitting Shylock, who then leaves the court. But, because of the Christian mercy shown by Portia, Antonio, and the duke, Shylock leaves without his pledge, but with his religion, his property, and his life intact. Then, having matched Portia's deeds to her beautiful speech advocating mercy, Oxford wraps it all up in a final act full of music, love, and laughter.

The Stratford man has a more practical view. He is impatient with Shylock's marvelous speech. The crowd will hate it—aside from being bored. And the final treatment of Shylock runs counter to his commercial instincts. "Alright, you don't want to boil him like Barabas, but, at the very least, we need to make fun of the Jew. He's got to get his comeuppance in the end, so the crowd can laugh at him." They compromise. Oxford keeps Shylock's "If you prick us do we not bleed?" speech; but he adopts the Stratford man's suggestion for the end of the court scene, in which the audience is to be delighted and amused at Shylock's staggering loss. Now, he loses not only his daughter, his ducats, and his pledge, but also his property. And worse, he is forced to convert to Christianity, which costs him his dearly held religion, as well as his livelihood as a moneylender, since that trade was (at least theoretically) forbidden to Christians.

Oxford questions whether the love and laughter of the final act fits with the devastation brought down on Shylock. The Stratford man assures him the crowd will feel no remorse for the Jew and will find his forced conversion quite funny. "After all, sir, it's supposed to be a comedy."

The actor suggests another new line that seemingly presents Portia as a hypocrite. When the prince of Morocco leaves, after choosing the wrong chest, Portia expresses the hope that all suitors of his "complexion" (i.e., black) will similarly fail. This is after Portia told him to his face that he was as desirable as any suitor. Oxford finds the new line offensive; but once again accepts the advice that the groundlings will love it.

Perhaps Oxford rationalizes his acquiescence with the hopeful thought that the dissonant lines may even sharpen what he has always considered a subtly underlying theme of the play—the hypocrisy of Antonio, Bassanio, and their entire class. With the newly suggested lines, even Portia, the heroine he had been reluctant to portray in a bad light, may be also perceived as a hypocrite, at least by discerning members of the audience—and maybe, Oxford thinks, that's not all bad.

But the play is not taken that way. The Stratford man turns out to have been right again. A few educated, sensitive souls are moved by Shylock's speech. But the groundlings roar with laughter at the Jew's humiliating end. Portia is viewed as a brilliant, witty heroine. No one notices the inconsistency between her rhapsodic advocacy of mercy one minute and her cruel denial of any mercy to Shylock the next.

And the crowd loves the line the Stratford man suggested for Portia, in which she hopes that all men of the same complexion as the black prince of Morocco will fail, just as Morocco did, in choosing the wrong casket to win her hand. Her earlier insincerity in praising the prince goes unnoticed.

Combining the superb work of the original playwright with the crowd-pleasing suggestions of the Stratford man, the play succeeds handsomely. So does a comedy Oxford writes two years later, possibly because of the risqué title suggested by the Stratford man. It's *Much Ado About Nothing*, "nothing" being Elizabethan slang for a woman's private parts.

Oxford has also been reworking *Hamlet*. It's now a very different version of the play Oxford wrote anonymously years before, when it was panned as silly and childishly melodramatic. The earl has reacted to this early humiliation by going in the other direction—turning the play into a brilliant dissection of a young man's innermost thoughts, opening them up to the audience in a way never achieved before. Oxford also wants the play to question whether the desire for revenge can ever justify killing. But the brilliance of the revised work goes on and on and on—for about four hours.

And it's a play highly personal to Oxford. To him, Queen Gertrude is his mother, who married relatively soon after his father's death. King Claudius is his stepfather. Polonius is his ponderous father-in-law Burghley. His poor, misjudged wife becomes Ophelia. His friend Rutland helps make the play authentic with real Danish names, like Rosencrantz, Guildenstern, and Helsingör.

The Stratford man tries to be tactful, but it's not easy. "The new version won't work," he tells Oxford. "It's not the same problem you had before. This one's much too long and too talky. It'll be dark before it's done; but it won't matter. The audience will drift away long before that. Remember, sir, there's no privies. And Hamlet talks us to death. He's almost girlish. We need to include more action that shows our boy's got a will. Rosencrantz and Guildenstern are too clever by half. Hamlet's got to turn the tables on 'em, get 'em killed in his place. He ought to kill useless old Polonius too and yell out 'I'll lug the guts into the neighbor room,' and then he should do it—just drag the corpse right off the stage. Then, when he kills the king, he can kill the queen and Laertes too, before he dies himself—all in one big, bloody scene. And let's change 'Helsingör' to Elsinore, so at least the actors can say it. Finally, when Hamlet dies, he can't just lie there and say 'The rest is silence.' He's got to groan, show us he's in pain—maybe cry out 'O, o, o, o,' so the audience knows he's suffering. But you know, sir, it's still going to be way too long."

Oxford reluctantly agrees to many of the changes. After all, he thinks, having Hamlet cause added deaths may lead even more of the audience to question whether revenge is such a good idea. But the earl will not yield on the play's length. Too many of the lines have personal significance; too many of the ideas are important to him. It is left to others, over the centuries, to cut the play to a more effective length.

Oxford is shaken and remains affected by what he considers the murder of Marlowe. Over the years, he works references to Marlowe's death into his own plays. In *As You Like It*, he speaks to Marlowe, repeating Marlowe's own lines: "Dead Shepherd! Now I find thy saw of might"; and through Touchstone, he tells us that when a poet's verse is not understood "It strikes a man more dead than a great reckoning in a little room."

In *Henry IV*, Part 2, he provides a comedic parody of Marlowe's famous chariot scene from *Tamburlaine the Great*.

In *The Merry Wives of Windsor*, he uses, almost verbatim, four lines from *The Passionate Shepherd to His Love*, a work by Marlowe of which he is particularly fond. As in the case of the Dead Shepherd speech in *As You Like It*, he knows the lines will be recognized as Marlowe's by many and considers them an homage to Marlowe, not a theft.

Oxford also writes some highly personal sonnets that he certainly will not turn over to the crass and common actor from Stratford. These sonnets are, in part, about his strong feelings for young Southampton. Oxford is not entirely sure just what those feelings are, or what he will do with these highly personal musings. He wouldn't mind reading some of the less personal sonnets to a few friends. He might even publish a few. But others are far too personal. They are just for him and the beautiful young earl. In some, he urges Southampton to marry his daughter—an arranged dynastic match that has nothing to do with love or with his own feelings for the young man.

On one occasion, Oxford, known for his quick temper, has a quarrel with Southampton. Some rude epithets are hurled, more consistent with "public manners" than the behavior of two highborn earls.

Always mercurial, Oxford is immediately sorry. He writes an apologetic sonnet to the young earl—the one we know as Sonnet 111. He blames his being ill provided for as the cause of his involvement in such ventures as the public theatre and the public sale of his poems and plays. Even though these pursuits are carried out under a pseudonym, they are the sort that tend to create "public manners." He even says that his own true nature has "almost" become what he "works in, like the dyer's hand." He is alluding to his recent display of foul temper. He offers to drink "potions of eysell" (vinegar) and asks for Southampton's pity. The sonnet grossly exaggerates, of course; but this is poetry, and there is such a thing as poetic license. Oxford's apology is accepted.

In one sonnet, Oxford can't resist a punning reference to Greene's letter warning against "Shake-scene," which still rankles him. "What care I," he writes, in Sonnet 112, "who calls me well or ill, so you o'er-Greene my bad, my good allow?" He goes on to claim that he pays no attention to either "critic" or "flatterer." Later, the printer drops the final "e" from "o'er-Greene," thinking it a mistake.

The years go by, and the "partners" bring out more and more plays. Not everything Oxford writes is turned over to the Stratford man. There are some plays with which he is not satisfied. He puts them aside for later revision—someday, when he gets around to it. He thinks he may abandon *Timon of Athens* entirely. It is too bitter and episodic. The disparate voices of the characters seem unclear and uncontrolled. He prefers *King Lear*, which he continues to revise, and still hopes to complete. Even though he recognizes the bitterness there too, *Lear* is starting to have a dramatic force that pleases him.

Oxford gets helpful information from his friends and relatives in writing the plays. His son-in-law Lord Stanley tells him about people and events in the court of Navarre. He uses them in *Love's Labour's Lost*. Oxford bases another character in that play on Stanley's dreadfully pompous tutor Richard Lloyd. Does he dare have the character Holofernes read a masque called "The Nine Worthies"? His family and friends all know Lloyd wrote an excruciatingly silly masque bearing that same title. He will! But . . . better to think on it for a time. He puts the play aside and finishes it later. Stanley also has a brother, Ferdinando, who's the ruler of the Isle of Man. He's a fine model for *The Tempest*.

In late 1603, Oxford completes *Measure for Measure* and *Othello*. After the holidays, he returns to work on *Macbeth*, a play he started earlier, but which he thinks will please the new king, who, after all, is a Scot. In the spring, he puts *Macbeth* temporarily aside and comes back to *King Lear*, which still needs some work, he thinks. He hopes to complete the two over the summer.

But none of us controls his destiny. In June of 1604, Oxford contracts the plague. After a short illness, he dies.

His friend and son-in-law Stanley looks through the earl's papers and finds a number of plays in various stages of completion. Stanley, who loves plays and the theatre, would hate to see these works lost to the world forever. Knowing of the clandestine arrangement between Oxford and the Stratford man, Stanley consults his lawyer Francis Bacon, the wisest man he knows. He is surprised to find that Bacon also knew of the arrangement and, indeed, had read and commented on certain of the plays at Oxford's request. Bacon recommends that the arrangement with the Stratford man simply be continued. He and Stanley agree that the undelivered plays should not remain in obscurity, but that, if they are to be performed or published, Oxford would have wanted his anonymity preserved, and this would be best for the family as well. They consult with Oxford's widow, who agrees. Bacon meets with the Stratford man, who readily agrees.

Fairly soon, Stanley supplies the actor with five new plays, *Measure for Measure*, *Antony and Cleopatra*, *Othello*, *King Lear*, and *Macbeth*. A lover of the classics who believes his title is traceable back to the ancient Romans, Stanley loves *Antony and Cleopatra*. He is uncertain about *King Lear*, with its unrelieved cruelty and suffering; but he decides it has brilliant moments and is ready for delivery. Even though *Macbeth* is shorter than the others, he considers it fit to be produced. He tells the Stratford man that Oxford may possibly have some more plays squirreled away, but that these could be the last of the lot.

The Stratford man is quite keen on *Measure for Measure*, *Antony and Cleopatra*, and *Othello*. He agrees that King James will fancy *Macbeth*, short as it may be. But *Lear*, he feels, is depressing and, at the very least, needs updating. He agrees to present it anyway. Money is money, after all. Still, before the play is produced, he adds a reference to "the late eclipses" to give the audience a current allusion they will easily understand. For the same purpose, he gives the drunken porter in *Macbeth* humorous new lines about "equivocators."

Other plays among Oxford's papers seem to Stanley not ready at all or give him concern for other reasons. Some are obviously incomplete. Others, he feels, are just not his father-in-law's best work. *Timon of Athens*, for example, seems almost as bad as *Titus Andronicus*, a completed play Stanley has long considered execrable. Loyal to Oxford, he blames *Titus* on George Peele, who wrote almost one-third of the play. Stanley thinks *Timon* may have been an early and unsuccessful attempt by Oxford to do what he did with far greater success in *Lear*. He finds *Coriolanus* strange and sometimes incomprehensible. He has similar worries about *The Tempest*, with its obvious references to his late brother Ferdinando.

But Stanley is not ready to give up on any of them. A competent author in his own right and by no means a "nidicock," he attempts his own revision of some of the undelivered plays, trying always to retain Oxford's distinctive "voice." He brings in other playwrights to complete the plays he particularly dislikes—Thomas Middleton on *Timon* and George Wilkins on *Pericles*. Stanley considers Middleton's additions adequate, but he deplores the early acts of *Pericles* written by Wilkins. Hoping to improve the quality of such revisions, Stanley and Bacon offer *Henry VIII* to John Fletcher, who writes much of the play as it exists today.

From time to time, Stanley asks Bacon to read and comment on the plays, just as Oxford did in his lifetime. As additional plays are considered finished, Stanley delivers them to the Stratford man, telling him he's "found" them among other papers at Oxford's home. The actor, no innocent, is skeptical. But the money is good, so he asks no questions. The "collaboration" goes on.

Stanley overcomes his concerns about *The Tempest* and delivers it. The Stratford man has doubts about its commercial possibilities. In his view, nothing really happens. He adds the line about the "still vexed Burmoothas" and other references to the recent shipwreck to give the audience something current to recognize.

Ultimately, putting aside his doubts as to *Timon*, *Titus*, and *Pericles*, Stanley delivers everything he has. The Stratford man receives them all, but feels that some simply cannot be produced and that others, like *Troilus and Cressida*, seem more suitable to private performances, or at least the Inns of Court, than to presentation on the public stage.

Finally, having put aside a significant amount of money and not expecting a flow of new plays for which to front, the Stratford man moves back home. If and when Stanley comes up with any more plays, he'll make the trip to London to deal with them.

In the interim, someone, somehow, gets hold of Oxford's sonnets. In 1609, they are published with no participation at all by "Shakespeare," but with praise for our "ever-living poet." Oxford is dead, and no one consults the Stratford man, now busily immersed in real estate dealings.

Oxford's family is stunned, including Stanley, who, after all, is married to Oxford's daughter. To them, the sonnets reek of homosexuality. They're all too conscious of how many people had remarked on Southampton's feminine beauty in his youth, and of the likelihood that the sonnets' expressions of "love" and even "passion" for the youthful earl will create new talk of an improper liaison.

This is particularly worrisome to the family since, during his lifetime, Oxford had been publicly accused by his cousin, Lord Henry Howard, of buggering young boys. He denied this, of course, and few believed it. But now, with these sexually ambiguous poems and that troubling, girlish portrait of the young earl, looking for all the world like a catamite, it could all come back.

They discuss this with Southampton and his family, who readily agree. They are all aware of the fiction that the Stratford man wrote the plays. Demonstrably a heterosexual and reputed to be something of a womanizer, he, rather than Oxford, must be perceived as the creator of these embarrassing sonnets. The fiction must continue. It must be reinforced and expanded. And any further editions of the sonnets must be suppressed.

The families decide to foster the concept of the Stratford man as poet and playwright whenever and however they can. These are powerful men, well able to accomplish the task. Oxford's other son-in-law is the earl of Montgomery, whose brother, the earl of Pembroke, is the Lord Chamberlain. Lord Stanley's own family has immense power and influence. Efforts are made to ensure that any manuscripts in Oxford's hand are destroyed, along with any notes or letters that might suggest that Oxford was the true author.

The Stratford man has no objection to any of this. He has no intention of disclosing the charade, but he rather enjoys the fact that all these entrenched aristocrats are terrified that he might. Perhaps some additional payments are made, providing added financing for real estate deals.

The death of the Stratford man in 1616 causes the families concern. Has he disclosed the secret in his will? In other documents? He has not. If anything, they conclude, his death removes a potential source of the truth's getting out and makes it even easier to carry out their plan.

First, they finance a monument to the Stratford man to be erected in Stratford's Holy Trinity Church. They also arrange—for a generous contribution—to have him buried in the interior of the church rather than in the common churchyard. Not bothering to visit Stratford, they are unaware that the actor's remains are not "within" the monument, as it recites, but beneath the floor of the chancel, under a stone bearing the childish doggerel the Stratford man had written before his death.

But they do achieve their basic objective. They avoid local derision by directing that the monument be given a deliberately ambiguous inscription in Latin suggesting that the deceased was an author, but not in language likely to be understood by the residents of Stratford. Instead of an open reference to the deceased being another "Virgil," they refer to his being a "Maronem" from "Moro," the lesser-known family name of the Roman poet—a name not likely to be known to the farmers of Stratford. Similarly, instead of "Nestor," they refer to "Pylium," since Nestor was the prince of Pylos. How many Stratford citizens would know *that*?

To further the impression that the Stratford man was an author, but, again, with studied ambiguity, he is to be portrayed with a quill in one hand, and with each hand on one side of a pillow. When the monument is completed and installed in Stratford, someone is to find and insert an actual goose-feather quill in the figure's right hand.

But the locals who handle the installation fail to do this, leaving the hand empty. It is more than a century before the omission is corrected. In the interim, the empty hands seem to be clutching what looks like a sack of grain. This is the way the monument is seen and represented in published sketches. It readily fits with the impression of the Stratford man held by his fellow townsmen—at least until publication of the First Folio seven years after his death.

But the monument is not enough. It is out in rural Stratford and will not be seen by the people whose opinions really count, whose gossip could pose a serious threat. More must be done to tie the authorship of the poems and plays permanently to the Stratford man and keep it away from Oxford. The families consult Bacon. Although a homosexual himself, he's a realist, and he understands their concern. Besides, Stanley is a valued client. Bacon recommends a bold plan. A compilation of "Shakespeare's" plays will be published in one huge folio, linking the poet and playwright firmly and irrevocably to the Stratford actor. The pretense worked well enough during Oxford's life and even after his death. Why not now, with the Stratford man dead and unable to reveal the truth?

Bacon makes an arrangement with Ben Jonson. Jonson will be handsomely paid by the family to oversee the project and to create an irrefutable record identifying Shakespeare as the Stratford man. Jonson is glad to do it. He never cared that much for "Shakespeare's" work, and what a joke it will be to tell the world it was all written by that crude actor from Stratford. Jonson laughs to himself, "I'll praise that money-grubbing 'gentleman' to the sky, and dance my way to the bank."

Permissions must be gathered from the publishers who hold the rights to the plays already printed. Manuscripts must be found and prior editions corrected. The project takes considerable time and money. But Jonson's backers are wealthy men, and, to them, it's well worth the time and investment. Family honor and reputation are at stake.

Jonson, of course, includes all the plays that have been completed either by Oxford before his death or by Stanley and others thereafter. With Bacon's valuable assistance, the families finally obtain the necessary permissions for all the plays. Jonson begins to feel some pride in the folio he's preparing. But he feels some of the plays need additional work—some trims and revisions here and there. An accomplished playwright, he makes them himself. At Bacon's suggestion, he revises *Hamlet*, making it consistent with Bacon's *De Fluxo et Refluxo Marit*.

The compilers face the issue of how to treat collaborative works. At first, Bacon and Stanley agree that *Henry VIII* will be included, but *Timon of Athens* will not. But, when they have trouble clearing title to *Troilus and Cressida*, they insert *Timon* in its place. Finally, they solve the problem of *Troilus* and decide to include *Timon* as well. Stanley, however, remains adamant about *Pericles*, much of which he considers the work of an untalented hack.

In the end, there are thirty-six plays. Their vocabulary is extraordinary. After all, they contain not only the thoughts and lines of Oxford, but also the contributions of other creative men, at least five of whom—Bacon, Stanley, Jonson, Middleton, and Fletcher—are intelligent and well read. Even the Stratford man, after years in the theatre, has suggested lines calculated to please the common theatre audience, as well as arcane rural jargon acquired in and around Stratford.

Jonson writes a poem for the Folio and includes another commissioned from Leonard Digges, making it as clear as possible that the poems and plays were the work of the Stratford man. Jonson also writes two letters to the same effect, nominally by Heminge and Condell, who are being well paid and perfectly willing to let their names be used.

The world is convinced. With the exception of a few skeptical souls, it has remained convinced ever since. Poet Laureate Sir William Davenant is sufficiently confident that the Stratford man, who sometimes visited his parents, was the great Bard, that he hints with pride at being the actor's illegitimate son. Countless academics and other "experts" are so convinced that, over the centuries, they dismiss the entire authorship issue as no issue at all.

Do I *know* this is what occurred? Of course not. It seems to me a logical explanation, the one that fits the facts we know most comfortably. But, instead of Oxford, it could have been Marlowe, hiding in Italy, or the brilliant philosopher-lawyer Bacon who wrote the poems and plays and gave them to the Stratford man. Or the Stratford man could really—somehow—have managed to write them all himself.

What I have described is simply my own opinion. It could be altered by newly discovered evidence; and it is only one of many possible solutions to this extraordinary mystery that has been with us for 400 years and may be with us forever.

INDEX

legal matters, knowledge of, 99–101
likenesses of Shakespeare, 195–97, 213–14
Lincoln, Abraham, 4
Lloyd, Richard, 263, 291
local references, 103–6
Lodge, Thomas, 63, 130
London, 41–42, 58
Looney, J. Thomas, 2, 209–10, 214
Lopez, Roderigo, 22
Lord Admiral's Men, 42
Lord Chamberlain's Men, 44, 60, 61, 167, 168, 218, 223, 245
Lord Russell, 6
Love's Labour's Lost, 55, 60–62, 80, 89–91, 96, 124, 163, 190, 229, 252, 255, 262–63, 291
Love's Labour's Won, 61
Lucy, Sir Thomas, 40, 104, 282
Lyly, John, 121, 202

Macaulay, Thomas, 203
Macbeth, 64, 161, 170, 220–22, 226–27, 229, 268, 291, 292
Mainwaring, Arthur, 128
Malone, Edmund, 7, 148, 237
Manners, Francis, 52, 268
Manners, Roger, earl of Rutland, 52, 259, 265–68
Manningham, John, 49–50
Marlowe, Christopher, 1, 13, 22, 58, 73, 75, 101, 105, 143, 167, 196, 227, 236–50, 259, 262, 271, 285, 287, 290
Marmion (Sir Walter Scott), vii
Marsden, John, 253
Mary, countess of Pembroke, 183
Mary, Queen of England, 15–17
Mary Stuart, 17, 19

Measure for Measure, 93, 98, 150–51, 156–57, 161–62, 222, 224, 291, 292
Mendenhall, Thomas, 242
The Merchant of Venice, 22, 61, 83, 86–87, 91, 93, 101, 105, 131–37, 143, 147, 157, 163, 190, 238, 241–42, 257, 287–288
Meres, Francis, 61, 63, 130, 202–3, 222, 246, 249
The Merry Wives of Windsor, 39–40, 80, 98, 99, 104, 151, 211, 221, 237–38, 290
metaphorical usage, knowledge of, 94–96
Meyrick, Sir Gilly, 65, 66
Michell, John, 184, 267
Middleton, Thomas, 75, 226, 293
A Midsummer Night's Dream, 5, 61, 150, 270
military matters, knowledge of, 96–99
Millar v. Taylor, 169
Milton, John, 75, 101
Monteagle, Lord, 65
Montgomery, earl of, 181, 232, 273, 294
monument (Stratford), 7, 174–79, 195, 279
More, Sir Thomas, 68, 69
Mountjoy, Lord, 27, 93
Mozart, Amadeus, 125
Much Ado About Nothing, 150, 169, 221, 289
Munday, Anthony, 68, 202

name, variations in, 6, 189–94
Nash, Thomas, 63, 166, 167, 254–55
naval matters, knowledge of, 96–99
Nestor, 175, 179
Non Sanz Droict, 47
North, Sir Thomas, 92